TRACY
50 Years, 50 Stories

Collected and edited by

RICHARD CRESWICK
and
DEREK PUGH

With a foreword by
The Honourable John Hardy AO
21st Administrator of the Northern Territory

TRACY: 50 Years, 50 Stories

Creswick, Richard: Author/Editor
Pugh, Derek: Author/Editor

Design and layout by Mikaela Pugh: mikaelaapughh@gmail.com

ISBN: 9780645737417
Printed – Paperback

Subjects:
Northern Territory History
Darwin
Cyclone Tracy
Cyclone Selma
The Great Hurricane 1897
The cyclone of 1937

Notes: Includes bibliographical references and index.

Front cover: Cyclone Tracy on the radar, 1974, (LANT, ph0026-0022).

NATIONAL LIBRARY OF AUSTRALIA

A catalogue record for this book is available from the National Library of Australia

Dedication

This book is dedicated to those who lost their lives in Cyclone Tracy; to those who have died in the intervening years, and to all of those who survived. It is also dedicated to the people of Australia who responded so magnificently when called upon for support and provided solace and succour to evacuees or helped clean-up and then rebuild a devastated town. On the fiftieth anniversary of one of Australia's greatest natural disasters we thank you.

Acknowledgements

The stories in this book are the personal recollections of more than fifty survivors of Cyclone Tracy or its immediate aftermath. This book has been a chance for them to record history as yet untold. They have written their stories, sometimes for the first time, for their families and for posterity generally.

Our thanks go to Hon. John Hardy AO, 21st Administrator of the Northern Territory, a Tracy survivor himself, for his foreword. Thanks also to the authors, and everyone who has been a part of the project. We have found it humbling, enlightening, and sometimes challenging. We hope the book's readers will share some of those emotions.

We acknowledge the Larrakia people as the traditional owners of the area that was devastated by Cyclone Tracy, and advise all Indigenous Australians that, as this is a history, it necessarily contains the names and images of people who are now deceased.

The publication of this book has been assisted by the Northern Territory Government through the History Grants Program.

Contents

Foreword

During Cyclone Tracy, John Hardy was a radiographer at Royal Darwin Hospital. He and his family lived in Cubillo Street in Wanguri. After the cyclone, John became the Superintendent Radiographer of the Northern Territory. A pilot for many years, John and his wife Marie started Airnorth in 1978, and in 1991, Hardy Aviation, providing much needed air transport to remote Territory communities. In 2014, he was sworn in as the 21st Administrator of the Northern Territory. His Cyclone Tracy story is well known – at the 40th anniversary commemoration he said: "We awoke to a badly damaged house and a city unlike anything I had seen before, I remember people making comparisons to Hiroshima, the devastation was so severe."

Christmas was approaching and many homes in Darwin were preparing for a joyful family event. Children in many homes, especially those with young children, became excited as presents began to pile up under the Christmas trees in their living rooms. Although we were now into the cyclone season there was little regard for the approaching storm.

There was a false sense of security in the air as only a few weeks earlier we had been put on alert by another cyclone, named Selma. This weather event came and went with very little drama and minimal actual damage. It was assumed that Tracy would be just as tame. Some people felt no need to worry or to go to too much trouble getting prepared but as the cyclone approached, like a lot of Darwin's population, we were on edge. We lived in the northern suburbs, about as far as you could get from the old Darwin Hospital to which I was on call. Of course, I was hoping not to receive a call, but the telephone rang anyway, and despite my reluctance to leave my young family, 'duty' had to be obeyed. I was quickly into my car and sped off to the hospital.

The storm had not yet broken but it was very close. It was now after 11pm and I quickly took the X-Rays of the broken leg I had been called in for and sent the patient and his pictures back to the attending surgeon. This all took nearly an hour to complete and just after midnight a furious Tracy had arrived. Torrential rain, hurricane force wind, lightning, and destruction!

I had to get home to look after my family on the other side of town, so I left the relative sanctity of the hospital and went out into the night, now without street lighting. The streets were strewn with downed power lines, some of which were alive and sparking. I was in constant fear that my progress would be halted by a fallen tree or power pole lying across the way.

Mine wasn't the only vehicle on the streets but probably like me, the other drivers were also desperate to get home!

My mind knew the way. I had done the journey so many times at all hours day and night, I knew all the twists and turns from the hospital: *go down Smith Street; use only streets leading to Bagot Road; keep away from the Botanical Gardens, too many trees that may fall... Bagot Road is straight until it becomes Trower Road; then there are several turns as it passes Casuarina High School and Casuarina Shopping Centre; right onto Vanderlin Drive; now close to home on Cubillo Street; made it!*

As I got out of my car I saw that nearby houses had already not survived the destructive force of the wind. There was building debris all about the street from houses all around us, but amazingly ours was still untouched.

My wife Marie and I were now under extreme stress as we gathered in our upstairs living room expecting the worst to happen very soon. All the children were told to put on shoes and socks as broken glass would be everywhere. The glass louvres gave way to the wind, and we expected the roof would go any minute. The seven of us all retreated to the tiny bathroom on the leeward side of the house and were trapped there while the house shook violently. Eventually the roof broke away and took with it the outside wall that was in front of us. We now had to scramble to the ground and get out. The older kids handed the babies out to the adults, and we made our way to the brick storeroom for shelter and safety. This was our only option. The rest of the house was whipped away by the wind but, alas, the storeroom proved to be no match for the strength of the wind either and it began to disintegrate.

Using my torch, our only light in the pitch black. I could see our three cars parked under the house between us and the face of the storm. The one closest to us was intact so taking care to avoid missiles whizzing past we all got into this car and out of the storm, it was dry inside and the lights worked. After the terrible and exhausting ordeal, we had been through everyone fell asleep and did not wake until the dawn.

As we all now know, Tracy was very potent and packed a deadly punch across the city of Darwin, causing death and destruction. Many surviving this dreadful night still live in Darwin and have put pen to paper to assist Derek and Richard to produce this fascinating book which I am sure many will read, appreciate, and discover what it's like to experience a cyclone's wrath.

The experience was not only about learning how to survive the storm but also the aftermath of living in a destroyed city. Our neighbours had been through the same horrible experience, and this brought comfort, strength, and confidence that we could live through this storm's upheaval and survive.

This book dispels the notion that the cyclone destroyed our lifestyles and caused everyone to leave town never to return. Although a few never did, this is not correct for all of Darwin. Most people wanted to return to their damaged homes, fix them and resume the lifestyle they previously enjoyed.

Darwin is a perfect example of this behaviour, and the authors can attest to its veracity. Darwin is a wonderful place to live, even with an occasional wild storm. There have been a few since Tracy, but they have never caused a population decline. Darwin still has much to offer, a tropical climate, beautiful gardens, and a friendly community. A tropical cyclone passing by will never be an excuse to leave town and live elsewhere.

The Honourable John Hardy AO
21st Administrator of the Northern Territory

Preface

Like the death of a princess or a rock and roll legend, or man's first steps on the moon, all Australians who were old enough at Christmas time in 1974, remember where they were and what they were doing when Darwin was all but wiped off the map by a cyclone.

Unlike in these days of virtually instant communication, 'Southerners' first heard of Tracy's devastation through their radios, and they had to wait nearly two days to see the first shocking images from Keith Bushnell's film. Later, as they read articles in newspapers and magazines, many donated clothing or cash to help the victims, and/or hosted Darwin's refugees. After Australia's largest ever evacuation, arriving with nothing except the clothes they wore, thousands of survivors were fed and housed in southern cities, sometimes for weeks or months. Many developed long-lasting friendships with people they would never have met otherwise.

Cyclone Tracy became the yardstick used to measure all natural disasters in Australia. There have been songs, documentaries, articles, books, and more books, and museum displays. Tourists want to know about Tracy, and they crowd into the dark room at the museum to listen to an actual recording of the storm. With their memories still somewhat raw, even after all these years, rarely are the victims of the cyclone willing to join them in that little room.

Tracy's fiftieth anniversary falls on 24 December 2024. Naturally, many survivors have passed on during the past fifty years and most likely, none will be here for the hundredth anniversary, so we asked survivors to come forward and write about their experiences while they still can. More than fifty took the opportunity.

There have been many books where survivors' stories have been compiled or included as part of the bigger story of Cyclone Tracy. This book is different. Not only are the stories in the book written in the survivors' own words, only lightly edited, they are the stories of 'ordinary' people who experienced extraordinary things. The stories have either never been published, or if they have, have never been seen by a wide audience so remain fresh.

We discussed whether our collection of stories should be restricted to *only* those people who actually experienced the cyclone in all its terrifying ferocity. But there is a group of people who were *adjacently traumatised*, despite not being in Darwin at the time. They had such a close connection to their Darwin homes and lifestyle that their suffering was also traumatic, and their stories legitimately belong here too. We have chosen three.

We have deliberately edited the stories from the perspective of historians. Our additional chapters place Cyclone Tracy, Australia's greatest natural disaster, into a broader 'Darwin disaster' context and deal with cyclones past and proximate. Our hope is that we, as a community, learn from the past and remember it in the future, and put Tracy into an historical context.

Richard has previously told his own story in *They Gave Us a Television Station to Play With* (2021), and in numerous newspaper articles, particularly in commemorative issues marking one or other of Cyclone Tracy's milestones. It is also recorded in the oral history collection of the Library and Archives of the Northern Territory.

When collecting these stories, we heard comments like: "Funny, no one has ever asked me for my story before" and "I have never been able to tell my story before this." One old friend begged to be let off. There was so much trauma that she could not revisit. "My memories", she said, "are about certain death and hopes that my very small children might survive and be found. I simply can't write about all of this".

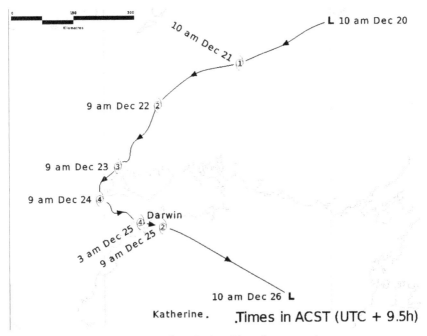

Figure 1: Tracking Cyclone Tracy (bom.gov.au).

Tracy was a single event, but every one of the more than 40,000 Darwin residents who experienced it has a different story. These pages hold just a few of them. The occasional small inconsistencies that appear in some of the stories are forgiven, when we remember that half a century has passed since the night of that terrible storm.

We hope that the 50th anniversary in 2024 will be an occasion for healing, if necessary, and for remembering friends and family.

Richard Creswick and Derek Pugh
Darwin, 2024

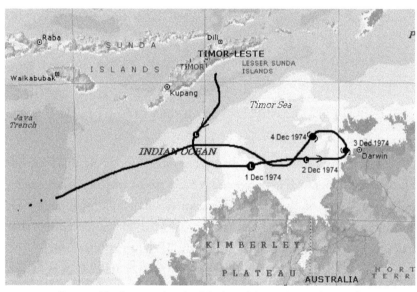

Figure 2: The 'near miss' path of Cyclone Selma in December 1974.

Cyclone Selma
A Warning Ignored
By Richard Creswick

Many of the stories from survivors in this book mention Cyclone Selma, a cyclone that briefly threatened Darwin a few weeks before Tracy. It had started forming south of the island of Timor on December 1, 1974, and it initially travelled south-west before turning due east on a track which, on December 3, saw it in Beagle Gulf between the Tiwi Islands and Darwin. The Bureau of Meteorology issued regular alerts and warnings for people to prepare for a potentially devastating storm while it was approaching, and some people did. But on December 3, Selma suddenly changed direction. It turned north then west, crossed the western tip of Bathurst Island, and headed southwest, away from the city. The storm crossed its original track a couple of times and eventually petered out south of the Indonesian island of Java on December 9. It was a near miss. There was a lot of rain and some trees had been brought down but nothing was too alarming. Like so many had done before, Selma drifted away to the west.

As Richard Evans notes in *Disasters that Changed Australia*[*] "near-misses" lead to complacency. "When authorities warn of a serious danger that does not eventuate," he wrote, "people can become fatally sceptical".

Barbara Pottle was acting Nursing Supervisor of Casualty and

---

[*] Richard Evans, 2009, *Disasters that Changed Australia*. Victory Books

Outpatients at Royal Darwin Hospital. Her comment is typical: "Some three weeks prior, Darwin had been subjected to Cyclone Selma which knocked over a few trees and made a bit of a mess around the gardens, so not too many people were fazed by another one, even though it could have chosen a better time to visit us, being Christmas Eve and all."

For Darwin residents, many of them new to the tropical north, Selma was their first exposure to the threat of a weather phenomenon that few had ever experienced.

However, there were some, including people whose stories you will read in this book, who took the warnings about Cyclone Selma seriously. They taped the windows with masking tape, filled the bath with water, tied down or locked away loose objects and ensured they had torches and working battery-powered radios.

A very few, with greater technical knowledge, went further by attempting to properly cyclone-proof their houses with tie-down cables fixed to concrete footings. However, bearing in mind that most residents were short termers here for a two-year stint and therefore renting their homes, such preparations were unfortunately rare.

As it turned out, such was the ferocity of Cyclone Tracy, that taping the windows was a joke. Not only was the glass in easily smashed banks of louvres, but the walls holding the window frames also disappeared. As for filling their baths with water as advised – intended as an emergency water supply should that facility fail – those whose baths actually survived often found themselves huddled in them as the rest of their house disintegrated around them.

And while the battery-operated radios undoubtedly proved of value later, there were no radio transmissions to tune into for a day or more. Indeed, one radio technician spoke of the eerie feeling experienced from spinning the dial across the transmission spectrum and hearing only silence or the hiss of atmospherics.

The fact that Cyclone Tracy developed and then hit at the height of Christmas celebrations undoubtedly contributed to the sense of complacency engendered by Cyclone Selma. Richard Evans writes of a 'sober truth' that is ignored by the subsequent gloss of Cyclone Tracy being described as the catalyst for a 'New Darwin' (the fifth Darwin, as he notes).

Evan's sober truth is that "The human suffering and its long-term economic and social cost – including the diversion of resources from other Territory towns and communities – could have been avoided if the sensible warnings of intelligent and responsible people had been heeded. Old Darwin should have survived Tracy more or less intact", he claimed. Tracy was not a freak event, as the previous destructive cyclones (1897 and 1937) had shown. A severe cyclone would again hit Darwin – the only question was when.

"Despite those warnings or lessons," Evans wrote, "the city in its physical and social structures was appallingly ill-prepared. In the wake of Cyclone Althea, the Department of Works in Darwin had recommended extra strengthening in houses, that cladding be better secured and that windows be protected with shutters and screens. But no-one paid much attention".

The trouble was no-one had experienced a severe cyclone like Tracy before, and no-one believed it could happen to them. The fizzle of Cyclone Selma can be added to that list of the causes of complacency that afflicted so many of those who ultimately survived Cyclone Tracy.

Figure 3: A house in the northern suburbs (Pengilly Collection, LANT ph0365-0005).

Joan Andropov

*After seven years living and working in Papua-New Guinea, imminent
independence seemed to make a return to Australia a wise move for Joan
and her family. Her husband, Simon had been offered a job setting up
course work and teaching civil engineering at the new Darwin Community
College. After a Christmas with family in Victoria they moved to Darwin
in January 1974, buying an older house in Rapid Creek that was shaded
by dozens of big black wattle trees.*

Earlier in December 1974, breakup parties on the last day of
school had been cancelled. The schools closed because of a cyclone
threat, but it came to nothing, so perhaps this one called Tracy would
do the same. The usual recorded cyclone warning on the radio was
first heard during lunch hour on December 24, and at frequent
intervals during the afternoon and evening. We were warned to
take bottles off bars, pictures off walls, fill the bathtub with water.
We were to open windows away from the wind, and close windows
facing the wind, adjusting them after the lull, because the wind would
change direction. Under no circumstances were we to shelter under
an elevated house but were to stay upstairs in the hallway, or in the
strongest room.

I filled the car petrol tank at 3 pm, bought kerosene, batteries,
and matches. We filled hurricane lamps and put the primus on the
stove in case of power failure.

The fridge was full of delicious Christmas food so we hoped the
power wouldn't go off. What a nuisance it would be to have a mess in

the yard on Christmas day!

Our friends from the college, Kerry and Elaine, were in Brisbane for Christmas holidays, so we were minding their utility and their labrador, Torah. Simon roped the boat securely and put the Mazda and the utility under the house, and we put the guinea pigs in their cage and covered them securely. Simon bought Torah and Laika, our Labrador, upstairs at 10 pm.

Our neighbours over the back fence were a policeman, Lance, his wife Dagma and their baby, Karl. Dagma rang to see if we needed help, as Lance had seen Simon struggling with the heavy, frightened dogs. We reassured each other that our houses were 'battened down' with nothing more to be done and I joked that if her house landed in our back yard, we'd have coffee ready and vice-versa!

We read stories and the children, Vanya 3, and Dima 4, nodded off to sleep as normal. A Christmas surprise was bright new curtains and bright coloured bedroom stools in each of their rooms, along with the presents placed around the Christmas tree in the lounge.

We went to bed, but I couldn't sleep, so I got up and dressed in jeans and a winter shirt, as I felt goose bumps all over. I kept my ear to the radio, and the ABC Radio said that they would stay on air all night for the latest cyclone reports.

But they went off the air in the stormy conditions, about 1.15 am. The last report was that the cyclone was 28 kms northwest and travelling southeast at 6 kms per hour. It was expected to strike the coast in the early hours of the morning, we figured about 5 am, but of course it had already started.

The front door blew open at 1.30 am and the wind was so strong I couldn't force it shut. The door was solid jarrah and the knob had made a big hole in the wall. Simon wedged a chair behind it, but it didn't hold for long.

Simon kept an eye on the roofing iron, as the front corner was lifting, and he suspected we'd lose it all.

Dima woke up because of drips of water falling on his face.

The new curtains hung from door height, but the louvres went up to the ceiling, and although they were locked tightly, the rain was coming horizontal, reaching right across the room and the bedspread was getting wet, so we shifted the bed away from the window, but this really didn't help. Vanya woke up too, frightened when the manhole in his room blew up into the roof space, leaving a big dark hole. I was relieved to see the roofing iron was still on.

The curtains were dripping, the sea-grass matting was floating, and water was spreading quickly over the floor throughout the house. I had planned that Christmas day wouldn't involve hard work, so decided I would leave the curtains hanging at the windows to dry, but the matting was going to be a heavy job, and blow the beds being wet! I took the boys into our double bed, thinking they might go off to sleep again.

A branch came through the louvres, and the wind, even from that small hole was frightening, the curtains were blowing up against the ceiling. I drew them and put a spare mattress against the windows.

All this time Simon was busy checking things about the house and under the house. The boat had loosened and was rocking, but the cars were ok.

At 2 am, Vanya really wanted to go to the toilet, so I tucked Dima in with pillows all around, and off we went down the hallway. We had just started back when there was an almighty crash of exploding glass all along the front of the house. We sank to the floor and stayed in the toilet while Simon raced to get Dima. Actually, Dima was halfway up the hallway and got a fright banging into Simon in the dark. He had received a cut ankle from flying glass but was being very brave. We wrapped his bleeding ankle in a towel, and it soon stopped. Simon got more towels, pillows, cushions, lounge cushions, life jackets, and blankets for protection and warmth, so sitting it out in the toilet seemed quite snug.

The hurricane lamp helped to keep us warm and cheery, although we were all soaked, and the boys had towels wrapped around their pyjamas. Simon dragged all the mattresses up the hallway to outside the toilet in case the walls collapsed. I held Dima and Simon held Vanya till the lull at about 3.30 am, when it was relatively calm for 10 minutes.

While the children and I stayed in the toilet, Simon raced about the house doing everything, including bringing the dogs from the back balcony into the bathroom, putting electrical goods into cupboards, and he brought a jug of milk, water, lollies and cookies into the toilet. We reorganised the wet cushions about us and prepared for the long sit-in thinking the second half couldn't be as severe as the first half.

The second half of the cyclone came from a different direction but was much stronger and really rollicked the house. It reminded me of an old Melbourne train doing a very fast express and bouncing about, noise terrific, deafening. As schoolgirls in the 50's, we enjoyed the thrill of opening all the doors and windows of these express trains South Yarra to Caulfield.

The toilet wall was moving so much I couldn't rest my head against it. Simon and I had to mouth words, lean close and yell to communicate. Simon managed to get out every now and then and bring back reports of the destruction as it progressed. Dagma and Lance's house had gone, half of Peg and Vince's house had gone. Our end bedroom wall was gone, and the lounge room wall was holed. It seemed unbelievable, sitting in the warmth of the toilet, rocking, and patting the boys, telling them stories right into their ears so they could hear. They were half asleep and quite calm. My stomach by this stage was in a nervous knot and I felt like dry retching.

The whole roof of the Dental Clinic, next door, our planned alternative if our house went, had landed in our back yard upside down and iron was twisted around the big stringy barks. The three big Black Wattles had gone, and Simon could see all the way to the high-rise apartments in Millner.

At first light, about 5.30 Simon said he should go and check on Dagma, Lance and baby, as he could see their house was completely wiped off the floorboards. But as the wind was still so strong and noisy, I urged him to sit for another half an hour, I didn't want the boys to feel the wind and experience the trauma if Simon should have an accident.

Our side neighbours, Peg, Vince, and their baby had only half of their walls standing, and had struggled, getting repeatedly blown over, through the cyclone to the nearby school.

At 6 am Vince pounded on the toilet door and said we should leave the house and go over to the school; they had found a safe dry room. I looked out and saw things still flying through the air, the wind still battering, a car tyre bouncing past; I decided to dig back into the toilet with the boys for another half hour. I was worried the cyclone might turn back and strike again. Above all, I wanted to protect the boys from the sight and sound of it all.

I think the boys and I would have stayed in there all morning had not Lance, Dagma and baby pounded on the door at 6.30 am. They were in shock as they had lain on their bare floorboards, protected only by their bathtub full of water.

When we finally emerged, the sight up the hallway where the end wall had been and through where all the trees had been was unbelievable. We realized we were on a hill, and for miles over the suburbs could see nothing but the colour grey and black Stringybark trunks, stripped bare. The effect of an atomic bomb, a bush fire?

We found the only iron left on the roof was one sheet over the toilet, and that was the only room in which windows didn't break. The Masonite ceilings throughout the house were intact, although sagging with running water and the rain and wind were still strong.

As the primus was on the stove ready to use, everyone got a cup of coffee. The uncooked turkey came in handy Christmas morning. We filled a big preserving pan with rainwater and made turkey soup with onions, barley and all the available vegetables.

As the fridge had warmed, just about everything went into that soup. We had the soup for Christmas dinner with a glass of wine.

Actually, soup was about all anyone could swallow, as our mouths were dry with nerves and shock. We had to position our bowls and glasses between the waterfalls from the ceiling.

The boys seemed unscathed from the night, apart from being pale and shadowy eyed. They found their Christmas presents in a sodden heap in one corner along with the Christmas tree and heaps of glass and garden bits. They didn't seem to mind everything being wet and had wonderful adventures in the rubble in the yard later on.

Simon first put a tent up in Dima's room, which seemed the least damaged and had a waterproof floor. We used that as our dry room for the next two days. In this tent baby Karl at last got off to sleep on Christmas day and Vanya and Dima also had a sleep in the afternoon.

Dagma and Lance spent time searching the wreckage under and around their house and found the baby photo album. It was very wet. Lance found his wedding ring but couldn't find the car keys or his Police pistol. It took him and Simon ages to break the steering lock in order to get it on the road, then luckily they found the pistol too.

I packed everything that was still dry from the cupboards into big garbags, and later stored them in the tent.

The insides of the cupboards were flooding fast, and it was a very hard job heaving wet blankets, bedspreads, sheets and mattresses downstairs for drying whenever the sun came out.

Things were very dirty and covered with leaves and glass and twigs, but I had no time or energy or water for washing things, so dried them dirty and packed them into plastic garbags. In that humidity I didn't know how much would survive the mildew.

As it rained and blew most of Christmas day, it was rather drippy inside. Ours, and the house opposite were two of the few in the area that didn't sustain too much damage.

All the roofing iron was gone, but the roof structure was in good condition and ceilings intact. Simon walked miles for sheets of iron straight enough to put up over the kitchen and tent room.

We had to bore holes in our jarrah floor to let the water out.

By far the highlight of our Christmas day was when 'Wob', our wallaby, came home to check us out. We had nursed her from when she was tiny after her mother had been killed on the road. Dima had taken her to preschool, and she was very loved. She had grown strong and had disappeared a month or so earlier, although she was often spotted down near the creek.

Christmas day she was outside on the road. Simon went down and picked her up and brought her into the house. She had grown even more, and looked healthy, she jumped around the house and then left. She returned the next day and then must have made her break for freedom.

By far the worst of our Christmas day was when a friend came to tell us his 9-year-old daughter had been killed. Our policeman, Lance, said the worst thing for him that day had been digging a whole family out of the rubble in the northern suburbs. We all felt sad but didn't know at that stage that they were also our friends.

Christmas night was spent in the tent without mattresses or pillows. The boys were disturbed but very good. I was up dry retching most of the night, and there was a terrible storm, clanging iron, lightning, thunder, and the rain was heavy on the ceiling. We were dry in the tent, but it afforded little protection if the ceiling or fan fell on us.

So, Simon brought a ladder and placed it above the louvres and across to the hallway wall, beneath the fan, then brought in beams from the back yard rubble and criss-crossed them over the ladder. He then brought two doors from downstairs and placed them right on top. He was soaking wet and exhausted, but he'd got his energy from somewhere. He laid down and was soon asleep while my eyes stayed wide in absolute wonderment.

On Thursday, the 26th, Simon was up at first light, dressed in immaculate long white trousers and shirt, a whistle tied in his lapel, looking very official. He said he was going to 'get' a generator, or the meat in the deep freeze would have to be thrown out that day.

He came back beaming an hour later, and the sweet sound of a little Honda soon filled the house, and the deep freeze light was glowing. Apparently when questioned upon removing the generator from the show room window he gave his name, address and car number plate, and said it was urgently needed out at Casuarina, and the police were wanting to know if any more were available.

Yes, there were four more, so Simon informed Lance, and the police sent a car to the show room for them. Meanwhile a few of the neighbours brought their defrosting meat into our deep freeze.

Vince, our neighbour, worked for Shell, so late that evening Simon and he picked up a few 44-gallon drums of petrol for the generator and the cars, and some kerosene for the lamps and cooker.

That night, we spent a more comfortable night in the tent, because I'd managed to get camping mattresses and pillows dry, although there were more electrical storms and heavy rain.

On Friday 27th. Simon continued to roof over the bedroom, kitchen, hall, and part of the lounge, even though it was really hard to find straight sheets of iron.

This was great as the heavy rains came every night, despite the clear and sunny days. We took down the tent and put two single beds with camping mattresses into Dima's room.

Dima's 5th Birthday was surprisingly happy. We made a big fuss over a birthday cake that I'd had in the deep freeze as an extra.

We spent the day carrying water from everywhere and anywhere for washing dishes, clothes, floor, and for toilet flushing, and we went to Rapid Creek for a lovely dip and hair wash.

We put our names down for evacuation, as women and children amongst such devastation were only burdensome, and once the families were away, the men could get down to business. If we could have got water on we may have stayed, but it was suggested that the whole city might be bulldozed or burnt, so we weren't to know at the time.

Simon kept checking the lists out, and he took the officials cold beer from our deep freeze. The beer was dumped on our nature strip every evening by Lance who happened to hold the keys to the brewery, so Simon was able to keep many workers happy, even the Salvation Army. Later on, boxes of beer were put in the fridge at the Community College as there were lots of people sheltering there after Tracy. This was to be the start of the Darwin Community College Social Club.

On Saturday 28th, we were told we'd be off in the afternoon. Three cases of dysentery were reported in the area, so they were clearing the evacuation centre. We weren't allowed to take any baggage, so I packed a suitcase with everything treasured for Simon to mind if everything was bulldozed. Then I went on a quiet walk with the boys to feel and see odd things. We handled the tops of electricity poles, wires, and streetlights, and saw roofing iron wedged deep into tree trunks.

Vince was now living in our house, and soon was to be joined by our friends Kerry and Elaine, as their house in Wagaman had been completely wrecked

They had been in Brisbane but had given our address, so were allowed to return to Darwin. Our little VW which had been in the showroom for sale, had been undamaged and Simon got it back safe and sound.

Saturday at 1.30 pm we left for Rapid Creek School and waited till the bus came at 4.30 pm to take us to the airport. On the bus we waited till 5.30 pm before loading onto the RAAF Hercules. At first the boys thought it was a great adventure, strapped into hanging canvas seats, all squashed up.

But no one could move from their seat and with 250 other hot, tired mums and crying children, no toilet facilities, no drinks, food or windows, waiting in the heat and humidity was almost unbearable. We were shut inside the plane while all engines revved, and at about 7.30 pm the babies were bright red and exhausted, so the mums had to pass them up to RAAF staff who were walking high up along the beams, through to the front of the plane for fresh air and drinks.

Two hours later, about 9.30 pm, we finally took off and with the vibration and noise, it was like sitting the cyclone out all over again. The Hercules is certainly not designed for passengers, but everyone was very uncomplaining. The boys had 300 mls of milk each when little containers were passed around, and later, half an orange each. They were still asleep when hardboiled eggs were passed around. Despite having both arms around the boys, I successfully got most of the shell off and popped it into my mouth. Well, I thought I might suffocate, as I had no saliva, and the egg was seriously hardboiled.

I don't think any mums got any sleep, and after 7 hours we landed at Tullamarine at 4.30 am, Sunday 29th.

The poor fellows who opened the back of the plane must have been just as shocked at the hot stink that met their noses as we were with the freezing cold fresh air that hit ours. They passed blankets in, and we really did look like a lot of refugees walking across the tarmac. Police and volunteers were everywhere helping to carry kids. One young fellow came up to Peg and me and said, "Now, you're my family". He was designated to us.

Doctors were available for those needing them, and every woman had to get checked by a registered nurse. All we needed was knickers, as just about everyone had thrown theirs in the toilet bin and we were pleasantly surprised to receive $80 cash and some warm clothes.

Simon's brother Nick got rung up at 5 am and he came to get us. I hadn't realised I was tired until I couldn't remember Nick's phone number, his address or even his suburb. Luckily he was the only N. Andropov in the book. We smelt to high heaven and sitting in the back seat of the car, I couldn't apologise enough.

We all had a hot bath and the boys slept but I was overtired and stared at the ceiling for ages.

A few days later we went to stay with my parents at Maldon,

unsure for how long. Then, in February I had a call from Simon saying he was coming down to Maldon. He arrived two days later after driving almost non-stop from Darwin. Laika, our dog, had sat on the front seat with her head on his lap the whole way, enjoying lots of tinned meat from our Darwin cupboards.

We had a couple of weeks more fun in Maldon, and finally left on February 14 for the long drive back to Darwin. Getting back was an adventure in itself. The roads in Queensland were closed by flooding so we put the car on trains and trucks and flew back. Vanya spoke for all of us, as the plane was circling over Darwin. "Ah, it's good to be back in Darwin again!" he said.

David Baker
The Flying Maternity Ward
With Richard Creswick

Several years ago, while researching stories around Cyclone Tracy, I came across a website called The Professional Pilots Rumour Network (PPRuNe) and a thread started in 2012 by a poster with the username 'Fris B. Fairing'. He was seeking to document all of the airline movements involved in the evacuation of civilians immediately following Cyclone Tracy.

One item in particular caught my eye. It was posted by a person calling themselves 'Teresa Green'. This would seem to imply the poster was a woman, but another poster noted Teresa was a variation on 'Trees Are' (Green) indicating the person was probably a man with a sense of humour. Subsequently another almost identical post appeared in which Captain David Baker identified himself as the author of the original post. The first post is quoted below. Additional information is included in brackets.

Captain David Baker was on leave on the north coast of NSW when the cyclone hit but drove to Brisbane in response to TAA's urgent appeal for extra crews, as most of the line pilots were already flying their bids over the busy Christmas period.

Myself [Pilot in Charge] and another TAA Skipper landed in DRW [Darwin] at 1100 hrs on the 27th Dec. [actually the 26th] in VH-TFF a F27 [Fokker Friendship], with the sole purpose of picking up the Ladies [sic] about to give birth from the Darwin Hospital. I spoke to the Base Commander, Air

Commodore David Hitchins, and got help to clear a path to the aircraft, as the ambulances arrived. We left at 1324 with 40 last-stage pregnant ladies [much to our horror] 2CC [Cabin Crew], 2 Nursing Sisters and one doctor, 2 cats in cages [they belonged to the hospital] and my memories are the total carnage, a DC3 firmly implanted in the Base Commander's house, and the fridge in the water tower [30 metres up!]. It was all downhill from there. Two ladies were in labour, so we went straight to Isa, no joy there, they were already packed from those who went by car, so running out of hours and ideas, I called up Mackay, and pleaded [No, threatened] that we needed help, and finally got in there vastly relieved, as the noises up the back were becoming terrifying to say the least. The other pilot and myself staggered to the nearest pub, for fortification. We overnighted Mackay and after refuelling flew back to Brisbane on 27th December and resumed our leave and I of course somehow ended up with the cats, who both lived to a great age and cost a fortune in Vet bills. I never did find the owner. (We refuelled at both Tindal and Mt. Isa)

Strangely, a review of the *Mackay Daily Mercury* of the time, shows that the newspaper missed this extraordinary story. They have nothing but a brief reference to a Fokker Friendship carrying 30 pregnant women and 27 babies, without mentioning it landed in Mackay .*

Late in 2023, I tracked down Arlys Baker, herself a long-time TAA and QANTAS employee, who confirmed that her late husband, David Baker – he died in 2021 – was indeed the pilot-in-charge on this amazing evacuation flight.

Arlys said when David finally retired with 27,000 hours of flying time, he described it as the worst flight he had ever made. Both he and his co-pilot had well-exceeded their legal flying hours and were exhausted. Even though there was medical assistance on board, many of the pregnant women were Indigenous, and some had never flown before. Between the sounds of women in labour and the wails of fear, the flight was horrendous. Adding to that was the stress of running

---

*   *Mackay Daily Mercury*, thanks to Pam Zaglas, Mackay Regional Council Libraries

low on fuel – which was why he told Mackay he was going to land whether permission was granted or not.

Arlys said her husband was not only a highly experienced pilot, who later became a training and check captain, he was a strict observer of flight regulations, and there were a number of rule infractions that day about which he was concerned. But, she noted, the evacuation process was an extraordinary time for everyone involved and there were almost certainly other breaches of regulation during Australia's greatest peacetime evacuation.

Alan Barham

*Alan Barham and his sister Patricia were children at the time of Tracy.
Alan's father, George Barham was the acting Gaoler at Fannie Bay Gaol,
while his mother, Nancy was the matron for the female prisoners. They
lived in Buchanan Terrace, Nakara.*

On Christmas eve, Mum and Dad were babysitting my eldest
sister Margaret Blackadder's children, in our home at Buchanan
Terrace, Nakara. About 11pm, Margaret and her husband arrived to
pick up the children to head back to their home in Alawa and we
retired soon after.

A short time later we were woken by water coming in through
the closed louvres. We had only recently moved into this new house, so
I was concerned about water on the new carpet. Mum and Dad were
both awake and up as well, and we got towels out to start mopping up
the water. While walking out to the kitchen to wring out the towels
I noticed that the corner of the roof of the outside balcony area was
starting to lift and told my father.

Dad suggested Mum and my sister get dressed, but he and I
stayed in our pajamas. We then made our way down the back stairs
and under the house to our car. Dad tried to reverse out to make our
way across the street to the Nakara Primary School. It was a brick
building and we thought that it would be a better place to shelter, but
the car would not reverse.

Dad was reluctant to drive forward as the backyard had newly
planted lawn and was boggy. He then told us to get out of the car,

as he was afraid of something being blown through its windows. We made our way to the laundry/storeroom area and my sister, and I sat in a cupboard and Dad shut the door. A short while later we noticed the back brick wall of the storeroom starting to flex and move, so we got out of the cupboard and moved into the laundry area. The laundry was open at one end with open breeze blocks at the other end. Dad used the door from the storeroom, which swung into the laundry, to block as much as was possible the wind and rain from impacting us.

During the cyclone's lightning flashes we could see wood and roofing iron being blown about. During one of these flashes of light we saw the roof of our house lying in our back yard. We were very much aware of the change of wind direction as the wind was now blowing directly onto the door that Dad was holding open. It was relentless – the eye missed us in Nakara. Dad held that door against the wind from approximately 0130 to 0530. Dad and I were both still in our pajamas and it was very cold.

When the wind started to die down (I think roughly 0530) we made our way out of the laundry and found the car was intact, without damage, we sat in it for about an hour to try to warm up and take stock of what had happened. There was roofing iron under the back wheels of the car, so it was blocked in.

As soon as we could, we started to walk to my sister's place in Alawa. On the way my brother in-law, who was on his way to get us in his work truck and picking his way through the rubbish on the roads, found us and we set off back to their place. When we arrived there everyone was safe. Their walls were still standing but there was no roof. After assessing everything we used the truck to drive to Delaney's Produce Store, their business in Stuart Park. We were relieved to see the store still had its roof on. Mum and Dad then went to Fannie Bay Gaol to assess the damage and start organizing things. I don't know where he found them, but Dad ended up with some dry clothes.

Christmas night was spent in the shop. The women and children slept on the back tray of the truck, and the men slept on chaff bags. We could hear rats scurrying about in the roof, but at least it was dry. We stayed there for some time.

Sue Barrel

Sue moved from Port Moresby to Darwin in late 1971 after her husband, Trevor was promoted to a job there with the Commonwealth Department of Works. She was employed by the same department as a library assistant, and she worked there until their first child, Gene, was born in July 1972. Their second child, Nathan, was born in 1974. They lived in Malay Road, Wagaman.

We were a typical Darwin family. While my husband went to work, I worked at home, keeping the household running and looking after our small children, a daughter 2, and a son 8 months. In addition, we had three guests for Christmas from 'down south': our nephews Carl Looper aged 13, Shane 11, and Paul 9 . We lived in a new, low set, house, built on a concrete slab in Malay Road, across from the Wagaman Primary School playing fields.

Our story begins a day or two earlier when the first warnings came over the radio and TV. Who can forget the sound of that siren? But there had been a similar warning three weeks before, so we really didn't take much notice. Overnight the sky became very cloudy and as December 24th progressed it got darker and darker, and started to rain.

The warnings continued to blare out of the TV, and although we were beginning to take it more seriously, we sat down to dinner and followed the usual nightly routine of putting the little ones to bed and enjoying the company of the older boys. When they went to bed we stayed up for a while longer. As the wind became stronger and began forcing rain through the glass louvres and across the room, we became more and more alarmed.

By 10 pm the wind had become very strong, and we could hear the nails in the roof sheeting starting to pull out of the beams. We woke the older boys and got them to put their shoes on, got the little ones up, and we all headed for the bathroom, the smallest room in the house, as advised in the warning messages. When the power went off, seven hours of fear then numbness began, as we accepted that we might not survive.

The boys were head-to-toe in the bathtub, we were on our knees and elbows, each holding a small child against our chests, my head was under the basin and my husband's bottom and feet against the door. The noise from the wind and the sound of the roof tearing off and debris hitting the house was like standing on the tarmac behind a 747 with its engines roaring. The flooding rain soaked the ceiling lining and it fell down to rest on the basin and the side of the bathtub. This was lucky, as it provided some protection from whatever the wind carried our way.

We communicated with the boys by yelling as loud as we could, checking on them regularly to make sure they were OK. When they told us they could feel something warm dripping on them, we were afraid one of them had been cut and was bleeding, but it was the warm water from the hot water system that had once been on the roof. Our little ones, sensing that this was a serious situation, remained quiet without complaining, even during the days that followed.

We could hear glass breaking and in the bright flashes of lightning see large parts of the house being torn away. Something that we laughed about, afterwards, was the smell of the various flavours of alcohol as the bottles broke in the high cupboard on the other side of the bathroom wall and the contents blew down on us. Also, our collection of expensive glassware was totally destroyed but the cheap glass wine decanter survived.

Eventually, the wind died down. It became eerily quiet, and we knew it must be the eye of the storm. It did not last long and when the wind came back, it came from the opposite direction. Silently, we stayed in our 'shelter' and waited for it to end.

As dawn broke the winds slowly subsided and the worst was over. We pulled the soggy ceiling sheeting apart so we could all sit up. We were unsure whether to go out or not.

Our elbows and knees were numb, we were completely wet, and we could see the sky above us. Eventually, we heard people walking across the debris, asking if there was anyone in what was left of the house. We called out to let them know we were all OK and were advised to go to the largely undamaged Wagaman Primary School which would provide a dry place to stay.

As we stood up we saw many holes in the bathroom door caused by wind-blown debris. The holes were above the level of our car, that was parked next to the hallway wall. This had prevented injuries to my husband's behind. Both our cars were sand blasted down to bare metal by the wind.

Outside, we saw that our entire world had changed. Although three walls of our bedroom were gone, the wall containing the wardrobe remained and we expected to find some dry clothing. However, opening the doors, we found everything soaking wet.

We checked on our friends next-door. They were all uninjured, and they had some dry clothes that were suitable for us all, as they also had a young daughter. (I returned the very brief denim shorts given to me by this friend on her 50th birthday, 27 years later, much to her surprise – neither one of us could fit into them by then.)

Planning to go to the school, we loaded the kids into my husband's work car, and it started, but we did not get very far as the driveway and street were covered in sheets of galvanised roofing and other pieces of houses. All the fences along the street had twisted roofing sheets draped over them.

The school had been constructed in two sections, one of classrooms and the other open plan, with a tuckshop and covered open area next to it. We settled in a vacant part of the open plan area and were soon surrounded by hundreds of others.

It was interesting to observe how different people handled the situation. Human nature was revealed, bringing out the good and the bad. A man who worked in the same office as my husband, and was known for being somewhat unfriendly, rose to the occasion and did an amazing job of organising the food supply. He had us pass the word around that if our fridges were still closed the food in them would be suitable to eat. Almost everyone had roast ham or chicken and other dishes cooked on Christmas Eve, because dinner was usually served cold in that hot climate.

Food soon began arriving, with people bringing anything they could find to feed themselves and contribute to feeding others. The boys watched the two little ones while we went back to the house and foraged for food left in our fridge and kitchen cupboards. Fortunately, this included tins of baby food and a large bottle of orange juice.

The man organising the food broke into the tuckshop to get large pots. Firewood was collected and a large fire was built in the open area and cooking began. It was no fancy recipe, just a big mulligan stew, with whatever meat and vegetables were available tossed in. As the pots emptied, they were refilled, and the cooking started again. This continued for days.

The next day, an Army truck arrived with food, sanitary products for the women, nappies, and cartons of cigarettes. When an Army water tanker arrived, we lined up with any containers we could find, and filled them with potable water. We were instructed to take turns guarding the truck with a rifle the soldiers left with us, and I took my turn. Sitting on a folding chair, I held the gun very gingerly because I had never held one before. I did not know whether the safety lock was on or off, or even where it was. I was much relieved when my 'tour of duty' was over.

We had been advised that looters would be shot on sight, and during the first night at the school, when we heard gun shots in the distance, we thought it was really happening.

It turned out that abandoned pets were being put down as there was nowhere to shelter them nor any food to feed them. We were relieved that no humans were being harmed but felt sorry for the people charged with this task.

The food and drinking water were sorted but as there was no water supply to the school, the toilets could not be flushed and were soon overflowing. Now, anyone who has served in the military would be familiar with the field manual on how to set up camp to accommodate hundreds, including latrine arrangements. Whoever oversaw taking care of this very necessary facility had obviously not studied that manual.

Instead of a long, narrow and deep trench that a person could simply stand over with a foot on either side, a large bulldozer arrived and scooped out a very big hole, at least 15ft wide, 15ft long and 15 ft deep. Star pickets were placed around this hole with hessian fabric attached to provide a modesty screen. Turns out there is no modesty while squatting at the edge of a big hole, trying not to fall in while doing your business.

Also on the second day, an army sergeant arrived and set up a table and chair, then asked if anyone had a typewriter. I had a portable one that had survived intact and provided it to him. He advised all of us that he was going to take down names and phone numbers of people down south who could be contacted and given a brief message to let them know we were OK. The lists would be flown to Alice Springs and the calls made from there. The army still owes me one portable typewriter.

My parents were staying in the USA and both my Australian nana and American grandmother were with them for Christmas. The west coast of the US was 18 hours behind us, and that meant that they woke up on their Christmas morning, turned on the TV news, and saw the first film of Darwin after the cyclone. It would be three days before they got the message that we had survived.

Afterwards they told us those were the longest days of their lives.

Our message went to a family member and then to my husband's parents in Brisbane, where our nephews' mother was also waiting.

During the night of the cyclone, my husband held onto a briefcase that contained all his paperwork and our passports. He had planned a trip to the US for his long service leave starting in February 1975. We would stay with my parents for several months. The first thing I asked him when we had settled at the school was 'would we still be going?'. The answer was yes.

The roads were cleared quickly, and my husband was able to drive into the office each day as his department was one of those responsible for getting power and water back on, plus clearing all the debris and many other public works that were required.

I looked after the kids during the day, the only drama being when one of the boys stepped on a nail that went through his shoe into his foot. Fortunately, there were tetanus shots available. My husband looked after the kids at night while I, who could not sleep, helped the nurse on duty look after those with injuries. I learned how difficult it is to help an older person, on crutches with a broken leg in a cast, to use a pit 'latrine'.

Four days after the Cyclone my husband took us into his office building which had not been very severely damaged. The huge water tanks on the roof were still full so the toilets flushed and the boilers in the tearooms held water we could drink.

We had a whole room to ourselves, with dry carpet to sleep on. Such luxury. We also found packets of instant soup, lollies and other treats when foraging through desks for which we thank those unknown occupants.

On the fifth day we were told to go to the YMCA to be put on an evacuation list. Buses came and we were loaded on and taken to the airport. My husband made it in time to say goodbye through the bus window. We did not know when we would see him again.

We were allowed one suitcase per family. Our photo albums

had survived in a cupboard, slightly water damaged but otherwise intact, so they went into the suitcase along with a christening blanket, knitted by Nana when I was born, plus a few other treasures found among the debris.

We flew out on a TAA plane. It was very clean and staffed by cabin crew in their immaculate uniforms. The passengers were packed in, the six of us sharing three seats, and having not showered for five days, the smell was malodourous, a mixture of fear and unwashed bodies. The flight attendants ignored it and did an amazing job of sharing out food and drink during the five-hour flight to Brisbane.

When we arrived, we were bussed to a government depot in Fortitude Valley where food and toiletries were provided. It was wonderful to wash faces and hands and brush our teeth. Salvation Army volunteers looked after the kids so we mothers could clean up. We were then given funds, so much per family, to buy clothing and other necessities in the coming days.

A taxi then drove us into Brisbane. We dropped the three nephews at their grandparents' house, where their mother, from Canberra, was also waiting and then went to my family home where my brother and his wife were staying while our parents were overseas.

We found clothing and nappies that had already been dropped off there by several friends. The little ones were bathed, dressed in new clothes, and put to bed. I then had the best shower I have ever had, before or since, and donned clean clothes. The top and shorts I had been wearing for days went to be washed while the sandals that had walked through a lot of dirt and other things, were immediately relegated to the bin. Sinking into a real bed with fresh sheets was the best feeling ever.

When I went to the chemist the next day, the staff took one look at me and asked if I was from Darwin. I had weighed eight and a half stone (54 kg) but then lost two stone (12 kg) in that week, so was looking a bit thin, drawn, and tired. I collected some toiletries and make-up, but they refused to let me pay.

A close friend loaned me her car. The generosity of people was amazing.

My husband arrived seven weeks later, and two weeks after that we left for the US where my parents looked after the little ones while we went on a long road trip, just what we needed to help heal the trauma of Tracy.

My husband got called back to Darwin to work in the Reconstruction Commission, while I stayed in the US, his boss having told me that it was no place for small children. We were reunited in Brisbane several months later, built a house and have lived there ever since.

My husband's job took us back to Darwin twice, once in 1978 for three months and again in 1979 for eight months. It was wonderful to see most of the town restored to its pre-Tracy condition and all the new houses out in the suburbs.

The most important lesson we learned from this experience was to live each day to the full, as you never know when it might be your last.

Figure 4: Wagaman (NT Dept of the Housing & Construction Collection 1975, LANT ph0026-0125.)

Fiona Bekkers

In 1983, Fiona's mother handed her a letter she had found when clearing out some papers. It was headed "16 Dudley Street (or what's left of it!), Nightcliff. Saturday evening, December 28, 1974" and was to be delivered by her evacuated sons to tell relatives interstate about the ordeal. It took a while for it to be delivered…

Just a quick note for the boys to take with them when they go sometime tonight or tomorrow (we hope). You know the catastrophe that has befallen Darwin and also that we are comparatively well off. Can imagine how worried you must have been about us, and there was no way we could let you know we were safe. I sent a telegram at the first opportunity but apparently you did not get that (story is that some drunk tore up the sheets everyone had written their messages on!) so just as well I sent another yesterday. And then Peter went to town this morning in response to an appeal from his department and managed to phone his mother.

As I said, we were lucky. We have lost the roof off the living room, kitchen, bathroom, and toilet, but that part over the three bedrooms is intact and the study is quite unharmed. We have not lost a plate or dish – the linen cupboard and the cupboard in our room got wet, in fact everything seems damp, and I spend a lot of time running in and out between showers trying to dry blankets, cushions, clothing etc. Just about all our trees (no more mangoes!) are down, so there is plenty of hanging space!

The living room wall is full of holes and the lining has collapsed inside, there is a huge hole in the kitchen, and the toilet wall and storeroom below must have been hit by something big. We can't use the toilet as the pedestal is off its mountings, so we go next door which is practically demolished – no bedrooms left, roof off the sitting room, but kitchen intact.

The neighbours on the other side have lost their roof so are sleeping with us and eating here. With no water, power, or sewerage and with eleven people things aren't easy.

Someone has given us a generator, so we have power for lights, and we have to go to various watering points for water. All drinking water is boiled on the barbecue where we also do our cooking. We've run out of fresh food and went over to the communal kitchen at Nightcliff High School to eat last night but have decided it would be more hygienic to eat out of tins at home. There is plenty of food and more coming in all the time.

We had to register for evacuation in the beginning and we had to re-register again today. We want to get the two younger boys away and I hope to come on Monday. Peter and John will stay until something can..."

But here the wind snatched the pages away and they were not found and posted until January 24, 1975. Fiona wrote the following more recently: The story of Cyclone Tracy really began some three weeks before when Cyclone Selma came within 55 kilometres of Darwin then veered north and passed harmlessly over Bathurst Island, bringing strong winds but little damage. An inspection of our roof prompted my husband, by a stroke of genius as it turned out, to double the insurance on the house. He was not impressed by the security of the nails attaching the corrugated iron to the timber battens and added a few of his own, at the same time re-bolting iron reinforcing bars that had been removed when we built a brick, air-conditioned study beneath the end bedroom.

Freda Brocker

Freda Brocker lived with her husband Nick, who worked for Darwin Colour Centre in Bishop Street and their baby daughter, Brenda. Freda was injured in the storm, and evacuated on the first Hercules to Brisbane, with many others who were injured.

We were going to have visitors over for Christmas Day, so I was busy getting things ready. Our daughter, Brenda 2, had been sick, so I had taken her to the doctor's that day to be told she had tonsilitis.

That night, as the wind got stronger, I was knitting a pink and white cardigan for Brenda with the television on, because they were going to televise the midnight mass from St Mary's Cathedral. But about 11 pm, the wind was so strong they told people to go home, a cyclone was imminent.

I didn't understand what the word meant, so I decided to put a thermos of hot water in the sink so, if the power went out, we could have a cup of coffee in the morning.

Then when the wind became very strong, I thought I had better wake my husband, Nick, and take Brenda to find a safe place to stay. First, we got under the bed in Brenda's room, thinking we would be safe, but we heard the sound of tin being ripped off the roof above us. We took the mattress and went to the toilet because they had told us it was the safest room. What we didn't know was the roof at the back of the house was about to blow off. All of a sudden there was an almighty crash into the wall of the toilet. The roof smashed in, and my leg was slashed by some tin.

I threw Brenda onto the mattress. Nick picked her up, screaming, and went to phone the police. No phone… no phone table… chairs everywhere. Everything was out in the back yard.

I ran after I was hit, but I don't know how I got out. I fell over in the mud but got up to run to Nick's work ute. We all got in, but then the windscreen shattered, so we escaped to our own car. We got into the back seat with Brenda on the floor, me on top of her, then Nick above us both. The car wouldn't start, but just as well because there were power lines across our driveway.

When it got lighter Nick looked at my leg and tore a piece off my dress and tied it around the cut. He said he would walk to the police station while I stayed in the car with Brenda. A little while later two guys came round and offered me wine.

Nick came back and this time the car started.

I don't know how I got there, but the next thing I remember I was in bed in the hospital. I believe they tried to put stitches in my leg and told me that I was being sent to Sydney.

I was flown out on the first Hercules. There were lots of people on stretchers, and doors being used as stretchers. On the plane I lay in one of them. There was someone above me on another stretcher. On the way it was decided that the plane was to go to Brisbane, not Sydney.

I thought my daughter Brenda was safe with my husband back in Darwin, but unbeknown to me, the pilot of the plane had told him to put her on the plane as well, so he could stay and help other people in Darwin.

In Brisbane I was taken by ambulance to the Royal Brisbane Hospital and had an operation on my leg. Meanwhile, without me knowing, Brenda was given to a Salvation Army lady named Beulah Harris. All Brenda had on was a nappy and a tag around her leg with her name on it, but she too, arrived in Brisbane safely.

While I was in hospital she stayed with John and Eva Fischle, a

Salvation Army family. They brought her into the hospital to see me while I was there, and when I came out, I stayed with them, at their place.

I went back to Darwin with Brenda on March 19, 1975, but I couldn't handle it with a 2-year-old. We only stayed for three days

Figure 5: Brenda Johnson (nee Brocker), aged 2, about to be evacuated on the Hercules. She was cared for by Beulah Harris, of the Salvation Army (Photo courtesy of Brenda Johnson).

before we all went back to Brisbane.

There, we decided it was best if we left Brenda with Eva and John again and returned to help out in Darwin. We picked her up later in June 1975.

While I had been in hospital, Nick had helped out at Ludmilla School, giving out food. After that, he went to Katherine and had a job making sure people had a permit to enter Darwin. At that time only Darwin residents with somewhere to live were allowed back in. He then worked in Darwin moving caravans around and checking people had somewhere to live.

Eva and John Fischle were like a nan and pop for us, until they passed away. We still keep in touch with one of their family, Grace.

Anne Brooks

Anne and her husband Chris were living in a half-built bush house at Howard Springs and had celebrated the arrival, four days before, of Chris's sister Liz, brother-in-law Nick and their three children, Michelle, Richard and Louise, who were immigrants from Kenya. Their luggage arrived a few days later but ended up spread to the four winds.

That fateful night we were invited to party at Barb and Viktor's place in Fellows Road, Howard Springs. At this stage the cyclone was expected to hit our area badly, but not impact Darwin so much. Uncle Eddy Dias pleaded with us to come and shelter in his house in Parap. Thank goodness we didn't. His family ended up in the bathroom. The rest of the house was destroyed, and we would have gone with it.

The winds really picked up around eight, along with the frivolity. Paul and Giselle were there as well with their newborn baby. Around nine I phoned my parents in Canberra, "Ringing to wish you a happy Christmas. Bad weather here with a cyclone on the way. The phones lines will probably go down but don't worry about us, we will be fine."

The lines went down shortly afterwards, and huge trees now blocked our escape. We sheltered in a demountable used as a bedroom. All six adults and seven children including the newborn baby. Viktor and Chris stood guard all night in the kitchen, hammers, and rum at the ready.

"German built, this place, Brooksie", boasted Viktor.

He was right. The winds howled and the demountable swayed but stayed on its supports. We survived the night reassured by the late-night presenter on the ABC urging us to "Stay calm Darwin. We will get through this together." Then around midnight a frantic call came over the radio: "We have to go. The roof's caving in." Footsteps echoing, smashing sounds and then an eerie silence. We were alone. Just us and the raging tempest outside.

Looking back on that night, I recall the fear and the feeling of helplessness as I lay on that bed cradling the four-year-old Sonya. I tried to distract my vivid imagination from dwelling on impending doom and the stacks of sheeting iron and other building supplies stored by Viktor up the hill. I had us all decapitated as the wind picked them up and used them as guillotines. Little did I know that families in Darwin were facing that exact danger as they ran for shelter dodging the missiles from their shattered houses.

Dawn saw relief and the chooks from the farm down below sailing up the hill, legs outstretched like paper planes in the jetstream. Once we managed to remove trees from the road Chris and I went back to see our bush house. Not much to see. Roof gone, just a few uprights. One with the telephone. It was ringing. Very strange since communication lines were down.

It was my friend Pam from McMinns Lagoon. She had escaped any damage.

"How are you? How is your house?"

"No house. Just a few posts and the telephone."

"Don't exaggerate Anne". The lines went dead.

I consoled Chris. "Don't worry, we still have our house in Moil. We will just have to move in with the newly wed Lois and Bruce. All seven of us. They'll be happy."

We had no idea that Darwin had been reduced to rubble. Imagine the shock when Viktor and Chris finally fought their way through fallen power lines to reach Moil. They described it as a war zone with shell-shocked people moving around.

Lois and Bruce had survived a night from hell cowering under their bed, the roof and half the house ripped away. Neighbours Denise and Glen much the same. Denise was eight months pregnant and was one of the first evacuees when the airport was cleared.

One upside was we had generators and scored gourmet Christmas food from our friends. About a week later Liz, Michelle, Richard, Louise, and I were flown out on a US Air Force Starlifter to Sydney. We were greeted like heroes and showered with goodies before travelling on to Canberra to my parents' home.

From there we went to 'Reynella' at Adaminaby, home of my brother John Rudd and his wife Roslyn who gave us wonderful care. Chris and Nick stayed to clean up and find us somewhere to come back to.

My story is trivial compared to that of many Darwinites who lost their house and loved ones. I can't imagine the horror they suffered running for their lives. That trauma will never leave them, and many could not face returning to our city. I didn't spend the night running and dodging missiles and my heart goes out to them. So many stories of bravery, resilience and tragedy.

Keith Bushnell

Keith arrived in Darwin in April 1972 to become a contract film cameraman for ABC TV News and other programs. His film of Tracy's destruction was the first to reach the outside world and won him the inaugural Thorn Award for television news film. It is also the film shown as part of the Cyclone Tracy exhibit at the NT Museum and Art Gallery.

Sure, we'd all heard the weather reports, for weeks, on and off. There had been a cyclone pass by only three weeks earlier. That one was also around for long enough to have earned the name 'Selma', but it had come with the associated warnings and gone like so many do, every wet season.

Through the door of The Don Hotel we could see the downpour. Some of the drinkers must have quit work early or like me were enjoying a long lunch with a Christmas party atmosphere. As well as some of the ABC's journos and other Post Bar regulars, I had in my company an old friend from South. Toni, an ABC employee from Adelaide had come for a holiday and was experiencing Darwin for the first time.

As I may have explained to my guest, the Cyclone called Tracy had been to the North of Bathurst and Melville Islands for a few days, while trending generally south west and for this cyclone to hit us with something like a bullseye, it would have to travel right around the west coast of the islands which, in effect, protected us, turn hard left before changing course to make a gentle right turn at just the *wrong* place in order to meet Darwin's coastal suburbs.

You'd never bet on such a sequence but, as we now know that's pretty much exactly what happened.

In a sober moment that afternoon, it occurred to me that, cyclone or not, it was probable that the electricity would be off during Christmas Day, if not sooner. The power supply, in those days, was susceptible to 'outages' and every wet season, streets or whole districts would be unplugged for unpredictable periods. I had a leg of lamb at home, planned for roasting on the morrow but, with the weather looking like it did, I proposed that we depart forthwith, head back to my place and prepare for our feast right away.

This was agreeable to Toni and her cousin, who also joined us at my third floor flat in Voyager Street, Stuart Park. Even then in the early evening it was raining, and gusts of wind pushed even a loaded Land Cruiser around.

Toni reckoned that we should heed the warnings that were being broadcast and bring in any loose objects from outside. Rubbish bins, of course and the 16mm film-processor was duly tied down on the balcony, still attached by way of garden hoses in and out but also fixed to the cast iron balcony railing.

We must have been home early enough to do it all because we enjoyed a fine meal, which included sparkling burgundy, supplied by my thoughtful friends.

I was sure we'd made the right decision about having our Christmas dinner early because although the louvred windows were tightly shut the candles flickered quite violently on the table – even needing shielding and re-lighting at times. I remember, when visiting the bathroom, seeing the water level rising and falling several inches in the toilet bowl. I'd never noticed anything quite like that before.

Things were crashing about, outside. Palm fronds, probably, but they're very weighty items and moving at speed, would certainly make some impact.

Toni's cousin, also a recent arrival in Darwin, became concerned about her own flatmates and wanted to be taken home.

During that excursion, which must have been about 10 pm, I saw that this was indeed a serious storm. There was little traffic and with stuff flying about in the gale where one could see very little past the windscreen wipers it must have been a risky trip.

Back at my place, close to midnight, Toni and I exchanged Christmas gifts. Mine was a Charlie Rich cassette tape that I didn't get to play because the power had already gone out. Not long after that there was quite a crash against a wall in the main bedroom.

Toni went for a look and approaching the direction from which the storm was coming, was concerned enough to hold a pillow against herself as she faced the window.

The glass was still intact, but she reported a large tear in the fly screen, beyond the louvres. I was about to have a look but standing in the hallway area and by hand-sheltered candlelight, I also saw trouble coming; I called Toni to "come and look at this". Above me, the ceiling in the lounge was 'floating', moving up and down a handful of inches. I expected there couldn't have been much in the way of roof above that and wondered would you hear it if your roof took off?

And then, in the same time it took to blow out the only candle, the ceiling disappeared, and some wall and glass fell inwards. It was a candlelit lounge room one moment and a big black hole, the next.

Automatically, we scrambled to get out of the rain, or save things from the storm and aware of the fragility of my new, *you-beaut* colour TV, I moved to wrestle with it when something told me not to bother. There was nowhere it could go.

Throughout the evening the storm had been banging away at our south side and the louvred glass wall flew into the room in many pieces. We dropped whatever we were carrying and scuttled into the second bedroom, which was across the hall and as far north as we could go.

I forced the door closed against the blast, shoving glass and small debris as it went. This door was hardly going to keep out much of anything because above us, and by the illumination of lightning, we saw there was only sky covering that room as well. The only space to have any cover over it was the built-in wardrobe.

As much because she was in the way, I shoved Toni into that wall cupboard and squeezed in beside her. There was just enough room to sit with legs folded or knees up to chin. I had the cupboard doors as closed as they would go while still leaving room for my fingers to hold them. And despite my direction to 'just run for it or make yourself invisible' Toni had carried with her my old Cine Special 16mm camera (It had never shot anything 'serious' for me, before or since, but it was dear to me, *even as a doorstop* and she knew it).

Through that inch-gap held by back-to back knuckles we watched a lightning-lit sky where my rented apartment used to be. My back was pressed hard against the rear of the cupboard: a rather flimsy structure although there should have been three walls between us and the gale, so where had they gone? The plywood back of this cupboard, motivated by the wind, punched and pushed us in the back for the next five or six hours. We could retreat no further. I tried to imagine what might become of us if the cupboard managed to detach itself from whatever still anchored it.

Always aware that we were on the top floor of a building which was coming undone, I told Toni that she should hang onto my leg because whatever happened, I wasn't going to let go of these cupboard doors and assuming that they stayed attached to the cupboard, where it was going, so was I. This was my only plan.

I don't recall us having anything like a serious conversation during the night. Except to say, that she had nothing to worry about because we were 'as safe as houses' in here which wasn't really funny, but Toni was a brick, and if you could say that that was 'facing death with a smile', I reckon that's what we were prepared for.

There really was nothing else to do but hang on and watch for any change, imagining the worst, which in our case the most likely would be coming to earth, still hanging on to some part of a flying cupboard.

The noise for those next few hours was like large trains thundering past with the occasional jet plane screaming through. But relentless and without a break. I also I had some thoughts for the cheapskate-builders of these units. Why me?

Having been a news cameraman for about 15 years, there were many times I'd been sent out to film 'The Aftermath'. Assignment boards would read; 'Fire aftermath; Flood aftermath' or (in our case) 'Storm aftermath' and off I'd go to film the pitiable and/or luckless victims of various Acts of God for that night's News. When I got there, passers-by might be standing in whispering groups; or neighbours, with arms around shoulders, talking bravely to cheer up the unfortunates who'd lost their roof or had their home speared by a tree or were flooded when the river rose – whatever it was.

Whatever it might have been, this time, God love us, it was me! Christ, would the ABC come around to my place and film *me* climbing out of my el-cheapo apartment in soaking wet clothes? How embarrassing. How undignified.

I learned later that most people imagined that it was only their place which was breaking up in this particular wet-season storm. You see, for the participants if it's just your place that falls over, it's a storm. Only in the light of day, only when you find that the whole neighbourhood was blown away do you know you were hit by a cyclone.

Another thing I was to discover: some people experienced a lull in the storm, a period when the wind actually died altogether only to find that it soon blew in from the opposite direction – and just as strongly. That would be the eye of the storm. Not so at my place. We experienced no 'eye'. Unless I 'slept' through it?

By the very first light of dawn, about 6 am, the wind had shifted around – not so much punching us in the back as trying to pull the doors from my grip – as it died in fits. For a while I thought I might loosen my grasp, have a peek out, and then the winds would almost rip them from me again. I held on. We outlasted them. Through the crack, past my fists, I saw that devil off into the sky and away from us. And we were still here.

I can't speak for my friend's first impressions, but I was stunned. I climbed very carefully from the cupboard space, steadying against a wall, hanging onto a door, whatever was closest but always moving toward the outside. I stepped through pools of water washing around lots of broken glass.

Two heavy roofing beams had crossed each other and rested on my colour TV and Charlie Rich was swimming under there somewhere but we, in wet clothes, had not a scratch on us. No *physical scars*. But if, anytime, somebody asks me to describe what I know about PTSD, I can now point to those torturous hours on the brink.

Wind and rain still blew in gusts, enough to frighten me when I found myself on the balcony. It was now missing the iron railing that I could've held on to yesterday. The railing had been ripped out of the concrete, leaving a rubble-strewn, rough-edged path about three feet wide.

Lifting my eyes from this precarious platform, the next unforgettable view was of a world with very little foliage. Here in tropical Darwin, one accepted lush growth as part of every scene. Not this morning. Not only had every leaf and frond been removed from sight but many whole trees too. I don't remember what particular trees had lived in my street, but I noticed that they weren't there anymore.

This is when I first saw that we'd been in a cyclone. I crept past next door's flat, hugging the wall (which was not an easy thing to do, I discovered).

A large part of the outside brick wall had fallen into the car park and a sizeable slab rested on the bonnet of my Land Cruiser. I pushed off the bricks, but she wouldn't start. Later that morning it did start but at the time, I believe it too had been 'in shock'.

The house on stilts, downwind from us, had gone. The stilts supported what looked like a polished, wooden dance floor, ten feet above the ground. The rest of the house was scattered downwind. I wondered if people had died around here. I saw no bodies – but nor did I look for any.

Below me lived a QANTAS steward. In the yard we found him, accompanied by friends or neighbours, beside a Christmas tree. They were wet and shocked, and everybody was drinking duty-free rum. Toni remembers me drinking some rum before leaving.

One of the men tried his car, and it started, and we agreed to drive away from there together, to see what we could see. We picked our way along the roads, between thousands of sheets of twisted iron. I'd get out of the car frequently and drag some off the road or lift power lines that dangled from twisted poles, over the car .*

Five minutes away, downtown, at the corner of Knuckey and Cavenagh Streets, there was something of an electrical/hardware-type shop. It appeared relatively intact, except the plate-glass window was smashed and a couple of people were there already, carrying stuff that might have come from that shop. A youth rode a brand-new bicycle in wide circles on the intersection – a bike that might have been a Christmas present. We said nothing to them, and they didn't seem to mind us driving by. It was still quite early, and I saw no one else on foot.

A cruise around town revealed the Anglican Cathedral largely caved in, and the equally ancient, sandstone Naval HQ on the Esplanade was a write-off. There was a ringing noise all around and as we moved through this dream it became clear that it was not just ringing in my ears: it got louder as we approached the corner of Bennett and Smith Streets and emanated from the Reserve Bank. Right opposite the police station, the alarm was ringing at the bank and the heavy, glass door seemed to be open, but there was no other soul in sight. 'Nobody was home' around here. It was weird.

Having seen that much of Port Darwin had taken the hiding,

---

* Keith had taken his CP16 film camera, and it was this film which was the first seen by the rest of Australia the following night – Ed.

we drove out to the airport and saw many light aircraft up-ended and variously tossed about. I shot some film as I went, more like a 'machine on automatic' than a cameraman

Ok, I thought, if our end of town had suffered so badly, there'd be lots of scrambling for alternate beds that night. Now I'm starting to think clearly, why not head out to the northern suburbs, where the ABC owned a number of staff houses and get in line for boarding?

We picked our way along Bagot Road, northbound, and I noticed a lot more traffic heading into town. They'd obviously heard about the smashed city and were coming in to have a look around, even on Christmas morning, even while it was still raining. My first thought was 'ghouls' but all of a sudden I shivered (and still do, at the memory): *all* of this traffic couldn't be coming into town to have a sticky-beak.

My God, could they have been blown away, too? Could they be homeless and looking to us for help? This could look like an exodus. If so, we could be in BIG trouble. That's a time when I was frightened.

Having discovered that the northern suburbs had, indeed, been comprehensively smashed we returned to Stuart Park and went our separate ways. I don't think I had ever met my driver before that day and have not seen him since.

Back at Stuart Park, I climbed up the still-scary flights and found Toni, no ceiling and not much roof above her, cleaning up! She actually had her arms in the sink, with her back to me, when I came through what would have been the front door and filmed her.

"Will your mum be worried?" I called, to get her attention. Toni turned, standing ankle deep in wet wreckage, rubber-gloved hands, and all, and smiled to the world. While I told some of what I had seen, Toni moved about salvaging what would later prove to be some very useful items. She was thinking more clearly than me, I reckon. After having already seen the enormity of this city's predicament in my most-vulnerable state, I might well have been nearer despair than most.

I wanted to contact workmates to see how they'd fared. So, now in my own car, I started out again. I visited the homes of several journalists seriously wanting 'somebody to hold the mike' in front of my camera. It would be more like normal if I could look at this world from the removed position through the viewfinder and see somebody who looked as though he knew what he was doing. There was nobody home. In fact, some of their homes weren't home!

A cameraman (particularly an ABC one) was supposed to keep a shot-list, a chronological account of what was filmed, shot by shot, and give 'names' and pertinent details, all of this for an editor, who would then cut the story. He would otherwise not know enough about what was filmed and why. I didn't much care to even look for a dry pencil and paper that day, but such things were on my mind and to excuse such unprofessionalism, I commented, once or twice, as I filmed, speaking barely loud enough for the camera-mounted microphone to pick it up, I gave such scintillating information as, "This is Smith Street". Brilliant. And I thought, for many years, and many times, 'What I should have said was...'

Of course, most of the journos had families and more important stuff to worry about. I don't believe any came looking for me that morning. I returned to the ABC studios in the afternoon. Inside the building that had suffered mostly water-damage, wives were collecting tinned food, feeding children, and making tea on camp stoves for people like me.

Either these people, who'd obviously been 'blown away' too, hadn't seen what I'd seen, or they were made of sterner stuff. And, in any case I couldn't imagine they or anybody would bother to clean up and rebuild Darwin in the same place.

Some of their men sat together on the front steps of the building, in the sun. Somebody had a portable radio and via its short-wave, I heard a little of the Boxing Day Test that was being played in Melbourne. It was most reassuring to know that out there, not so far away, the world still functioned normally.

It was a great lift. But then the fall. Soon after and for the second time that day, I felt a wave of fear. The radio picked up a news service. In this 'News break', and I don't think it was even the lead item, was broadcast a report on the storm:

"Darwin was, last evening, known to have been approached by a cyclone but there have been no reports... And now, here are the cricket scores..."

Holy shit! They just think the lines are down. Here I was, nearly a day later, expecting the cavalry to be coming over the horizon at any moment to save us and they didn't even bloody know!

I felt very much alone just then. And still do, when I think of that time, no matter what company I'm in. Maybe those intact families were well off in many other ways. They were together offering some sort of mutual support.

At night, our Newsroom (and the Darkroom/Editing-room – my own 'personal space' at the ABC) was occupied by a variety of families and other bodies. Toni and I slept on a bench-top with a foot-thick stack of newspapers under us. Not at all comfortable.

The next night we moved into a caravan which I had towed from Sydney and lived in when I first came to Darwin, and which I knew to be unoccupied. Some windows had been ripped out by the storm but, for at least a night, Toni and I slept on its damp beds. Mostly sheltered by a monster Banyan tree, this little oasis also sported a bathtub or laundry-trough which, sitting in the open, had collected enough water to bathe in. Nice. A day or two later we abandoned that place, and an ABC colleague was thrilled to be offered such accommodation.

On the evening of December 25th, I drove out to the RAAF Base and met with Commanding Officer, Group Captain Dave Hitchins. He was a good sport whom I'd met on a number of film assignments. I wanted to be rid of it, so I handed him a cardboard box which contained a roll of exposed 16mm colour film and a scribbled note addressed to whoever finds this bottle tossed in the ocean: "please call my parents at this phone number and say that I'm OK and may be seeing them soon".

The small parcel was taped shut and with a marking pen I wrote on it, 'ABC TV – ANYWHERE'. I knew he was a busy man because, earlier in the day, I had filmed among other things, a DC3 – his personal transport – which had been tossed into his own garden.

In the early hours of the 26th, though I'm starting to lose track of days and nights, I was later informed a RAAF Hercules landed safely and had taken my roll of film.

I went back to the ABC this day to find quite a few people in the Newsroom. Some of them I'd not seen before. They were busy. Mike Hayes was at a typewriter. Dick Muddimer and Richard Creswick were back at work, too. A stranger moved around appearing to 'direct' other strangers. They were southerners; journalists and cameramen who'd arrived that morning. They were the first wave of them.

We were not even introduced when one bloke said that he'd "left Brisbane in a bit of a hurry" and he'd like to know where he could buy some cigarettes. There must have been many cartons of very wet Christmas smokes washing around the whole Top End right then, but I replied by asking, did he, by any chance, have an extra pair of dry socks? He turned on his heels and walked away thinking, no doubt, that there was something wrong with me!

The news stories being written were being shuttled down to the wharf, where the State Ship *Nyanda*, had recently come into port. They were sending their stuff out using the ship's short-wave radio. I did ask whether there was anything that I could do? Any film assignments for me? There weren't, apparently. It was as if I was in the way. I didn't feel at all friendly toward these 'intruders' but, like it or not, they were probably better equipped emotionally to shoot 'our aftermath', than we were.

I drove around, called upon some close friends, and exchanged 'information'. I had also spent time getting the car and my friend ready to take a long drive.

The absence of solid news or 'public instruction' bred rumours in the coming days. Some were quite frightening. For example: it was supposedly reported that hundreds of dead were being bulldozed into pits, somewhere. There was also the sight of tons of rotting foodstuff everywhere you looked and the likelihood of disease spreading from bodies of animals (and people) seemed to make more than a little sense.

Now, this became all the more sinister when it was added, "The Government's covering it up y'know. They don't want to spread panic." OK, I didn't believe that one, but I wouldn't have needed much of a shove to panic. A lot of people believed it, some still do.

As it turned out, the 'official' death-toll added up to 66.

I reckon there could have been a few Aborigines who would not have appeared on anybody's list. I don't believe the story which said that the Blackfellers knew what was coming and left town.

At this time, I'd been in Darwin for about 3 years, but I felt like an outsider to some degree: not actually being one of the ABC's staff. I was a mere contractor. One, incidentally, who was now clearly out of business: no longer having a film processor to fulfil a contract for a TV-station no longer on air. I would not expect *The Corporation* to look after me and I had no family there. A working telephone soon informed me that if I wanted to leave, the News Editor, 'down south', had approved it.

Soon there were vehicles of many a battered shape, overloaded and heading down 'The Track'. I'm sure we both were keen to join them. Toni was supposed to be back at work in Adelaide eventually, though I'm sure they would have covered for her.

I filled the car's long-range tank and several Jerry cans with petrol at a bulk fuel depot. I reckoned we'd get a safe distance with what I carried. And just as well because here's where I heard another rumour: "Oh no, mate, you won't be able to fill up in Katherine. They've been blown away, too!"

I was sure that a cyclone couldn't travel that far inland and still be so fierce. But, in any direction one looked – as far as the eye could see – there was wreckage. How could disturbed minds be certain that the whole world didn't look like this?

We loaded everything we could into the 'cruiser and set off that evening. Toni had squashed garbage bags full of soft, wet stuff into every corner. What was in the bags, I didn't ask or care to know.

As soon as we were on the Stuart Highway we found ourselves in a convoy. Through the night, many of them racing, were vehicles that might have driven straight into the Mad Max movies. Some had been crushed by falling who-knows-what but underneath, apparently, they were mechanically sound enough.

Whole families crouched in crumpled, tin boxes on wheels. More than one had the boot-lid removed and there, standing very heavy in the arse-end, rode a 44-gallon drum, full of petrol I supposed. They'd have gone off with a bang. Many cars without windscreens had a desperate man at the wheel. He might be surrounded by wife, children, and pets, heading south as fast as he could go with what they'd saved.

The atmosphere in this one-way rush encouraged the stronger cars to overtake the weaker ones. Obviously, there was next to no northbound traffic, so why not use the extra lane? When one moved out to take that space, another followed. People were doing some dangerous things.

I couldn't help but join in what felt, at times, like a headlong rush. Some must have believed that they were running for their lives but being there, one was swept along. It was frightening but I also felt some relief. I gripped the wheel and was a part of it.

In the last light of that day and into the night, we raced through showers with lightning cracking a whip at our tails. We had all funnelled into this 'only-road-south' and Katherine was the next town, 220 miles distant.

At Katherine, some vehicles turned right and pointed 'home', for Western Australia. They had a long way to go. Queenslanders had about 650 miles to go before turning left!

Unsurprisingly, Katherine was not even a refreshing pit-stop. We paused only a short time, but it was long enough to see that there were no 'stables for rent' that were more comfortable than the one we drove. I met a rather distressed friend there: an 'ABC casual'. We had yet to learn that cash wasn't a problem for those south bound. And an introduction to a motel owner was enough to get her comfortably accommodated. She planned to stop overnight before setting out for Geelong: about 2,300 miles between there and her mum. She had only a large dog for company and, moving with the flow we met each other a couple more times before reaching the South Australian border. Toni and I drove out of town and stopped along the way for a bit of a sleep where we sat.

After dawn we drove into Elliott, 450 miles from Darwin, which had a public telephone near the petrol stations. There was a queue of people lined up to call south. Most of their families would still know nothing except that a cyclone had hit Darwin, the town where loved ones lived. So it was with us.

When I got my turn on the telephone, which was a free call, I was told by the operator to "keep it to two minutes". I called my parents in Adelaide and asked them to phone Toni's mum. We were safe and out of there. That's all.

It was still cloudy, but we were mostly clear of the showers and as the day grew hotter we had to travel even more slowly. I had discovered the previous night that a leak in the radiator would require frequent (if brief) stops. I'd watch the temperature gauge until it got to that certain point then I'd kick her out of gear, freewheel to a stop and top up the water from the cans I carried. The crack at the top of the tank was a result of the wall falling on the 'cruiser's bonnet.

At the day's hottest, I found that I could only drive a careful 14 to 16 miles before I'd have to repeat the procedure. At this time of year, luckily, we could pick up water lying in pools here and there.

Between those, what we carried and the occasional bore-tank in a farmer's paddock, we limped into Tennant Creek.

At Tennant, there was a refugee receival station. Hastily scribbled signs on the highway directed Darwin refugees (that's what we were, though it still sounds strange), to the CWA Hall. We went, not only because we were curious but because the police obliged us to. They wanted to register everybody who was on The Track and so shorten the [no doubt, being-assembled] 'missing persons list'.

Also, we were all checked for cuts and injuries and given tetanus shots, if deemed necessary. Inside the hall were long tables overflowing with clothing. Quite a few refugees were being cared for by many of that town's residents. I remember a woman sitting quietly against a wall with a kitten and a saucer of milk on her lap. We had tea and biscuits and were asked if we needed anything else. I don't think we did.

We were encouraged to take advantage of the offer of accommodation in someone's home, but we declined. Thanks anyway.

Here, for the first time probably, some people broke down and wept. This first 'safe haven' for some of that frightened convoy, allowed them to let go, relax enough to lower their guard and they cried for all manner of personal reasons. One woman in our hearing wept openly and was comforted by an old lady. When asked what could be done for her, the woman said between sobs that she wanted a bra.

She'd probably kept a brave face on losing her house, home, and everything else but now she wanted a bra, and it was very important for her. The old lady told her that that would be "no problem" and showed her a way through the piles of clothing that had been instantly donated by the good people of Tennant Creek.

All the way south there was petrol at no cost for Darwin refugees. Running repairs and much more were very useful, and thanks and credit should go to many organisations and citizens along the way.

I had the radiator leak fixed and they threw in a new tyre. We were tired but chose to be on our way. I didn't want to break down in public (or even private, come to think of it) nor be an extra burden to these folk who would, no doubt, have lots more-serious cases to deal with.

As we continued south, at each of the longer pauses in our journey I began to notice Toni spreading stuff on the ground. She'd haul her garbage bags over to the nearest bushes and drape clothes and linen and stuff. At each stop (while I saw to the car or whatever) she'd do it over again. There was at least one bag for 'sopping wets' another for 'damp' and a third was 'saved'. Even a short stop saw, for example, my sodden passport, weighted with a rock, each stop probably had a new page turned. That's a good idea. "Thanks Tone".

Not far north of Alice Springs we decided to camp for our first good sleep. We were clear enough of the monsoon's clouds that, at night, we could see a sky full of stars. A timely full moon lit the place where we pulled off the road. It was quiet. The first 'real quiet' we'd felt for days. By the light of that moon, we unloaded a little more than usual from the vehicle.

I made a fire and set a frying pan on rocks. Toni broke out our provisions. In the esky, sloshing around with the last slivers of ice and water was a packet of bacon, some steak, and the last bottle of sparkling burgundy. Until then, I didn't know what we had saved.

It was a peaceful oasis on such a night; we were two exhausted but relieved friends. Steak fried in bacon fat, and that beautiful, cold bottle of red; Mate, you'd have to go a long way for a taste that good again. And we slept.

Next morning, we drove on down to Alice Springs and were, once again, directed by signs to go to some marshalling area. Here we chose to be 'allocated'. We were introduced to different groups who were responsible for different needs. I made it clear that we were mostly self-contained, and I was confident that we could make it to Adelaide after this attention.

However, while responsibility for the vehicle was taken from me, we were 'billeted out' and received by a man and his lady-friend who'd made their home available to refugees.

Almost every home in The Alice was doing the same thing. He was a schoolteacher and at his place we were given an enormous dinner. They plied us with drink and gave us a room complete with spotless beds and anything at all that would make us more comfortable. That extraordinarily kind gent and his lady could not do enough for us.

As we emptied one bottle of whatever it was, he produced another. Up to and including a collection of 'miniatures'. I think we drank everything they had in the house before getting another good night's sleep. Still sober, as I recall.

If, somehow, that couple ever reads this, thank you, most sincerely, from Toni and me. In fact, thank you to all the townspeople of Alice Springs.

Around the Nation, in the following weeks, many organisations and towns collected money to help cyclone victims. I forget what the population of Alice was but if you want some idea of how much was collected from every man, woman, and child in a town like Alice, think of a number and triple it. They might've been a thousand miles from Darwin, but they were also Territorians. It's a family thing.

A lot of worry was behind us but there was a fair amount of dirt road to come beyond the South Australian border. The worst stretch, as I remembered, was a filthy couple of hundred miles which wound out-of-the-way, via Kingoonya and around the Woomera Rocket Range – a prohibited area. Having driven Adelaide/Darwin a few times, I dreaded that neglected section of track the most. And it was 'neglected' because they were sealing that last section of dirt and hadn't used a grader on that bit for a long while.

As we approached The Range, near Mt Eba, a sign directed ex-Darwin traffic to go 'this way'. They'd opened their locked gates for us. Through the range! What a relief. It must have been nearly a hundred miles shorter and bitumen all the way! When we drove into the Woomera township we were, once again, shown spectacular hospitality. We only stopped to fill up and fill up, I did.

There was a large room full of food. Toni remembers me finishing another giant meal with an embarrassing number of Government-issue, trifle desserts. All for free.

It was downhill (easier going) from there, sealed road all the way, a few hundred miles to Adelaide. Toni presented me with three garbage-bags full of dry linen and soon after, went back to work. I visited the ABC there and felt like something of a novelty for five minutes. My film had been well received and I heard something of 'the flap' that greeted its journey to Queensland.

When that first RAAF Hercules had returned to Amberley Air Force base it was pounced upon by TV-types who knew that Bushnell was in Darwin at the time and, if he was alive, would probably have shot something and got it out.

But whoever had escaped on that 'first flight out of town', knew nothing of any film. With sunken hearts the empty plane was searched one last time (so the story goes), until some ground crew-type then announced, "Is this what you're looking for?" It was.

The film was raced off to film laboratories, processed and transmitted around Australia, intact. That ten minutes of film was, for a whole day, the only pictures anybody had. I'm told that 'the Commercial Stations lined up' at the ABC and insisted on a copy for their own use. I'd love to have seen that. There was talk about its 'being in the national interest' and all that sort of stuff. The ABC had got it for free and eventually, everybody got it. Did anybody pay for it? I still don't know.

Although I wasn't aware of it at the time, it was reckoned that there'd be some freelance, *Tracy Aftermath* to shoot for a while before that work would inevitably evaporate. I was still not playing with a full deck, but I sped back to the Territory. Do you know, those Woomera characters wouldn't let me go through their place northbound! The whole story was different now.

A day or two later, at Three Ways, there was a roadblock. I was asked to prove that I had 'a place to live in Darwin' before I'd be allowed in. There were similar challenges along the way, and it was the camera that got me through.

Of course, at that time, they were evacuating as many people as they could. There was going to be a gigantic job to feed, supply, and house all the construction and other emergency workers that were needed.

Either way, I reckoned they had 'no legal right' to block our way, I still don't think they really did, and I probably said so.

The ship *Patris* arrived and tied up at the wharf. She was used as a floating hotel for quite a few hundred of us 'workers'. I didn't make much, as usual, but a lot of these construction people made big money and we played a lot of poker in the evenings. I did better at that.

For the next few months, I shot a lot of the cyclone aftermath for most networks and a documentary for ABC Sydney's 'Chequerboard'. ABC-Darwin had no plan to re-engage us for local films because they were now taking their news from Queensland via the microwave link.

On the morning of 1 April (was the date significant? I wondered at the time) I got a phone call from the 'News Director' in Sydney. There was talk of my/our cyclone film having made the shortlist for an award and would I care to come down to Sydney for the presentations, a couple of weeks hence? Why not? I called QANTAS and confirmed the flight details: one freebie airfare and a night's accommodation in Sydney. It only took me a couple of days to decide that, after this, I'd look for a new place.

At 'The Awards', held at the Journalists' Club, I met a few people I knew. Some camera crews were there to make a story out of the event, particularly those stations who expected to win something, I suppose. I had my hair cut very short for the occasion. In my child-like state, I probably thought it was 'putting on my Sunday best' or could hear my father grumbling, 'Get your hair cut'.

Before the presentations, I was interviewed and asked how it felt to win the first "Thorn Award for TV-News". I answered, honestly, that I hadn't won it yet, had I? (Though I should have known: the air-ticket from Darwin and all). I must have embarrassed the Journo, who'd obviously been given the tip. I remember going on at great length for a radio interview, trying to justify my belief that it was Gough Whitlam becoming the new Prime Minister that was the cause of Cyclone Tracy. Surely, somebody must have seen that I was missing some cards. But nobody told me.

After the 'runners-up' they called my name, gave me a cheque for $250 (I think) and an order for a free Thorn-TV set, to be delivered anywhere I wanted. Whereupon I promptly sat down. After a little shuffling and the suggestion that a speech would have been in order, I got to my feet again and said, "Thanks to Jack Gulley, for entering my film in The Awards". I told somebody they could contact my parents in Adelaide and let them know they could collect a new TV. And that was that.

With the help of a couple of friends, I drank the $250 that week. Then (because I hadn't been there before, I went for a couple of weeks' holidays to Tasmania with Toni who, presumably, was still owed some holidays. I was still in a bit of a daze. We stayed with another old friend, David Flatman (then fronting the current affairs programme, TDT) and soon Toni went back to Adelaide.

I didn't know what to do or where to go next. I called an old friend in Canada, and she said, "come on over" and I was on a plane the next day.

In Toronto, they took a long look at me and my crumpled passport. They even took me into one of those rooms used for grilling undesirables. I wonder what we talked about? A couple of weeks later, I got a job shooting news for Global-TV-network. And just days later, I woke up and found myself married! You want to know about pain and suffering? As Toni had warned, now I was really in trouble.

Postscript: The driver was Bill McGuinness, a TAA engineer who now lives in Victoria. After their filming travels, Bill delivered Keith back to their damaged units then, seeing a TAA Fokker Friendship circling over Darwin, he reported for duty at the airport. This plane, piloted by Ray Vuillermin and Tony Burgess landed late on Christmas Day. It was the first 'heavy' aircraft to land on a hastily cleared section of the main runway. Bill performed services and checks on the plane to ensure it was ready for departure the next day. Ray Vuillermin's story also appears in this book.

Graham Butterworth

Graham retired from the Army with the rank of Major in 1973. It was a distressing experience, after nearly twenty years of service, but with retraining and assistance from his senior staff officers, he became the road/rail divisional manager with Ansett Freight Express in Sydney. It was while working at Mascot that he was offered the position of Darwin Branch Manager.

August 1974 was a massive time training in Adelaide for the new role in Darwin, while also finalising affairs in Sydney and Victoria but, at noon on Monday December 23, 1974, my wife Barbara and I stepped off the plane at the old Darwin Air Terminal to begin a new life and lifestyle in the Top End.

Because the outgoing Manager, Max Eaton, and his wife, were still occupying the company house in Larrakeyah, we were booked into the Poinciana Motel. We settled in and hired a Mini-Moke from Hunters in Smith Street and drove out through Winnellie, to Berrimah (the end of the road) for a "look-see".

After that we returned to the motel, parked the Moke under a huge poinciana tree, had dinner in the motel restaurant and hit the cot. Next morning, we walked down to Mindil Beach and while we were there it started raining; when we got back to the motel, we were saturated, the rain was getting heavier, and the sky was becoming darker – but about what was to come, we didn't have a clue!

After dinner that night, we were enjoying drinks with Mick, the licensee and his two barmen when about 11 pm, Mick said "It's getting a bit windy – I think we'll close up for tonight", so we returned to our ground-floor suite.

Shortly after, the howling wind and the noise of things striking the building became very scary. I went to the window, looked out and all I could see was tree branches, palm fronds and sheets of corrugated iron flying past from right to left. The noise was horrific.

Then suddenly, Barbara panicked and tried to get out of the room, so I had to physically drag her from the door, toss her between the bed and wall and sit on her.

Moments after that, there was a tremendous bang and the room was filled with choking dust – we later learned that the big air-conditioning unit was blown off the roof. We stayed down by the bed and then it became quiet for about half an hour, so we thought it was all over. HA, BLOODY HA! Without warning, all the noises resumed so we again dived down between the bed and wall and stayed there.

At dawn we went outside and joined other confused residents. The big AC unit was in the motel pool, and foliage, wreckage and rubbish was everywhere – including a very flat Mini Moke under a large branch from the poinciana tree.

The rest of that day was spent in a daze, wondering what the hell we'd been through and what was coming next. The motel manageress kept us all supplied with tea, coffee, nibbles and kindness!

In the following days we met and got to know our first four locals: Leo Venturin, Brad Lawson and Michael Griffiths from Bradlaw Agencies, and Michael's dad, who provided us with copious quantities of XXXX beer, stories about Darwin, and past cyclone events. We all went to the High School Distribution Centre, to receive our first packs of foodstuff.

One week later, we were all "ejected" from the motel, because the Department of Transport and Works took it over to accommodate some of the incoming emergency reconstruction workforce.

Leo Venturin came to the rescue for Barbara and me, providing us with temporary accommodation in a house he owned in Hudson Fysh Avenue, Parap, until we were able to move into what was left of the company's Manoora Street house. There was the downstairs area and laundry, and the kitchen, bathroom, part of a bedroom and the bare lounge floor and landings upstairs. As a roof, these splendid facilities were totally covered by many huge green tarpaulins provided by AFE and Wridgeways, which at that time was a company subsidiary.

At the same time, fellow company managers George Kreuger, Trevor Grieg, my foreman Dick Stewart, and I had tracked down some of the AFE and Wridgeways staff and resumed almost-normal transport and storage operations, while also reconstructing much of our damaged premises in Winnellie.

During this period, we met and became friends with some marvellous people – outstanding in my memory are our Larrakeyah neighbours Paul Sweeney and Tassy Graham, other Company Managers including Fred McCue from Ansett Air; Cec Van Der Velde of TNT; Wayne Foster from Brambles, Kwikasair's Bob McNaughton, and their families, plus the well-known character, Carl Atkinson from Doctor's Gully.

In March 1975, my brother Noel, his wife Nadine and their children Vicki and Mark, arrived. They brought our mum, Bessie, with them for her first and only trip outside of Victoria, and sadly, this was the last time we saw her alive – she went home to Victoria and passed away in March 1976. Mum was besotted by the frangipani trees and the blossoms in our yard and around Darwin.

My stepson, Lee Hubble, also arrived from Sydney, and several of these family members joined me at AFE, working temporarily to reestablish our operations, while I tried to employ new full-time employees which wasn't easy at the time!

When we eventually completed the rebuilding process, Wridgeways resumed their separate operations, AFE built a new depot on the adjoining block.

In 1978, I resigned to become manager of a new aged-care

facility known as Tracy Lodge, in Woods Street.

There have been many changes in the life and lifestyles of Darwin following Cyclone Tracy, some magnificent and some less fortunate. For me and my family there have been mostly enjoyable changes in residential, employment and social factors. We still absolutely adore living in this wonderful place.

Pamela Cameron

Pamela was 14 years old and the oldest of five children. They were living at Larrakeyah Barracks because her father was a supply officer with the army. Their house was destroyed with them in it.

After settling Mum and us children in the toilet Dad ran out to grab the Christmas presents from under the tree and put them in the hall cupboard. We children told him to bring his present back because we had bought him a large torch for fishing. We were then able to sit with a light on and check the time on his watch. This was very comforting. Dad sat on the loo and held a mattress over us for most of the night. When bits of debris fell in, he pushed them aside.

We didn't get the cyclone eye at Larrakeyah, so when daylight came Dad called out to some army personnel who were checking houses to help get us out, because we thought it was all going to happen again.

After the initial shock it was an adventure. My brothers recall hacking through a fallen wall in the house to crawl into the wardrobe crushed below it. They retrieved clothing and other saturated belongings and remember this as being a lot of fun.

We were due to leave for a posting to Brisbane on January 9, so most of our belongings were packed already and sitting at Grace Removals at Winnellie. Dad's boat was ok but most other things were destroyed.

We spent Christmas night on wet stretchers in the roofless Officer's Mess.

I recall being shocked by the devastation in Larrakeyah. It was surreal. I remember crying and shaking when we first got out of the wrecked house and saw the ruins, but the silence was welcome after the roaring and screeching noises all night.

My parents were very practical people and they took it all in their stride. Mum and we five children were put on the first Hercules on Boxing Day with the seriously injured. On the bus trip to the airport to board the plane the scene was amazing. We couldn't believe the widespread devastation.

It was a very long and noisy flight to Amberley! I had Mum's sewing machine wedged between my knees. We were very fortunate to have the army look after us and we received clothing and linen on arrival in Brisbane.

We then turned up in a taxi at my grandparents' house unannounced because they didn't have a phone. We don't appear on evacuation lists.

Because Dad was a supply officer he stayed on in Darwin for a few weeks. He said his biggest challenge was arranging good food and cold beers for the poor army guys who were going door to door emptying fridges full of rotting meat, etc. Imagine that job in the Wet!

I loved our time in Darwin and went back at 20 for my first job as a registered nurse, staying on for most of the next 31 years. My three children still live there. Darwin has a special place in my heart.

Carol Conway

Carol Conway (nee Willson) arrived for her first job as a teacher at the newly opened Nightcliff High School in 1970. Darwin's laid-back tropical lifestyle and frontier feel presented much that was new, unique, and slightly quirky. It was very different from her lifestyle and experience in conservative South Australia and Carol and her friends relished exploring and sharing this new place with camping trips and amateur theatrical performances. An interest in theatre brought Ken Conway into her life, and they shared Cyclone Tracy together in Hinkler Street, Fannie Bay.

The day began quite early since I had lots to do. Foremost on my mind was my challenge to make the entrée for the planned communal Christmas lunch next day. Somewhat foolishly in my enthusiasm for everything French at the time, I had offered to make a chicken liver pate and a terrine of pork, veal, and pork liver as my contribution. Getting out my newly acquired cookbook "Pates and Other Marvelous Meat Loaves", which still survives to this day, I embarked on the process.

I gave little thought to the cyclone warning, and I didn't even have the radio on for most of the day. We had experienced Selma a few weeks before and had made some rudimentary preparation, but it hadn't come to anything. We even went down to the rocks at Nightcliff Beach to watch the waves during the day.

So, the process of attaching the antiquated grey metal meat grinder to the edge of the kitchen table, and the squeamish feelings I had in my gut as I forced the livers through the appliance occupied my thoughts totally.

Later in the day Ken came home from Brown's Mart, where he was executive officer for the Brown's Mart Trustees. More preparations for Christmas Day were made. We were to buy the wine and orange juice for the next day, so the shopping was done, and liquor duly stacked in the antiquated fridge we possessed.

Maybe the word "antiquated" needs explaining. We lived in a little old low-set fibro shack/donga in Hinkler Crescent, Fannie Bay. It had been built after the war and just about everything about this house needed the skills of a carpenter or a tradesman, so taping up windows that didn't close anyway was not a high priority.

Even the weather during the day was not alarming. Ken said he even thought about taking the tape off the louvres in the back office of Brown's Mart that he had prepared for Selma. Our cyclone preparations were minimal, but we did have food and drink and later in the day we put on some warmer clothes as it was wet and rainy anyway.

Still lulled into a false sense of complacency, we even agreed to go to the Fannie Bay Pub about 9.00 pm when our mate Ted Whiteaker turned up and suggested going for a drink.

It was getting blowy by then. The drive to the pub was an adventure, with the wind whipping tree branches around and the windscreen barely being cleared by the wipers going at full pelt. Ted still managed to get us there in his old Holden, but it did feel more like being in a boat as water splashed up the sides of the car.

The front bar of the pub still had a few bedraggled clients when we arrived, and we obviously were a good fit to join them after staggering out of the weather. The front doors faced seaward, so they kept blowing open, and spray from the now constant rain wafted over us, even as we sat at the end of the bar furthest away.

About eleven we thought maybe we should get ourselves home. Conditions were getting a bit rough in the bar, and more was to come on the way home to Hinkler Crescent as we repeated an even more boisterous journey.

Once home, Ted and Ken decided a game of Scrabble might be the go. By this time, I was feeling anxious as I looked around my "antiquated house" and saw leaks appearing and the glass flexing in the living room windows. I had the feeling that I wanted to shelter in a smaller, less open room.

The game was abandoned. Ted decided he would drive home despite my worry that things were too dangerous to do that now.

Our next concern was to go to the "safest" place in the house. The bathroom. We were joined by Keith and his dog. Keith lived down the backyard in a caravan under a big mango tree. Our bathroom, or the "ablution block" as I called it, was three sets of cubicles made up of toilet, shower and bath and basin – which was where the three of us took up our positions. Ken and I down one end under the basin and near the door, Keith and dog, alongside the bath.

The blow began in earnest and kept up until after midnight when we experienced the "eye". Things quietened down for a bit. Enough for us to use our torches to see how things were around us. I noticed some ceiling damage above us and decided to find something to protect us more from falling debris. Keith was still in position beside the bath which gave him protection from stuff coming through the outside wall.

Ken, much to my concern, went out to the back yard to see how things were out there. One of the things he discovered was my brand-new Honda Civic crushed under a tree, a fact he decided not to tell me at the time. My worry was that he wouldn't get back before the storm started up again. The noise of the storm could still be heard in the background during the eye.

Following up on my fear of debris falling on our heads, I went into the bedroom across from the bathroom. This room was still pretty much intact, and we had a small metal-framed single bed with a mattress in there. When Ken came back from outside, we manoeuvred one end of the bed through the bathroom door.

This gave some protection for our heads and upper backs, as we stretched our legs along the side of the bath towards where Keith was positioned. I have no memory of what happened to his dog.

After the eye things really got rough. The noise was all-enveloping. Ken and I were lying side by side, heads together and there was no way we could hear each other speak. Water backed up through the drain in the bathroom floor, so we were very cold lying in water for the rest of the night, as it wasn't safe to move from under the bed.

I had long hair tied back in a ponytail. The wind whipping through the bathroom blew strands of my hair up into the metal springs of the bed and twisted them around so when I did have the opportunity to move my head, I had to lose a few strands to do so.

Lying wet, in darkness and completely immersed in the huge noise and bluster everywhere around me, I was scared for us. I did think we might not survive and wondered how long it could possibly go on for. When I look back, I wonder what I could have thought about for all those hours we were under the bed. I certainly didn't go to sleep. But perhaps I have blotted out some of that time from my memory. For many years after the cyclone, I couldn't talk about it without tears pricking in my eyes. And even now as I try to remember the details, I feel teary.

When light came the next morning, the intensity of the wind was lessening. Very gingerly we made our way out of a bathroom that had remained fairly intact, except where pieces of debris had punctured holes in the wall and roof. We had to clear a big piece of 4x2 which had speared through the exterior wall just above our legs and had lodged in the opposite wall. We had not heard this hardwood missile miss us by inches because the cyclone noise had been so loud, and we felt very lucky it had missed our exposed lower backs and legs.

When we went outside, there was a wall of chopped up vegetation mixed with debris about 2 metres high surrounding our house. I was extremely thankful for it because I think it protected us to some extent. My current house, built on the footprint of the old shack, is surrounded by trees and shrubs.

The view onto the street showed a mass of debris along the road, a tangle of vegetation everywhere and houses with damaged walls and roofs. Basically, the houses were still standing. Our back yard revealed the crushed Honda Civic. It didn't bother me because we were just happy to have come through. Some, like the guy over the back from us, took their frustrations out with expletives, but shock and disbelief were paramount.

When we were in a position and mood to compare, Fannie Bay had stood up well compared with the devastation of the northern suburbs. Factors like the path of the cyclone and the bare layout of the housing in those suburbs obviously played a part, but I'm in favour of more trees around the house. They took the brunt of our damage.

Ken still had his VW Beetle parked in the street, but the roads were clogged and blocked by debris. Phones were not working, so to find out how your friends had fared, walking was required. So, later that morning, that was what we did. We walked to Parap, calling in on our friend Ted on the way. He had survived the drive home from our place the night before, and his house was completely intact bar a couple of broken louvres. It became a haven for us and other friends in the weeks to come.

Our Christmas Day lunch did not get wasted. That night after Tracy there was a big party at Ted's. We brought whatever we still had in the fridge that was useable. My pates made an appearance along with the wine that we had bought the day before. Not a bottle broken! There was a tremendous feeling amongst our gathering that we had shared something that had shaken us to the core, but we had survived.

The first few days after Tracy, Ken and I stayed at Ted's, sleeping where we could find a bit of floorspace. I went back to the house in Hinkler Crescent and sifted through our belongings every day. I dried out wet and damp books and other belongings.

I hadn't lost everything like some of my friends. At least I had the opportunity to search through my stuff. So many others didn't get to do that and lost precious photos and memorabilia.

The directive to move people out of town as soon as possible was almost absolute. There were good reasons for that when shelter, food, communication, healthcare etc. were in short supply. But I didn't want to leave, and I didn't want to leave Ken.

I felt I could still be useful if I stayed. But being an unmarried woman, I felt pressure to leave town. I reasoned I had somewhere to live, and I had a job as a high school teacher, so I stayed on, and I felt very grateful that I wasn't one of those evacuated at short notice.

For many, evacuation was the only option, but I felt I suffered less dislocation than some who were loaded onto airplanes and hurried away to uncertain destinations.

After a few days it became obvious there were practical things to be done in a town without services anymore. Water supply was an issue. Fire hydrants in the street were places to gather buckets of drinking water and to take a bath, but pipes were broken all over the place and water meters in houses needed to be turned off.

Ken and Ted somehow got enlisted to go around turning off water meters. People were asked to help by some kind of "bush telegraph" or by just happening to be in the right place at the right time because early on communication was limited.

Ken was a case in point. He was out and about when his old English teacher, the NT Director of Education Hedley Beare spotted him and asked him to work alongside some of his Departmental staff in the Evacuation Control Centre.

There, he worked with Terry Kenwrick, senior art teacher at Casuarina High, for several weeks, dealing with the people who had to leave and those seeking permits to return to Darwin.

Schools were an important resource during this time. They were first and foremost cyclone shelters that then became evacuation centres that gave food and shelter to people who had to leave town or who stayed. Some school principals and departmental staff took on the organisational roles of controlling the flow of evacuees to the airport in numbers that matched the numbers of aircraft that were arriving to take them to southern cities.

But, despite the best efforts of the control centres, chaos was inevitable, and many evacuees suffered, some spending hours queuing in the tropical heat and humidity on the airport tarmac.

As a teacher I was also called back into head office to report for work. I was set to work in the office doing clerical work for a week or two, after which I found some work at Ludmilla School, looking after a small group of children and providing children's activities: the rubbish dump was a mine of all kinds of water damaged goodies which had much potential for art and craft activities. I even found a set of Australian flags, which I rescued, and assembled along the living room wall (or where the living room wall had been) in our donga back at Hinkler Crescent.

With the benefit of a 'cyclone loan' our new house was finished in 1977 – after we had gone through 3 building companies in its construction. This one isn't a donga. It even got a mention in 'Vogue Living' in 1979. And we are still here. My memories of Tracy are many, some are still fresh and poignant, while others get hazier by the day.

Yvonne Corby

Yvonne was a WRAN (Women's Royal Australian Navy) Communicator posted to Darwin on December 9, 1974. She arrived at HMAS Coonawarra on the Stuart Highway with no family and no friends to speak of. Worse, she found a "Dear John" letter from her boyfriend in Canberra awaiting her when she arrived to join the 1RS (Receiving Station). But, as she writes, mateships made because of the cyclone are stronger and more resilient than ever, even after 50 years.

I vividly remember Christmas Eve because the watch supervisor had been keeping up with Tracy's movements via radio, and he predicted this would be no ordinary cyclone. At 4 pm when I finished my shift, I walked back to the WRAN's quarters. The sky was literally black with storm clouds.

A Christmas Eve function had been organised at the Junior Sailors Mess. When the bar closed, because of the weather, we were ordered back to our quarters, instead of making what had become the usual trek to the Berrimah Hotel.

Around midnight we were instructed to leave our cabins and take shelter in the recreation room which was then in the old WRANS quarters. As the winds increased and the door could not be held closed anymore, we were moved into more sheltered rooms where we spent the first part of Tracy.

We could hear the winds howling outside and then, with a massive crack, the whole top floor sheered straight off. Some of us had been up there only moments before to make sure there were no girls still up there. I can remember one of the girls opening the louvres and saying, "there goes my wardrobe". At one stage the door flew open and there was a family with three children from the marriage patch (the nickname for the Married Quarters) who had already lost their home.

When the winds died down during the eye, we walked down the street to the Junior Sailors Mess. I remember holding onto the hands of two children and walking them there. At one stage, there was a crack of lightning which lit up the sky as we passed the Captain's house. You could see straight through the roof to the sky.

When the second half was upon us, the Captain took charge at the Junior Sailors Mess and ordered every adult to have an alcoholic drink. To this day, I cannot stand the smell of Bundy and Coke.

It seemed like the whole of the depot was there, sailors, wives, children, dogs, cats. At one point the roof started to bounce above us. A broom was quickly found, and holes were knocked in the gyprock to release a ton of water. We were sitting under tables at that stage, surrounded by wives, children, dogs, and cats.

When the Captain announced all clear, sometime after daybreak, we went back to our cabins to clean up the mess. Everything was topsy turvy! There were buildings strewn all around the street. A boat had wedged itself under someone's house, but he didn't own a boat!

I was fortunate. My cabin was still intact except for some daylight, visible through the roof above the wardrobe. Even though I was on the top floor there was at least a couple of inches of water in the room and my camera floating in it.

The next few days were a blur: dragging corrugated iron to the tennis courts so that it could not fly around should another blow occur; operating the industrial dryers to get blankets dry for the families; offering cups of tea and reassurance to some of the wives who believed they had lost everything.

A few stories that stand out: one fellow woke up on Christmas morning in his bed but with nothing else around him, roof and walls completely gone; another rode out the cyclone in the big industrial dryer; and one sad story: "Stevo" who was on duty that night asked if he could go home to check on his family, a request that was denied. During the eye, his request was granted, and he found his wife and two children had perished, crushed under their bed.

On the bright side, the sailors who regularly hung off the bar were the first to get their hands dirty. The RAN commandeered graders, tractors, and trucks very early in the piece. These lads used whatever heavy equipment they could to clean up the houses on the marriage patch and the aerial farm. It was not an unfamiliar sight, seeing them racing graders and tractors across the aerial farm. We didn't see them for days and when we did, they were exhausted!

We spent the next days and weeks cleaning up and getting the depot back to fully operational status. It was all-hands-on-deck: everything from drying blankets to clearing out fridges on the marriage patch – which was not a pleasant task with most fridges full of Christmas fare and two weeks of no power.

Through all this the unspoken navy *all in this together* and *watch your mate* ethics shone through. Mateships, now lasting 50 years, have come to the fore and are stronger and more resilient than ever.

While I was working for ABC Radio between 1989 and 2007, I became the custodian of the sound recorded at midnight mass in the Christ Church Cathedral. You can hear it in the Cyclone Tracy exhibition at the NT Museum and Art Gallery. I still cannot go into that display.

Living in the tropics, I have now experienced a few cyclones. Nothing is more terrifying than hearing that sound, like a freight train getting closer. That was a night that will be forever etched in my memory.

Figure 6: Cyclone Tracy damaged Navy homes (Ken Doust Collection
LANT, ph0821-0012).

Norman Cramp

After their marriage in Sydney in March 1974, Dr Norman and Christine Cramp travelled to Brisbane where they stayed for a few months, before hitting the road in their 1960s Kombi van. Sadly, the engine in the Kombi threw in the towel at Camooweal, Queensland and they had to ship it to Darwin on the back of a truck. They arrived in Darwin in August 1974, planning on a short stay to see friends before leaving for an extended holiday in the UK, Europe, and America. They are still here.

We planned to continue our round-Australia trip when we returned from overseas, so to cover the cost of repairs to the Kombi's engine, we both found jobs – me at the Stokes Hill Power Station as a fitter and machinist and Christine as an administration officer with an insurance company.

We rented a ground-level, two-bedroom unit in a block of flats on the corner of Alstonia and Bougainvillea Streets, Nightcliff, and finalised our plans to leave for the UK in mid-January 1975.

We were both at work throughout the 24th of December and both of us attended workplace Christmas parties that afternoon before heading home to prepare for a small party with some friends from Sydney and my workplace.

That evening, we were joined at our place by Dennis and Tina May with Sky, their 10-month-old baby; Gary Kulmar, and a workmate named Allan and his wife. Dennis and Tina lived on the top floor of our block of units, Gary Kulmar was visiting from Nhulunbuy and Allan and his wife were staying overnight with us.

It had been raining for days and the wind gusts were strengthening by the time we all arrived home after work. Although there had been numerous warnings about the possibility of a tropical cyclone going near or hitting Darwin, none of us took much notice as we continued to party and get ready for Christmas Day.

Dennis, Tina, and Gary left around 9:30 pm and we were all in bed by 10pm. But by 11 pm the wind was really strong and howling – we lost power, and we could hear crashing sounds. It was the sound of the wind and the huge gusts that had us all out of bed, dressed and alert by about 11:15pm.

Around 11:45 pm Dennis appeared at our glass front door with a terrified look on his face and when I let him in he said most of the roof of the block had been blown away, rain was pouring in and there was limited shelter for them.

Even though the wind was howling, and the rain was belting down, I went upstairs with him and helped them move to our place. As we were doing this, a Greek couple who lived in the unit next to Dennis asked if they could come down as the roof had also gone from their unit.

We all trundled down to our place. It was made more difficult because the Greek lady was heavily pregnant, and Tina and Dennis carried a lot of stuff to care for Sky, but we got to our place safe and sound and huddled in the main bedroom at the back of the unit.

While in that room we watched the roof of the block of units behind ours peel off like a can of sardines being opened. Allan and I knew another of our work mates and his wife were on the top floor of that block and Dennis and I agreed we would go and get them "when the wind eased off a bit."

I don't recall when it happened, but there was a huge gust of wind and one of our front door panels caved in and I'm sure the whole brick and concrete structure shuddered. By then we were all terrified, we had emptied the bathtub of water and made a bed for the Greek lady there and we had all moved into the bathroom and toilet. I think most of us took turns to sit on the dunny to get off our feet for a while.

Even though it seemed the world was coming to an end, we men managed to slip out of our shelter to get a few beers every now and then – because they were cold, and we needed to keep our fluid levels up!

As the eye of the storm passed over us, Dennis and I went to Col's place to get him and his wife to join us because, even though one of the front door panels had gone, we were dry and as safe as we could be. They joined us in the bathroom/toilet area and the 12 of us rode out the cyclone.

Once the storm had passed Allan and Col, their wives, and the Greek couple left our place. Allan and his wife got their almost new Kombi going, and somehow managed to get to their flat, gathered as much of their personal property as they could find, and left for Adelaide where they came from straight away.

Later that afternoon, Christine, Tina, Dennis, Sky, Gary and I gathered a few things and went to the power station as I was on call. I think we were concerned the cyclone would come back! We spent Christmas night there and returned to the units on Boxing Day. It was a major problem travelling from Nightcliff to Stokes Hill and back as there were power poles, trees, parts of buildings and vehicles across the roads. But somehow we did it.

Christine, Tina, and Sky were evacuated on the Prime Minister's RAAF jet about three days after the cyclone and Dennis, Gary, and I two or three weeks after them. After 10-days R and R in Sydney, Dennis and I returned to Darwin and Gary to Nhulunbuy.

Dennis immediately packed their belongings in their Holden ute and went back to Sydney – never to return. Gary remained in Nhulunbuy for many years before returning to Sydney to live out the rest of his life.

After our return to Darwin, I went back to work at the power station, then transferred to the Darwin Hospital at Myilly Point and then to the Mechanical and Electrical Workshops at Parap under the management of Frank Geddes. Christine returned to work with John Vanderval, but took a position in the Commonwealth government a couple of years later.

Christine and I have lived in Darwin ever since our arrival in August 1974 and have no intention of moving.

Patsy Creswick

Patsy was a teacher at Wagaman Primary School which had opened the previous year as the Territory's first 'Open' School, exploring what were then new child-centred teaching and learning methods. Being school holidays, she and a friend, the teacher librarian at Wagaman Primary, were on holiday.

On the evening of December 24, 1974, I was sitting with a friend outside a small losmen on the edge of a volcanic crater in Bali. Meditating. Absolute serenity and calmness. We were teachers on holiday, my first visit to Bali. I was entranced by the customs of the people, the ceremonies, the daily offerings, the beauty of the landscape, the sensory richness of colours, scents, sounds, tastes. All was right with the world.

The next morning, we descended into the coastal area and joined a murmuring crowd at the Denpasar Poste Restante. In those days, this was the address visitors used for incoming mail.

People were talking about a cyclone destroying Darwin and we initially thought they were referring to Cyclone Selma which had by-passed Darwin several weeks previously. There was much confusion, but it soon became clear that something very, very serious had happened.

We caught a bemo back to the village of Batuan. We were staying in the family compound of a Balinese teacher who had been on exchange at Wagaman Open School, where I had taught since it opened two years previously. Agung Putra was listening to an

Indonesian news broadcast and immediately began translating for us. We heard the words "death, destruction and disease."

My friend and I walked in different directions outside trying to process this information and to think what it meant for us. Our husbands were there. We decided that we must get accurate information and find out how to return.

"Ha ha," laughed the smiling men at the airline office throwing their hands in the air, "Darwin Kaput."

So began our daily routine: bemo to Denpasar Poste Restante to send telegrams and aerograms to everyone we could think of: husbands, family, workplaces, consulate, embassies, Red Cross. Then, on to the central market for a breakfast of mie-goreng and to purchase things that we thought we might need on our return. I bought fabric and had some clothing made. Then again to the airline office, still "ha ha."

Indonesian news continued to focus on death, destruction, and disease with reports of looters, dogs being shot, and armed police patrolling the streets. We could only function with the belief that our husbands, Richard, and Harry, were alive. In my letters and telegrams to Richard I was saying I would stay in Bali until I heard from him or until he could join me. It was such a confusing time and communication options in Bali at that time were very limited.

We thought someone on a yacht in Benoa harbour might have English language news on short wave Radio Australia or the BBC World Service, so we made our way to the harbour and eventually managed to hear a BBC broadcast. Unfortunately, and very frustratingly, it was only cricket. We also tried to find a boat that might be going to Darwin. No luck with that. It was a long shot, but we were exploring all options.

Ten days later news finally arrived for me in a telegram marked "National Disaster Emergency" from Richard and a letter and telegram from my mother. I was very relieved to know that Richard was alive and driving south in a convoy, down the west coast to Perth.

My next and final visit to the airline office was to change my ticket destination from Darwin to Jakarta then on to Perth. No more "ha ha!"

I arrived early morning in Perth and was met by my in-laws, who were concerned about how skinny I was. I was recovering from a bout of dysentery. They were pleased to give me news about our three cats. They had been taking care of them after Richard had managed to get them to Perth.

At 5am I phoned my mum in Geraldton, and Richard answered! He had been with her for a few days while she washed things that he had salvaged, including a hand stitched double sided patchwork quilt that she had made for me. We reunited in Perth and after a few weeks R and R catching up with family and friends, we had some big decisions to make.

While we were in Perth we saw the documentary, *When will the Birds Return?* made by Film Australia. It was my first opportunity to really get an idea of the extent of the destruction the cyclone had caused.

Figure 7: Patsy takes her first look at her destroyed home.

We knew we could both get work in Perth again, and we had family and good friends who encouraged us to stay, so it would have been easy to resume our life there. However, during our three years in the Northern Territory, Darwin and the lifestyle had somehow captured my heart. We had also put a deposit on a block of land in the rural area. I felt strongly that I couldn't abandon this special place in its time of need. We decided to return.

With the permits system we were required to have a job and accommodation. The Education Department notified me that there was a job for me, and a friend offered us accommodation in his factory. We applied for permits. There was no problem for Richard who was an ABC journalist, however my approval hadn't come through. Eventually after tears of frustration from me in the government office and a phone call to Darwin, I received my permit.

We returned to Darwin at the end of January to a wonderful sense of community and generous sharing as we all got to work to clean up and restore our broken town. It was a time of joyful reunion with friends but also heartbreak as we saw the extent of damage.

My first job involved cleaning up schools in the northern suburbs and salvaging whatever resources we thought were still usable. We also helped with cleaning up evacuation centres and salvaging tins of food from water-sodden boxes. By early February 1975, there were enough children returning to enable the opening of the Northern Suburbs Primary School in the front building of Casuarina High School.

By then we had moved into a flat in Eden Street, Stuart Park (mould and more mould!) which had been reroofed by the navy, and we had the luxury of hot showers and meals at the ABC, where Richard worked.

There were daily broadcasts about which streets were about to be cleared. Before the bulldozers moved in, defence force people helped individuals with the salvage of personal items. I was in tears when I found an earring that my father had given to my mother. We found some bits and pieces that we stored, wrapped in newspaper, in a rubbish bin. Unfortunately, someone helpfully put the bin on the kerb when the council's rubbish collection resumed, so goodbye again!

Despite the necessary public emphasis on clean-up rather than salvage, we decided to salvage as much as we could. With friends we gathered everything we could, including the proverbial kitchen sink. I also salvaged many, many garden plants and they grew well in the ongoing wet season.

Later in the year, we moved to our block in the rural area and lived in a caravan while building our house. We were able to use many recycled items, such as plumbing fittings, sinks, toilets, louvre galleries, bathtubs, and swapped with friends doing the same thing.

We all learned many new skills in that time, including changing tyres, the result of so many punctures from nails and screws on the roads. There was very much a "can do" attitude, combined with a determination to get on with life in the place we loved.

Postscript. A few years later while on another holiday in Bali, this time with Richard and staying with friends, I met a New Zealand woman who had married a Balinese man in the seventies. I was telling her about meditating on a mountain while Darwin was being blown to bits. With further discussion we realised that I had been staying in the losmen owned by her father-in-law. The family hotel subsequently built on that land is a place we love to spend time. It's still a perfect place for meditating.

Murray Dawson

Murray arrived in Darwin in 1971 when he and an army mate, seeking fame and fortune, took up prawn fishing in the Gulf of Carpentaria for six months, after which he worked for AGC Finance Insurance Company. He met his wife, Lyndy who had moved to Darwin in 1971 for the opening of the Commercial Television Station, NTD8 and to be with her parents. They married in June 1973 and lived on the corner of Dripstone and Trower Roads in Alawa.

We were planning to build our own home in 1975, so in the interim were living with Lyndy's parents in their two-level Government house. Her father, Ray Wilkie, was the Officer-in-Charge of the Bureau of Meteorology in Darwin.

I was employed by AGC Finance Insurance Company, but on Christmas Eve I was moonlighting at the shell service station on the corner of Trower and Dripstone roads. After work, I went home, which was just across the road, had a drink with my neighbour, Brian Clark, and when he left about 10 o'clock we went to bed.

Soon the wind was so strong it was bending the glass louvres in the upstairs windows so that water was coming in. Lyndy, her mother Joan, and I got towels, and were mopping up but after a while it became apparent that the wind wasn't going to stop and that we were in quite some danger being upstairs in the house. So, we went downstairs and stayed there for the duration of the cyclone.

About 1 o'clock the top of the house was blown onto the roof of the bottom part of the house. That effectively protected the bottom part from blowing away, so the three of us stayed there with the cat, which was pissing itself in fear. We were in several inches of water the whole time, shivering cold. For Christmas I had bought a Lyndy a big, thick, woven cotton wall hanging for our new house, so I crawled through the debris to get her Christmas present, and we wrapped ourselves in it for the duration of the cyclone.

Sometime in the early hours, a family of neighbours arrived to shelter in the downstairs dining room with us. One of the adults was so drunk he slept in a chair throughout and in the morning going outside to pee. '*Fuck*!" he said. "What happened?'

At dawn we were able to see the extent of the damage. My next-door neighbour's house was almost completely destroyed. I went over to the fence and called out to him until he finally heard me. He and his wife had retreated to the bathroom and were trapped. I climbed up onto the floorboards of the elevated house and kicked a hole in the wall to enable them to get out.

After that we were quite concerned about Ray, who was in the bureau in the MLC building in town. He told us later that the wind was so strong it was bending the building so far out of alignment that curtains which would normally hang say, 6 inches from the wall, would be 18 inches from the bottom of the wall in the strongest gusts before straightening up. But the building remained intact.

In the morning when he was able to drive home, Bagot Road was just chock-a-block full of all sorts of debris, but he was able to pick his way through it, although I think he got several punctures from the nails in the timber from the destroyed houses. Eventually about 10 o'clock, he arrived back at the Dripstone Road house, much to the Joan's relief.

Surprisingly, Ray's baby grand piano survived, as well as the Christmas presents we had put on top to keep them out of the water. The piano gave many years of service when they eventually moved to Brisbane.

With part of the house still usable, we were able to camp there using cushions from the government-issue cane lounges to sleep on. One night it rained, and we slept in an inch of water, but it was all part of the fun of the whole thing.

When it rained the gutters were running, so we broke some downpipes and put rubbish bins underneath to collect water to wash with or flush the toilet.

We had an upright freezer which started to defrost. Starting with the food out of the fridge, we cooked a large pot stew on a wood fire out in the yard and kept topping it up as food thawed.

Eventually we salvaged a couple of beds, dried out some mattresses and were able to go to the end of the house where it was sheltered, after we blocked up the shattered windows. Later we bought an electric shower rose and enjoyed warm showers for quite a while.

The Wilkies were later allocated a house in Rapid Creek, and so that's where we all moved. Lyndy and I stayed in Darwin until February, when we used our government R and R tickets to go to Brisbane for two weeks. Lyndy was working for Ansett, and they needed her back and AGC Finance also had plenty of work for me to do in Darwin, chasing up damaged vehicles which were under finance.

I subsequently moved to MacRobertson Miller Airlines, by then an Ansett subsidiary. We returned to Brisbane permanently in 1979.

Jan Fanning

Jan Fanning (nee Lovegrove) was born in Alice Springs where her father, Creed Lovegrove, had been posted as a patrol officer with what was then the Welfare Branch of the Department of Native Affairs. In 1972, her father was appointed head of the renamed Department of Aboriginal Affairs under the newly elected Whitlam Government and moved to Darwin. Jan married John Wauchope, from another well-known Central Australian family and they had two children at that stage. She was 22 at the time of Tracy and was staying at her parents' house in Tambling Terrace, Wanguri.

My husband, John, and I had just moved to Darwin at the start of what was to be a round-Australia trip with our sons, Paul 3, and baby Danny, 11 months. We were looking after my mum and dad's home while they went to Sydney for a holiday with the youngest two of my four brothers. The other two brothers, Douglas and Richard and one of their girlfriends, Natalie stayed with us. Being Christmas Eve, we were busy getting ready for Christmas putting presents under the tree and roasting chooks in the oven.

The elevated house in Tambling Terrace, Wanguri was newly built, and my parents had only moved in six weeks before. The street was then the most northerly street in Wanguri, so it looked across the road to bush.

By 9 pm the house was beginning to shake with the strength of the wind and rain was blowing in through the closed louvres. I had put the kids on a mattress on the bathroom floor as we were advised, the bathroom being the strongest room with the smallest windows. I filled the bath with water as also advised.

My husband and I sat in the lounge room with our chairs shaking like we were on a train. We decided to go and check the kids about 11 pm and as we walked through the dining room the whole house exploded: walls peeled away, windows went flying and I could see electric cables blowing wildly in the wind.

I dashed in and picked up the two children, one on each hip while John went and got the other three out of bed. We made for the shower recess where we squatted squashed together, knees up under our chins, unable to hear each other even when we screamed at the top of our voices, the wind and other noises being so loud. At one stage the linen cupboard fell on top of me, a large piece of wood banged under my arm and the bathroom floor kept rearing up as the wind caught beneath it.

For about 5 hours I had my baby, Danny, in my lap and for at least two hours I sat there thinking he was dead because he didn't move or make a sound. I thought I must have suffocated him! Eventually, I placed my wet finger under his nose and felt his warm breath on my cold fingers! What a relief! Paul meanwhile sat with eyes like saucers not understanding what was happening.

Part way through the night the wind died down a little, and one of my brothers tried to go downstairs. He found a way for all of us to go, even though many floorboards were missing, and we all made our way down to the windowless concrete-block storeroom where we found, in a trunk, some umbrellas and blankets – all very welcome items. The floorboards above the storeroom were missing so we put up the umbrellas and snuggled into the blankets as it was very cold.

As dawn approached the wind died down and we decided to venture outside. We couldn't believe our eyes. For as far as we could see there was devastation; no houses left standing, cars and caravans overturned and blown along the roads. It looked like a graveyard. There was not a leaf left on a tree, no bushes or shrubs or grass anywhere; everyone's gardens had gone with their houses.

Sheets of roofing iron draped over electricity lines, like pieces of cloth on a washing line, and instead of tall, straight electricity poles, they were whipped around in spirals as if they had been strands of spaghetti. Across the street we could now see the distant sea at Casuarina Beach. All the children's Christmas presents had been blown away!

After a while, we began to think about what we needed to do to make ourselves safe and comfortable. We found some mattresses, a couple of tarpaulins, and a big pot. The men walked about picking up the VB cans they could see strewn everywhere. With lots of wood everywhere, we built a warm fire and using the slowly thawing meat out of Mum's freezer we cooked up a big stew. We made a shelter under the house, put the mattresses there and that's where we slept for the next couple of nights.

Later that first day, Paul, my three-year-old, was looking towards the back wire fence when he saw a flat, red parcel which had blown up against the wire. It was somebody's Christmas present that had blown into our yard, so of course, I let him open it. He was delighted to find, of all things, a kite.

We set it up for him and flew it in the gentle breeze that was now bathing Darwin. A photographer happened to be passing by, saw him and took his photo. This photo, captioned *Childhood Resilience*, was later published in Major General Alan Stretton's book about Cyclone Tracy. It also hung in the Darwin Museum for many years and was used on the front cover of a children's book called *Disasters*. Paul is quite famous!

Over the next three days we slowly tried to salvage what we could of Mum and Dad's belongings, which wasn't much, but we took what we saved to friends down the track whose house was undamaged. We also dragged our caravan out from where we had lashed it to the concrete piers under the house. Although the walls from the lounge room had fallen on top and damaged the caravan's roof, they had held it in place and protected it from worse damage. The most important thing to me was my sewing machine, which we found three days later in a puddle of muddy water hidden under a sheet of corrugated roofing iron. We dried it out, got it working later and it lasted another fifteen years.

Figure 8: 'Childhood Resilience', Paul and Danny Wauchope still have their copy of *Disasters*, with the picture of Paul and his kite on its front cover.

Soon after that we packed everything up, hitched the van to the sandblasted car and left Darwin, accompanied by my brother in his damaged, but drivable car. We all felt it was not safe to stay with small children.

Thousands of people had the same idea, so we joined the convoy of hundreds of cars, trucks and vans – most with some degree of damage – making their way to Alice Springs. They were all packed with belongings. On the top of one well-packed truck sat a young boy! I was reminded of scenes from the *Grapes of Wrath* by John Steinbeck.

On our drive to the Alice, everyone was so kind. There were food stations set up and we could get free meals, most fuel stations gave us free fuel, lots of charity organisations had clothes, toiletries, baby gear and other essentials. We were so grateful for all that care.

It was such a relief to get to Alice Springs where we had family and friends and what we thought of as civilisation.

Over the next few months, we repaired the damaged caravan, sold it to buy a smaller one and in May 1975 we returned to Darwin where my parents – my mother having finally been able to return to Darwin with my two youngest brothers – had moved into a house in Stuart Park. We decided to stay on in Darwin at that stage, but because of a lack of suitable accommodation in Darwin, we moved to Goulburn Island (Warrawi) where John worked for the Warrawi Housing Association.

Peter Garton

Peter, and his partner Pam, were in New Zealand when Cyclone Tracy visited Darwin, but as an insurance assessor he rushed back to Darwin to get back to work as soon as he could. They lived in a duplex in Nightcliff with Peter's parents. Adding metal rod tiedowns to his house in the weeks prior to Cyclone Selma saved their house during Tracy. As an environmental activist, one of the outcomes of Peter's post-Tracy years was the building of the Humpty Doo Solar Village project.

In 1974, I was living in a duplex in Nightcliff with my partner Pam, and my parents. The building was designed for tropical living by a friend in Adelaide and I had subcontracted to various trades to complete the structure. There was no "cyclone code" at the time and I was aware of the fact that the fixings from roof rafters to walls were designed to hold the roof up, not down, also the tropical design meant there were lots of louvres.

My parents occupied the back half of the duplex. Pam and I lived in the front. Pam was an occupational therapist working at the Darwin Hospital with many Aboriginal people. I was working in the family business of insurance and loss adjusting.

We had become active in the environmental movement and had also developed an interest in the colourful history of the Top End. Our interest in the region and its climate meant we knew Darwin had been struck by serious tropical cyclones at thirty-to-forty-year intervals. Around the dinner table one night we were discussing this history and the fact that the last major cyclone to strike Darwin was in 1937. So, in 1974, we were due for another one.

Some of Pam's Aboriginal clients told her they noticed features in the local flora and fauna that indicated a cyclone was coming. As we were running an insurance assessing business we knew we would be exceptionally busy if there was a cyclone, so we resolved to rectify any structural deficiencies in our house before one arrived.

The idea became relevant in early December when there was a warning of the imminent approach of Cyclone Selma. There was no time to redesign the house, so we fixed lengths of steel pipe along the eaves and tied them to blocks of half a cubic metre of concrete at several locations along both sides of the house using steel rods. We also made plywood shutters for each of the louvred window frames.

Cyclone Selma turned out to be a bit of a dud, but we felt we were equipped to deal with the real thing if it came.

Pam and I had arranged to spend Christmas in New Zealand and left Darwin in mid-December. We were woken up on Christmas morning in Rotorua by our hostess and told that Darwin had been destroyed by a cyclone. We immediately arranged to get back to Australia. The stewards on the QANTAS flight from Auckland to Sydney were aware of our plight and gave us special attention. In Sydney we were able to establish that my mum and dad were OK, but we faced difficulties getting back into Darwin as the place was being evacuated. Fortunately, my uncle was a senior executive in one of Australia's major TV stations and he arranged for me to get back to Darwin aboard a private plane carrying his news crew. Permits were impossible to get and despite the fact that Pam was an allied health worker at Darwin Hospital, she was not able to get back for another ten days

The arrival in Darwin was nothing short of shocking. As we descended through the clouds to land, the view out over the city was one of complete devastation. There were no leaves on the lush tropical vegetation usually visible during the wet season. The newly built public housing in the northern suburbs was reduced to street after street of rubble.

There was evidence of surviving structures in the city itself but clearly nothing had completely survived the intensity of Cyclone Tracy.

The press plane I arrived in parked on the Darwin Airport apron, along with a number of large passenger aircraft loading residents who were evacuating. This meant there was a wall of people between the apron and the terminal building, and to get into the terminal I had to climb a barrier fence, push through the crowd, then climb through a broken window. Only then could I get into the carpark and out onto the Stuart Highway and hitch a ride to Nightcliff and the family home.

Our house was mostly intact, apart from the front bedroom which had been crushed when the roof of a neighbouring house had lifted off as a complete structure and landed on it.

Mum and Dad were in surprisingly good spirits. They had planned to have a few guests around for a Christmas dinner but when it became apparent that a severe cyclone was on the way they put up the shutters and prepared for the worst. Their guests did arrive on Christmas Day, but as refugees from the destruction of their own houses.

Mum and Dad's end of the duplex was undamaged and there was lots of food to be consumed, as there was no electricity to run fridges or freezers. Most of the guests were moving on to evacuation centres, but Christmas lunch was served. Someone dug some trenches and erected screens in the garden to provide toilet facilities and to bury the food not eaten. We had gas stoves and cylinders, so cooking was not an issue.

Mum had followed the recommendation to store fresh water in the bath for emergency use, but unbeknown to her, one of the visiting children had been given a tube of bubble bath in her Christmas stocking, and the presence of a bathtub with lots of water in it was too much of a temptation. Never mind – it rained for days and there was plenty of fresh water to be collected from the intact roof.

The conversation over Christmas lunch switched from families recounting the horror of their experiences the night before, to their concern about how they were going to manage for the next few days without reticulated power or water. I discovered sometime later that Mum tried to lift spirits by demonstrating how to maintain personal hygiene by stripping off her clothes and washing herself under the copious flow of water from the roof. Never one to give in to adversity, my mother.

To prepare for the work ahead of us, me and a mate named Bill, who had stayed in Darwin during Tracy, began setting up our city office. The nearest place you could get food from the city was a temporary kitchen set up at Darwin High School, and we went there to get something to eat around lunch time. There was hardly anything left, but as we were leaving the duty copper told us to clean the latrines and the empty kitchen.

No doubt, we looked like a couple of blow-ins on the bludge, but we told the copper that we were busy getting my office re-established, until he began to insist that we obey his command. We started to walk away, but stopped when we were surrounded by six or seven armed police from an interstate force. Bill then lost it and told the coppers that we were not going to be intimidated. His exact words were "we are not going to help you because you're too f....g heavy."

I grabbed Bill's arm, jumped into the car, and drove off. No charges were laid. To this day I am not sure whether my refusal to assist was genuine, or a reaction to the fact that the only food left was a piece of cake, and that was not sufficient reward for the task demanded.

Being an insurance assessor in such circumstances was an experience to remember. Many of the property owners were first generation Australians from Mediterranean countries; they had a colourful way of negotiating to which I had to rapidly adapt. Most of them were in the building trade and had built their own commercial properties. They had an accurate idea about the cost of reinstatement, and it was their job to extract as much as they could for their loss. Negotiations were sometimes animated and at times tearful, but always entertaining.

Most private dwellings were underinsured. We developed the 'drive-by assessment' technique. I didn't even have to get out of the car to know I was looking at a total loss, because many houses were just a pile of rubble or a timber deck on piers. Unfortunately, the heap of sodden furniture and contents strewn about the yard usually cost more to replace than the sum for which it was insured. One problem we had was the identification of insured premises because street signs were missing or damaged, and street numbers obliterated. Local knowledge was essential.

I had only been in the insurance assessing business for three years at the time of Tracy. It was certainly a baptism of fire.

Uncertainty about the future of Darwin was at the core of the chaotic government response to Tracy. This provided those of us who were active in the environment movement with an opportunity not to be missed. The focus of our activity was a fossil fuel-free future and we tried to inject the idea of a low energy future in the design and re-construction of Darwin. That ambition was overtaken by the engineering response. This resulted in the replacement of the elevated lightweight tropical buildings with concrete boxes, which required air-conditioning.

The Darwin Reconstruction Commission graciously dismissed our suggestions with an offer for us to "show them how it could be done." They offered a piece of land just south-east of Darwin for us to use for a low energy development based on solar power, but the Australian Army now occupy that land.

Prior to Tracy, the Federal Government had given financial support to the Environment Council N.T. to employ a project officer. We were fortunate to find a well-known local journalist named Barb James, and she started the ball rolling by publishing a journal called *Solarwise*. Her research connected us to Steve Szokolay, an academic who studied tropical housing in the Architecture Faculty at Queensland University.

Steve offered to assist by setting our solar village objective as the project for his honours students. The students delivered a comprehensive report on the feasibility and design for such a project, but no Government financial support was forthcoming. However private support was building, so we decided to put together a less ambitious project with local participation. Several of us combined to purchase land at Humpty Doo, south-east of Darwin, and the Darwin Solar Village Project was born.

Andrea Gordon

Andrea and David Gordon lived in Waters Street, Rapid Creek, and ran the Nightcliff Pharmacy. The couple remained behind in the city's ruins as emergency services officers.

Trade at Nightcliff Pharmacy was brisk as usual with the added sales of last-minute purchases of gift packs for Christmas. The dispensary was particularly busy with customers coming in with prescriptions to be filled before they flew out in every direction to celebrate the New Year. Many of the locals had already left to have Christmas with family or friends elsewhere.

We were all aware that there was a cyclone warning, but this was not unusual for this time of the year. However, late in the afternoon customers told us that the cyclone had been upgraded, that it was teeming with rain outside, and the wind was picking up.

Around eight o'clock my friend Yvonne Worrall, a deputy matron at the hospital, rang from the hospital to say that they were 'on alert'. We had arranged to meet to go to midnight mass at the Anglican Cathedral. Yvonne said she would ring me later that night at home to reconfirm arrangements.

The pharmacy closed at 9.00 pm and I went home to prepare dinner for David, my husband, who was the pharmacist, and our friend and fellow pharmacist, Peter who lived with us at that time. Whilst preparing the meal I turned the radio on and became fully aware of the cyclone warnings. The instructions were to tie everything down, make sure that pets were safe, make sure everyone had enough drinking water and, preferably, stay home.

Yvonne phoned again saying that the hospital was now on 'high alert', that the wind was horrific in central Darwin and that the staff at the hospital were staying put. We arranged to meet for the Christmas morning service instead. I rang David and asked him to come home as soon as he could because of the worsening conditions, the scripts that had to be finally coded and sent to Canberra could wait.

Peter phoned around 11.00 pm, stating that he was staying at a friend's house because conditions were too bad for him to travel home. By this time the rain was lashing against the windows, and although the louvres were firmly closed and there was an external veranda at the front of the house protecting the passage and bedroom windows, water was coming in. The passage floorboards were awash. I grabbed the mop and kept on mopping, but it didn't make any difference.

Prior to the water coming into all of the rooms, I had collected the Christmas presents I had for my cousin June and her family from around the Christmas tree, and placed them onto the lounge to keep them dry – the lounge and the presents were never to be seen again.

We lived in Waters Street, Rapid Creek, in a typical elevated house situated just in from Rapid Creek Road and the tidal basin, it was on a large block that was bordered by five neighbouring blocks. The block had the usual sturdy wired fence surrounding it and an open driveway from the street.

In the early hours of the morning the wind was horrific. It was howling and screaming, and the house started to shake. There was water everywhere. Around 2 am on Christmas morning we could hear roofing being torn off and the house shook violently.

David said one word "run". I grabbed my engagement ring, a photo of my parents, and a crucifix which had been awarded to me when I was a teenager. We ran down the passage. It was now ankle deep in water.

There was only one exit from the house at that time and that was down the front stairs. David went first, and I followed clutching the rails for support as the strength of the wind tried to blow me away. The engagement ring was on my finger, the parents' photo and crucifix were down the front of my pyjamas.

A small flat had been built under the house where Peter usually slept, and we went into that, pulled the mattress off the bed and sat on the floor as far away as we could from the windows with the mattress over our heads. We had nowhere else to go. Huddled there clutching one another, we heard our house being demolished and I prayed fervently that the cross beam above us would hold and that we would be spared. I will never forget the screaming of the wind, the tearing of roofing, and the sound of things bashing into the walls before they too disintegrated.

Dawn came, it was still raining but the screaming wind slowed. We emerged wet through and very cold. The front stairs were still attached to the house, but it was now a shell of a building, with just a few, holed, walls left. The roof had gone. The lounge wall, together with the main bedroom wall, had completely disappeared as if someone had cut around the edges to remove them. I clearly remember saying to David, "I always wanted a view to sea, but not like that". We could see straight across to the mouth of Rapid Creek tidal basin and the beginning of Casuarina beach. Everything that had remained was sodden with water and dirt.

We learnt much later that we were luckier than many; our house had been privately built and was relatively solid compared to others, although it was damaged and shaken so violently that even the concrete pylons had moved, cracking the concrete floor downstairs. We were alive, and that was all that mattered. I couldn't find our cat and I knew that if I found her dead I would surely 'crack up' because all I felt at that time was numbness.

People in our street started to emerge from the rubble that was strewn everywhere. We all checked on one another to see if there were any casualties and to help where we could. Everyone was dazed and in shock, there was debris all over the road as far we could see, our concern now was to get to the Pharmacy to see what was left there.

We found some wet clothes, changed into them, and started walking in the drizzling rain, picking our way through the debris to Nightcliff, it was eerily quiet.

On arrival at Nightcliff, we found the front glass window smashed in, part of the roof missing and stock all over the floor. Everything was wet through and lots of broken glass and debris was over everything. However, the concrete wall the divided the front shop from the dispensary had remained intact so many plastic bottles and jars were not broken. This proved helpful when a man staggered in with part of his face cut open because I was able to cleanse the huge cut with Dettol and use butterfly clips to hold his face together. I advised him to get to the hospital as soon as he could and he asked, "how will I get there" and I replied "walk".

At that time on Progress Drive there were some flats that were still standing, and several young mothers came in to ask if we had any baby formula and bottles for their crying babies. The baby formula was in tins and the plastic bottles were ok, so we gave whatever we could salvage out of the rubble to anyone in need. Then the looters arrived, disgusting as they were, but they left quickly when they saw we were in the wrecked building.

Jan and Ron Natt lived not far from the pharmacy, and they arrived to see what they could do to help; Jan was our 'head lady'. We found some sheets of roof iron in the surrounding rubble and put a barrier across the front of the shop to stop further looting. We were told weeks later by friends who owned Nakara Pharmacy, that they had arrived at their shop to find people filling up garbage bags with stock, Homy Ped slippers and perfume seemed to be the favourite items to steal!

The following days seemed to merge into one another. There was so much to do in trying to filter through the rubble at home and to try and clean up the street so that cars that were still working could be used. One of the men who lived in the single storey flats that were across the road from us used a bobcat to pile up rubble on the side of the road.

Food-wise we were alright because the refrigerator downstairs was still there and although there was no electricity, all of the food that had previously been bought for Christmas celebrations with friends at our house was still edible for a couple of days. We sent word along the street for anyone to come and eat it up before it went off.

We filled a milk crate with tins of soft drink and beer and created a pulley system over our covered swimming pool to lower the crate into the water and try and keep the drinks cool. The pool had sheets of iron, wood, parts of trees and greenery in it but that didn't affect the tins.

One of our neighbours at the back had a very large caravan which had been picked up by the wind, blown over the top of our backyard shed and had landed in another neighbour's back yard. From this wrecked caravan we were given a small portable gas stove and bottle to use and some dry matches. In the following days I cooked tinned food and supplied something to eat for anyone, however small the serve was. Plates, knives, and forks were found in the rubble but, where needed, fingers were used.

Peter arrived home with his friend whose house had blown away. We all slept for a few hours of a night on the sodden mattresses under the shell of our house. To wash we used a broken fire hydrant on Rapid Creek Road.

My cousin, June and her family arrived by car after weaving their way through the rubble to check how we were. She said she planned to evacuate and drive 'south'. They were then able to get a message to our frantic parents and families in Adelaide and Perth that we were alive but not evacuating.

In the following days we learnt that evacuation was taking place and that Major General Alan Stretton had taken command, and that there was a daily broadcast of what to do and where to go to be evacuated. A transistor radio was found, and we would all huddle together at the specified time to listen to the broadcast and await further instructions.

In the meantime, an emergency centre had been set up at Nightcliff High School and the local doctors were treating the injured there. It was also a central hub for people to gather for shelter and was an evacuation centre. David and I were registered as emergency service workers and from our pharmacy collected the typhoid, cholera, and tetanus vials for injections, as well as bandages, antiseptics etc. that were wrapped in plastic and had not been damaged.

When we had cleaned up the rubble from our house, backyard, and street we concentrated on the Nightcliff shopping centre area. Many days were spent on the end of a shovel and sorting through rubble. One of the stark memories of that time that I have is of a very tall, broad, bare chested, moustached policeman walking down the lane way behind us and asking what we were doing and why was I still here if women were to be evacuated,?

I replied that I was classified as essential service. The policeman had a shotgun in one hand and a string of bullets over his shoulder. With his long dark hair, he looked like someone from a Mexican Western; his role was to keep out looters from the surrounding properties telling us that he was sickened with what he had seen and that he 'would shoot the bastards' if he caught anyone else.

Back in Rapid Creek, the Navy arrived and took over the corner house next to us as their 'hub' for crews to go out and start repairing houses.

We were told that a helicopter was bringing crews of men at daylight, landing on a suburban oval and then transferring them into jeeps to go to their 'hub'. The jeeps had previously been brought across from the ship by helicopters and remained at the oval overnight.

I cannot remember exactly when the drizzling rain finally stopped but whenever it was we pulled the sodden mattresses out into the sunshine to try and dry them. Most of the clothing found was so wet and dirty it had started to grow mould. We didn't need much but I did learn that one can go days without a lot of clothing or food but not long without water.

The sailors were coming back to the house next door, red like lobsters because they worked bare chested replacing iron onto roofs of the Government houses and the sun was now shining. I spoke to the office-in-charge and offered the sunscreen we had at the pharmacy. I respectfully suggested that the men should start using it and wearing hats. He thanked me and said that the comments were noted. We gathered all of the sunscreen and gave it to them the next day.

Some days later the officer called me and said that as a 'thank you for your kindness' his men would put a flat roof onto our shell of a house and patch it up as much as possible. He asked David and me if we would participate in a short Navy film about the work they were doing to clean up Darwin. We managed to see it on T.V. later that year.

Some of the sailors told us that when the news had come through that Naval House on the Esplanade had been destroyed, no one believed it because of the thickness of the bricks/mortar used in its original construction. However, that office, plus Brown's Mart, the town hall, and Christ Church Cathedral were in a similar situation.

Speaking of Christ Church Cathedral, months later I was speaking to Anglican Bishop Ken Mason about the cyclone, and he commented that he thought that there must have been more prayers sent to heaven that fateful night than ever before.

The days rolled on: we went to get supplies of food from Darwin High School relief centre and took only what we needed to survive. We were sad to seeing some people abusing the system by filling bags up with more tinned food than they would need. Most of the people who had to be evacuated had left by then and the population, we were told over the transistor, was about 10,000 people. There was no need for anyone to be greedy. The cyclone certainly brought out the best and the worst in people.

We were ruined financially by Tracy. We had been married for two years and had contracted to buy three pharmacies including Nightcliff Pharmacy. It took 14 years of solid hard work to get on our feet again, but we managed. Where there is a will there is a way.

Rodney Gregg

Rodney Gregg and his twin brother Ashley were 9-year-olds during the cyclone. They were living with their parents in one of the new elevated houses in Nakara. The boys were joined by the rest of their family from 'down south' for the first family Christmas together for years.

In 1973, we lived in Geebung, a suburb of Brisbane until Dad had a job transfer, and we packed up and moved north to Darwin. Dad was an engineer for Trans Australia Airways (TAA), Mum had retired from nursing, and there was me and my twin brother Ash.

Our older brother, David, was in the Royal Australian Navy and based in Sydney, while our sister Sue-Anne was newly married with two small children and was living in Brisbane at this time.

For the first few months we lived in a rental house in The Narrows, while our new home was being built in Nakara, in the northern suburbs. We moved into our brand-new home in late 1973, and encountered our first "wet season". There was lots of rain but typically, life went on as normal. Ash and I went to St Mary's Primary School in Darwin. The bus journey in those days seemed to take forever.

Life was good for our family. We made friends with our neighbours and spent many days riding our bikes and exploring the suburbs around us. If we were home before the streetlights came on, our parents were happy.

In December 1974, we were experiencing our second wet season, it was common to have big storms with lots of wind and lightning, thunder and, of course, the rain. Sometimes, the wind was so strong that the rain was horizontal when it hit you. About three weeks before Christmas, the first cyclone of the season was named 'Selma.' I remember lots of thunder and heavy rain. It was heading towards Darwin, but before it hit land, it veered north and petered out to a rain depression.

Around this time, our brother David and sister Sue-Ann arrived in Darwin to spend the holiday season with us. We were now a whole family again planning to spend Christmas together for the first time in several years.

'Tracy' formed a few days before Christmas, and as it was tracking the same route taken by Selma, many thought it would continue to go the same way though it looked like Christmas Day would be a wet one!

Christmas eve for us was like in every other home in Australia. We had a tree up and there were lots of presents ready to be opened the following day.

I remember, the rain and winds starting to increase in intensity from about lunchtime on Christmas Eve. Unbeknown to us, the city of Darwin was in Tracy's direct path.

During the night, the wind increased to the point where Dad, with the help of our close neighbours, braced the sliding glass doors at the front of the house with timber beams. But, not wanting to alarm us, he told us it was "time for bed". So, like many excited nine-year-olds before Christmas, we headed for our room at the other end of the house and went to bed.

I'm not too sure how long we were asleep, but around 1a.m. Dad came into our room and wanted us to get some of our things together. He said we had to move downstairs and take refuge in the laundry. As I turned to look at our bedroom for the last time, I saw one corner of the ceiling was starting to lift and flap.

Ash and I grabbed some of our presents from under the Christmas tree and the family headed for the back steps.

It was only then that I realised how serious it was getting.

As we headed down the back stairs, the rain stung every part of our bodies. The power had been out for some time, but the lightning outside was so intense that it lit up the whole back stairs and yard with every flash. We were nine very frightened people making our way down the stairs. We made it into the laundry, and we were in there for a short time before Dad decided it would be best for us to get into the car. Mum and Dad sat in the front seat of the family station wagon, our brother and sister took the back seat, and Ash and I jumped in the rear. Dad tried unsuccessfully several times to start the car because he wanted to take us to the safety of the cyclone shelter at the Nakara Primary School, about 1.5km away. Not being able to start it, in hindsight, saved our family's lives. The suburb and all of Darwin, was slowly disintegrating under Tracy's fury.

At about 1:15am we heard the front glass doors explode. The wind then pushed the roof and walls across the floor and deposited them at the rear of our house. In doing so, destroying the stairs that had led us to safety only a few moments before.

The sound of a town in terror, is something that we will never forget, the scraping of hundreds of iron roof sheets, the howling wind, the thunder, and the rain.

At some stage during the night, parts of houses around us began hitting our home and car. The rear window smashed, and shattered glass covered Ash and me. We both jumped the seat and sat huddled, cold, scared and shivering, to wait out the long night of devastation. Iron roofing sheets were hitting the pillars near us with so much force they began wrapping around them, and that gave the car some shelter and protected us, as Tracy's fury continued.

Suddenly there was a calm, the rain eased, and a lot of the noise faded away. 'Was that it?'

No, we were in the eye of Tracy. She hadn't finished with us yet. Gradually, the screaming of the wind and rain returned, but this time there was an even greater intensity, as she weaved her way around the northern suburbs of Darwin.

As dawn broke on Christmas Day, the wind and rain had finally ceased, we could, for the first time, see what remained. There was total destruction, as far as the eye could see. Also, there was an eerie silence that came with our first impressions of that morning. Everything that we owned had been blown away. The scene, that we have never forgotten, was destruction in all directions. Whole suburbs were reduced to rubble.

There was an eerie grey light for several hours. We made our way up the front stairs and could not really comprehend the destruction laid before us. Later, Dad was able to start the car first go that morning, As a family, we often spoke about that through the years, and firmly believe we were meant to survive. It was our Christmas gift from a higher being.

Sometime on Christmas Day, we made it to the Nakara Primary School, and our first night was spent in a makeshift cubby house in one of the classrooms, with desks pushed together to form a roof.

Ash and I were airlifted to Brisbane two or three days later. Dad washed us in a rubbish bin filled with rainwater and we changed into our Christmas clothes and made it to the airport. The last thing Dad did was to slip a $10 note in in each of our pockets, and he said, 'I'll see you boys soon'.

It was a crowded flight to Brisbane, no one spoke, everyone just stared blankly ahead and tried to comprehend what we had all just experienced.

After disembarking the plane on the tarmac of Kingsford Smith Airport, we were guided into a hanger filled with rows of clothing and household items. We selected clothes and presents. We had brought no luggage with us.

Close family friends met us, and we stayed with them for about a week in Brisbane before relocating temporarily to the central coast of NSW.

We couldn't return to Darwin until the middle of 1975, and

only when the living facilities were suitable for families to return. Dad had spent the six months making our house liveable. What once was the floor of the house became the roof, and we slept in a caravan under it. The eating area and TV room was fully enclosed, and we had a running shower and toilet. Dad had done a great job renovating what Tracy had left us on Christmas day, so we again had a home and were a family again.

We returned to school and commenced grade five at St Mary's Primary School. I joined the Jingili Soccer Club and trained twice a week at the school. Our matches were held at the Gardens Oval. We had goals, but no nets and we tried to return to a normal life. At the end of 1975, we left Darwin and our family moved to Redcliffe, Queensland where we finished our schooling.

Alan Haines

Alan, 20 and single at the time, arrived in Darwin in August 1974. Living in Adelaide, he was enticed by his brother Phil's suggestion of "let's go to Darwin". After a very cold winter in Adelaide, adventure in the tropics seemed ideal. Alan, Phil and his wife Annie packed the car and left Adelaide the next day. 3,000 kilometres later, a thousand of which was a very rough dirt track, they arrived in Darwin. Alan found work quickly with Spraypave, a Shell-owned company. Alan's job was to do whatever was necessary to keep a camp of about 50 men fed and working. In 1974, Alan lived in a mobile camp as they worked on parts of the Stuart Highway. He returned to Darwin on Christmas Eve and sheltered from the cyclone at Temira House, with his sister, a nurse.

I was due to fly Ansett to Melbourne at 9 o'clock on Christmas morning to attend the wedding of my dear friend Rosemary to Philip, in Ballarat.

My sister, Vicki, a third-year nurse at Darwin Hospital and I went to midnight mass at St. Mary's Cathedral, but the wind was already howling around outside. Just after communion had been taken there was a loud and very sharp bang followed by darkness. The mass was completed by candlelight.

To appreciate conditions at that time it is best to go to the Museum and Art Gallery's Tracy exhibit where the sound used was actually recorded at the church around one o'clock.

The last radio message we heard before the ABC went off air was some advice to 'get to shelter now' and 'do not attempt to drive down Bagot Road'. It was reported live power lines, and the odd light aircraft were presenting obstacles to accessing Nightcliff and beyond.

Consequently, as I could not get to my flat in Nightcliff, I stayed with Vicki at Temira House, the three-storey nurses' residence at the hospital. There were thirty-two rooms on each floor: thirty bedrooms, a lounge and a hairdressing room which had an air vent in one window. This vent was our saviour. The air pressure differential in a cyclone can cause buildings to collapse inwards and then the force of the winds does the rest of the damage. The air vent in this room meant there was little pressure differential.

The end windows of the central hallway on each floor of the building were blown away. The wind gusted at a frightening pace right through them but despite this, we managed to get the nurses into the hair-dressing rooms just in time.

A long, terrifying night ensued with a brief break as the eye of the cyclone passed. Calm came about dawn. I looked across the road to the Burnett houses. All appeared intact although the second house had been lifted in its entirety off its pillars and deposited on top of several vehicles parked below. The remains of demountable buildings at the hospital were strewn everywhere.

The hospital matron knew of me through my visits to my sister and arranged to have me and other men stay on each floor of the residence. The next week was spent doing whatever was asked of me around the hospital.

These days my brain is reluctant to detail accurately what happened during that week. Traumatic things occurred and were seen but I don't need or want to revisit them.

I do remember spending about 36 hours in the middle of that week at the Airport assisting with the evacuation of women and children.

The evacuations took place through the wartime hangar which was the passenger terminal and it had been considerably damaged.

People were bused into the terminal and anyone who had not

departed at the end of the day when the flights stopped had to stay at the terminal overnight.

Flights recommenced at first light the next morning. I spent a night with about 800 women and children while a storm raged. The desperate bravery shown by mothers fearing it was another cyclone is etched in my memory.

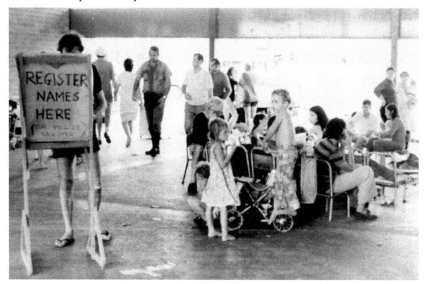

Figure 9: Registration centre after Cyclone Tracy (Bert Wiedemann Collection LANT, ph0611-0020

Returning to the hospital, which by then had been without running water for several days, I remember the joy of finding a large bottle of Fanta which was shared by many as we clamoured to clean our teeth using as little of the liquid as possible.

The oil terminals on McMinn Street had all been damaged. Authorities determined that the Shell terminal would be repaired so that fuel supplies to Darwin and the Top End could be guaranteed. Much of the technical expertise to get the terminal operational was supplied by naval staff who returned to their ships each night.

My employer had relocated the mobile bitumen camp to Darwin and set it up in front of the Shell terminal in McMinn Street. The camp accommodated the staff necessary to operate the terminal, and to distribute fuel throughout Darwin and the Top End. I returned to my role as a general dogsbody requisitioning food, alcohol, and clothing to keep a camp of about 50 men comfortable.

One day I took a break and drove out to the northern suburbs. Having passed what was left of the Casuarina shops I stopped the car at Henbury Avenue and stared towards the Dripstone cliffs. All that was left of Nakara was a forest of concrete pillars.

Every resident was given an R and R evacuation flight. In February 1975, I took advantage of mine. Shell had organised a transfer for me to its Adelaide office. My bank book and driver's license had disappeared in the cyclone, but I did still have my Ansett Airlines ticket. I went to an office in King William Street to register my arrival from Darwin. The registration office staff spoke to Ansett, and I was directed around the corner to the North Terrace office of the airline. They immediately wrote a cheque to refund the full amount and organised for the ANZ bank next door to cash the cheque.

I returned to Darwin for brief stints in '75 and '76 and then returned permanently in 1987. Sometime in the middle of 1975 I did deliver my wedding gift to Rose and Phil.

Trish Hansen

Trish Hansen (nee Munro) arrived in Darwin in 1957 at the age of four when her father took a job with the Commonwealth Public Service, partly (as she says) to escape his family and partly because it offered a government-supplied house for his own growing family. At the time of Tracy, Trish was in her first year of teaching at Darwin High School. She lived in Cooper Street, Fannie Bay with her parents and brothers.

When we were kids roaming the streets of Parap and Fannie Bay, my five brothers and I used to dream that one day a cyclone would come and blow our neighbour's house away. Mr Stiller was a local teacher whose garden had manicured lawns, perfectly pruned shrubs and two long rows of pineapples bordering our fence that we looked at longingly but never dared touch.

Our house had a few dreary trees, waist-high spear grass and a large mound of topsoil that my father ordered and never spread. We Munros wanted Stiller out. Of course, it was wishful thinking because when we were growing up, cyclones would form ominously over the Arafura Sea, warnings would be issued, winds and rain would increase, the cyclone would hover and then, somehow miraculously turn away.

That happened with Cyclone Selma so not surprisingly, many locals ignored the warnings for Cyclone Tracy. We shopped for Christmas presents, turkeys and hams, filled the fridges with stubbies and a bottle of Barossa pearl for the ladies and public servants knocked off at lunch and went to boozy office parties that lasted well into the night.

I was in my first year of teaching at Darwin High School, where I had been educated as a somewhat unruly teenager. Being school holidays, on Christmas Eve, I hopped in my little Datsun to go out to Lim's on the Rapid Creek foreshore for a few celebratory drinks with friends.

I noticed the winds were strong and I remember thinking this cyclone might actually hit. But nothing could deter a young 21-year-old from having fun on Christmas Eve. When my boyfriend and I arrived at the veranda bar at Lim's, it was pretty deserted. We settled in for a few and watched a barman battling to put up some hessian sheets to keep out the wind and driving rain.

At 11.00 pm we set off for Darwin Hospital to drop my boyfriend at work. He was a fourth-year medical student and was completing an internship. It was uncharacteristically quiet at the hospital, so the supervising Doctor told my boyfriend to go home and come back the next morning. '*There'll probably be a few extra patients with cuts and bruises from this storm,*' he said confidently.

Just before midnight, we set off down Gilruth Avenue towards home at Cooper street, Fannie Bay. As I drove, I had to steer almost into the wind to keep my little Datsun on the road. We had no idea that the cyclone was about to hit the northern suburbs.

When we arrived home, the wind was ferocious, and our elevated government house was shaking but we all headed off to bed. Three of my five brothers and boyfriend were in the end bedroom and when their wall started to shake uncontrollably, they retreated to the middle room with me. We huddled together under mattresses expecting each gust of wind to blow our fragile, fibro house away.

We agreed that if the house started to go, we'd head down to a large EJ holden parked underneath. The boys would carry my father who was paralysed from a recent stroke. I would follow with Mum.

Eventually, the winds eased and there was an eerie silence for about ten minutes. We were terrified to venture out because we knew it was only the eye, a brief respite before the winds picked up again, more savagely than before.

Those last few hours were terrifying and as the wind howled and screamed, the house shook and swayed, and debris smashed our roof, walls, and louvres.

The wind eased as dawn broke, and we struggled out to assess the destruction. Miraculously, our house had suffered minimal damage: a few loose roofing sheets, holes in the fibro and numerous smashed louvres. A large length of 4 by 2 timber was embedded in the window of the EJ holden, my little Datsun was covered in debris but apart from a few dents was fine.

Others had not been so fortunate. Most houses were either totally or partially destroyed. Trees were stripped and some were uprooted. Power poles were distorted steel sculptures and their lines snaked threateningly across roads and the remains of our properties.

The Stiller's house had almost disappeared; my brothers and boyfriend rescued Mrs Stiller from their FJ holden where she had sought shelter. She had spent several hours in a car covered in debris, alone, because her husband was in Adelaide.

I thought she'd be a quivering mess, but she announced brightly that: "We are now part of history, Tricia'. The trauma often comes later. Other neighbours crawled out from under the wreckage, dazed and bewildered at the extent of the damage. Many of us were unsure of what to do, so we set off on foot to check up on friends.

As we walked the extent of the destruction was overwhelming. I felt a dreadful inertia, where do you start when confronted with so much devastation?

When the winds picked up in the late afternoon, we became extremely nervous. We feared our damaged house would not survive a second battering and without power and water living there with Dad would be impossible, so we slowly made our way in my brother's panel van to Darwin High School, as I knew it had been designated as a cyclone shelter.

When we arrived, the school was crowded with people.

A few policemen were trying to organise things, but it was apparent they were hampered by their lack of knowledge and access to facilities at the school. I quickly swung into action. As a teacher and former student, I knew every nook and cranny and had a key to many storage rooms and cupboards.

I was able to provide access to basic first aid equipment and gave the police access to gym mats to distribute as mattresses. I also gave them a loud hailer for crowd control. Like many large government public buildings, the school had suffered minimal damage, so people were herded into classrooms and offices.

Despite the fact that there was no air-conditioning and only one small window for ventilation in each room, people were relieved to find somewhere safe. The only rules were that people had to be sober (some had spent the best part of the day celebrating Christmas), and pets were not permitted.

Pets were to be locked in cars. The latter was a particularly contentious issue with some families angry that their precious pets were being treated so cruelly. Worse was to come, within a number of days, many 'pets' which had either run away in the cyclone or had been left behind by their owners were shot to stop the spread of disease.

On boxing day afternoon, some senior executives in the public service came to the school and informed us that most of the population was to be evacuated by plane as soon as possible. Only those who could assist with the clean-up and restoration, or maintenance of basic services, were to remain. There was a clear order of priority for the evacuation.

The sick and injured would go first, followed by pregnant women, then married women and their children and the elderly. Married men, single women, and single men were last on the list.

I was among a number of public servants tasked with establishing a fair and orderly system of evacuation based on the priority list. Many locals decided they were going nowhere and returned to their damaged houses to look after themselves.

As the evacuation could take some time, we also had to establish the school as a safe place to live for this large homeless population. This meant sending out trucks to bring in food and essential medicines, setting up a temporary kitchen to feed people, and digging trenches for toilets and rubbish.

Police immediately asked for volunteers, and I noticed that Indigenous people, many from old Darwin families, agreed to the less desirable tasks such as digging trenches and cleaning the already overflowing school toilets. It was amazing how quickly people rallied to action. Twenty-four hours later we had some basic food and medical supplies, outdoor kitchens with large barbeques serving meals, toilets dug and a system for rubbish disposal established.

The phone line took a while to repair and buses began arriving without notice to take evacuees to planes destined for particular capital cities. We endeavoured to fill them as quickly as possible according to the priority lists. My parents and youngest brother were evacuated very early, as my father needed ongoing medical support.

The first call on the phone came one night as I was working in the school's front office. I answered immediately, expecting to hear from the evacuation command centre about incoming buses, but it was someone from the Sturt Football Club in South Australia, wanting to contact their star player, who was holidaying in Darwin.

Disasters bring out the best and worst in some people. Many wanted to help in some way and worked for hours clearing debris, sourcing supplies, preparing food or cleaning. Others simply refused or were unable to help; they lay around in rooms waiting to be evacuated. A few tried to be pushed up the order of evacuation, insisting they needed to leave Darwin immediately and became angry when we refused.

After a few days, a doctor arrived to inoculate us for typhoid, cholera and tetanus. I lined up for this shot on my 22nd birthday. The days passed in a blur of constant activity, I slept little and with no water I wiped myself down each night with disinfectant.

I remember two things: meeting Gough Whitlam, and a young woman coming in to tell me that a 'hippy boy' from down the street had stolen my car which I had left parked in our front yard. I responded to both events with a shrug.

Towards New Year's Eve my brothers left to drive to Sydney for a long-planned holiday. My boyfriend, having worked day and night for four days, was no longer needed at the hospital and rode his motorbike home to Brisbane.

So, I was alone and becoming increasingly anxious about the very male dominated atmosphere at the school. A few fights broke out over silly issues and there were reports of looting in the community. The police told me of a nurse who had been sexually assaulted walking home. With no lighting, Darwin was no longer a safe place at night.

When education department personnel arrived and told me that the NT police at the school would be relieved in the new year and replaced by NSW police, I decided to go. Twenty-four hours later, I boarded a plane for Sydney.

I quickly visited my father at Concord Repatriation Hospital and as I was walking out, I noticed a young man being wheeled in on a stretcher. It was the hippy guy from down the street. I chased the stretcher shouting, "Hey mate, where's my car!"

He apologised profusely; he had panicked and needed to get his mother out and thought we had left Darwin. In his haste to evacuate, he'd written the car off just south of Berrimah. His mum was fine, but he had a badly broken leg and was being admitted for a second operation.

I returned to Darwin in early February, which was no easy feat. I had to get a permit from government officials in Brisbane who only allowed me to go because I had a job, and a place to live.

While it was good to be back as the power and water were restored to most habitable dwellings, there was still much to do. It was September before I got round to making a claim for the clapped-out car I had never rescued. I wrote on the claim form that I'd been driving out to see my sister in Howard Springs on Christmas Eve and the car stalled in the heavy rain and I abandoned it.

It was damaged by debris and abandoned near Berrimah where I told the Insurance assessor he could find it. The assessor arrived at the school some weeks later; he didn't believe my story and said coolly, "That car was damaged while being driven". I then told him the true story. He looked at me for a long time then said, "No one could make that up," and signed the form.

Darwin changed after the cyclone. It grew to be a more ordered and beautiful city. But it lost something. Those carefree late nights at our old haunts like the Sea Breeze and Fannie Bay Hotels were no more. Houses were more closed in with fewer verandas and louvres and the old neighbourly barbeques where anyone dropped in as long as you brought a loaded esky seemed to diminish. The old laid-back *she'll be right attitude* was not so convincing. We knew that sometimes things did go horribly wrong. Old Darwinites still often refer to events as being before or after the cyclone: Tracy marks our history.

John Harrison

John was on his way back to Melbourne from London via India, Thailand, and Bali and accompanied by a Swedish woman named Jill he had met in Hong Kong. They stopped off in Darwin for a couple of days and John was looking around the law courts building one day, when he ran into an acquaintance from his days in PNG. The acquaintance worked for the Crown Law Department and said the Department was short of prosecutors. After the briefest of interviews, he was offered a job.

In early October 1974 I took up my new post as a prosecutor with the Crown Law department in Darwin. At the time of the cyclone, Jill and I had not yet found a permanent place to stay but we were minding a small government flat in a large complex at the corner of Smith and Daly Street. The apartment was on the ground floor of a three-storey block. It belonged to a couple who worked at the law courts and were on holiday. We moved in expecting to stay for a month or two until they returned from their trip.

December 24, 1974, was a workday but, about midday, people commenced their Christmas drinks, and I joined in enthusiastically. I was completely unaware of the approaching cyclone until about mid-afternoon when I was talking to a guy at one of the parties. He told me there was a cyclone on the way and that he was about to drive to Bachelor airport to tie down the gliders owned by the gliding club.

I promptly forgot about the cyclone and carried on drinking for the rest of the afternoon. I was aware that it was becoming windy, and there was some light rain as well. Jill and I went to Charlie's for dinner and then returned to the apartment.

We had been invited to Christmas lunch the following day at a house in the northern suburbs. Apart from arriving with alcohol, our job was to prepare the brandy pineapple dessert from a list of ingredients and detailed instructions that were provided.

I remember a large pot and quite a deal of stirring and, during the rather uncomplicated process of preparing this dessert, we somehow managed to have an argument fuelled in large measure by alcohol. I don't remember how the argument started or what it was about, but the upshot was me ending up in the spare bedroom for the night.

I went straight to sleep with no further thought of any approaching cyclone. I woke up somewhere between midnight and 1 a.m. when the fan stopped working, with a rather serious headache. So, I went to the bathroom where I took some headache pills.

There were no lights on anywhere and the water was just dribbling out of the tap. For a while I stood looking out of the small louvred window. There was constant thunder and lightning, and I could see sheets of roofing iron flying past the window.

It was particularly scary. I needed some company. I poked my head around the door of the main bedroom and tentatively asked Jill if she was okay. She came running out with a terrified look on her face and said no, she wasn't okay. Following our reunion in the spare bedroom, I slept quite well the rest of the night.

In the morning we discovered the top two floors of our apartment block had been blown out and the residents were nowhere to be seen. The only damage to our apartment was three broken louvres in the lounge room and quite a bit of water on the floor.

There was a lot of roofing iron on the ground outside. Almost all vegetation had been stripped from around the apartment blocks. My car was pushed back about 10 metres to the other side of the car park. There was a small dent in the bonnet, but it was basically okay.

We went for a drive around town to survey the damage and then we drove out to the northern suburbs to check on the house where we were supposed to be having lunch and also on its occupants. We did not bother to take the brandy pineapple with us.

Finding the house was particularly difficult because most of the signposts had been torn down and nothing looked as it had the day before but, somehow, we managed to find it.

The house had collapsed in a heap onto the floorboards. There was a car in the carport, but part of the floor had collapsed onto that, and it was badly damaged. The downstairs fridge contained a turkey and a ham already looking in bad shape. The parents and their two children had run away when their house was blown apart. We discovered them at a nearby primary school sleeping on a concrete floor with a large number of other displaced persons.

The father's back had been sandblasted and was extensively covered in a large red rash. They were all severely traumatised.

The next day we were joined in the apartment by two other couples who had also lost their houses. They brought with them what food and alcohol they had at home – mostly drinks and nibbles, so for the next few days our diet consisted of warm beer, biscuits, crackers, smoked oysters, sardines, and baked beans. I still can't believe I was able to drink warm beer in Darwin.

Within a couple of days, the supermarkets in town moved large amounts of stock to Darwin High School where anyone who remained could take what food they needed without payment.

By this stage the airlift of the majority of the Darwin population had commenced. Within a few days the population was reduced to about 10,000. Jill left Darwin during the exodus, but I stayed on for a number of weeks before going south, and after a short stay in Melbourne, I returned and stayed in Darwin, on and off, for the next 10 years. Jill returned and stayed for about 18 months before returning to Sweden.

Peter Hartney

Peter arrived in Darwin two months before Tracy, to find work there as a stepping-stone to hitting the Hippie Trail through Southeast Asia. He found it a 'revelation', and moved into a share house in Eden Street, Stuart Park with several other people.

I was swept up in the weird troppo craziness of Darwin at that time. I rubbed shoulders with travellers from all over, locals, 'long grassers' etc. It was the build-up period to the wet season when things got a little loose.

I remember the Don Hotel as the main meet-up place for all and sundry with many crazy characters, eccentrics, freaks, hippies, bushies and so forth.

The debauchery came to a halt suddenly at Christmas 1974 with Tracy. Someone said '*we should get stoned and go down to the beach to watch the waves and wild weather*' some hours before the cyclone hit. Thankfully, we stayed home at our house in Eden Street in Stuart Park.

When the winds started to pick up, we raced around securing stuff, then windows started blowing in and then the roof started going. Somehow about eight of us held on until the cyclone eye came over and we scurried over the road in the short dead calm period to what seemed to us to be a safer house, where about thirty people were holed up.

Then the real damage came with winds coming the other way to the already loosened-up structures. The roof tore off, glass doors/

windows exploded, some people got swept away but survived by somehow getting into a car.

The rest of us ended up in a bedroom with only the walls remaining, pushing against them for dear life. There was wailing and praying, and my mate Rex and I looked at each other saying 'this is it brother'. The sound was surreal: an unearthly screeching, howling, tearing cacophony, with loads of roofing iron blowing around.

Anyway, we held on, and it calmed down by dawn. We staggered out to massive devastation all around and made our way through the rubble from Stuart Park to another house near the CBD, which was intact, having been sheltered between office buildings.

I think the next day we went to a school which had been set up to feed and shower people. A day or so later, at the school, I stood next to Margaret Whitlam. Gough was there too.

We lined up at the Post Office and I called home to let Mum and Dad know I was alive!

I was involved in some work clearing streets and some of the others went to the hospital to volunteer there. It became a bit frantic and intimidating with police flying in to patrol the streets with guns to stop looting.

I ended up catching an evacuation flight out, with about six others on a jumbo jet evacuation flight, a week after the cyclone and we got stuck into the abundant booze that was laid on. It developed into a round-Australia sojourn for a few weeks. In Sydney, us bunch of raggedy wasted hippies were ushered into a warehouse with piles of clothes and groceries donated to survivors. Coming out, we were a dapper to bizarre mob in our new clobber! We were put up in a hospital for a few days and then, because free flights were available to us to anywhere in the country, we decided to fly on to Canberra because one of our group came from there. We were feted accordingly as Tracy refugees.

After some shenanigans in the Capital we flew to Cairns, where we thought we could stage our return to the Top End – there was talk of possible work on Groote Island but this fell through, and after more adventures capitalising on our refugee status, we flew back to Sydney where I stayed with old friends. I retrieved my old BSA Thunderbolt motorbike and fell back into the Sydney freewheeling lifestyle for a bit. By this time my Darwin mate Rex 'Ozzie' Wilson had arrived in Sydney, resplendent in his new wardrobe, and we decided after a week or so to fly back to Darwin to get work.

Postscript: Peter Hartney returned in April 1975 to the Hayes Creek region about 150km south of Darwin to work for BHP Minerals Exploration. He left for Southeast Asia in October 1975. In February 1984, he returned to Darwin with a growing family, working for the North Australia Research Unit of the ANU until 1988 when he embarked on a management career with Queensland National Parks and Wildlife, for 27 years.

Steve Heal

Steve Heal was the son of an architect. His family of six lived in Buchanan Terrace in Nakara. They had an especially horrifying night when Steve's two younger siblings were blown away in a bathtub.

We emigrated to Australia from rural Somerset, England in 1969. Dad was a young British architect lured to Darwin by the Australian Government with the promise of an exciting life in a new country.

I was aged 13 at the time of Tracy, with three younger siblings. We lived in Lovegrove Street and then Wonggu Court, Ludmilla for the first four years, finally moving to Buchanan Terrace in Nakara. In December 1974, I had just finished my first year at Casuarina High School.

On Christmas Eve I worked a shift as a bag packer at Coles and rode my bike home in torrential rain that afternoon. Dad was glued to the radio for cyclone updates. We had already 'cyclone proofed' the house and yard and were just waiting for the inevitable. Tracy was on a collision course and was going to arrive around midnight.

We still had to go to bed, because otherwise Father Christmas wouldn't be visiting and despite all the anxiety of what was coming, I fell asleep.

The first I knew of the storm was being woken about 11 p.m. by Mum to say that we had to take shelter in the bathroom. Getting out of bed I stepped into an inch of water on the floor. The driving rain was making its way through the gaps in the doors and louvres.

This was starting to look very serious. When the electricity failed, we were plunged into darkness.

We all moved into the bathroom... and waited. There was nothing we could do except brace for the impact. Mum and Dad sat on the bathroom floor, and I sat under the basin. My ten-year-old brother and seven-year-old sister were in the bathtub. My youngest brother, who was only three, was held in my mum's arms.

We could hear it hammering down outside as Tracy built to a deafening crescendo. The whole house creaked and groaned and lots of banging and scraping went on outside. I'll never forget the howling roar as it was upon us nor the eerie 'popping' noise of the roofing nails as it lifted our roof. The screaming winds were relentless, and the walls were heaving under the strain. I remember Dad opening the bathroom door at one point and saying "My god, our roof's gone"

At that point I think we all started praying, well I certainly did. I watched in sheer terror as the bathroom walls that were protecting us finally gave way – almost in slow motion.

The next thing I remember was dangling and swinging in mid-air from the end of my mum's outstretched arm and her screaming to me at the top of her lungs that she had to let me go – but I landed safely, and Mum followed soon after with the young one.

Dad finally joined us, his face a mask of horror. He said that bathtub with the other two children in it, had been swept away and had disappeared into the night.

They were gone.

We managed to make our way under the house and found refuge in the shed. It was already stuffed chockers with everything we'd cleared from the yard and under the house. We had been told that even the smallest stray item would turn into a deadly projectile in the strong winds of a cyclone, and Dad had ensured we cleaned the yard up as well but now there was hardly any room at all. I sat on the lawnmower. We were all cold, wet and very scared, and Mum was crying as she clung to the youngest.

Dad went outside, crawling around the house commando-style, desperately searching for his kids, screaming their names in a faint hope they were still alive.

At one point he returned and said he had seen what he thought was the dress my sister was wearing. It was flapping on a nail in the wind. I'll never forget this.

An eternity later, Mum and I thought we heard the faintest cry through the wind. Did we imagine it?

Suddenly Dad burst through the shed door. He'd found them. The bathtub had been blown to the back corner of the yard and overturned. My brother and sister were sheltering under it. They were safe.

During the long hours of the night and the rest of the cyclone, we huddled together in the tiny, packed shed. Then, when the winds finally started to die down and the first light of dawn appeared, we gingerly emerged from the shed to a scene of total and utter devastation. For as far as my eyes could see our neighbourhood was completely and totally destroyed.

For some reason, throughout the entire storm I thought that this was only happening to us. I was amazed. We had survived.

The days after Tracy were spent fossicking around in bewildered amazement and shock, salvaging what little we could and locking it in the shed. At one time I suffered through a delayed shock reaction and shook uncontrollably.

Nakara Primary School had survived the ordeal – much to my father's delight, as he was its architect. The classrooms became the emergency shelter for the survivors in our area. We received medical attention there for cuts and bruises and stayed a few nights in one of the large open classrooms. Sleep was hard.

We went to the Casuarina shopping centre and Coles where I had worked just days before, to help gather food supplies for everyone. The roof and ceiling of the supermarket had lifted and blown away and the sun was shining on the food aisles.

Groceries and tins of food were strewn about.

Eventually we were transported to the airport for evacuation, and I was gobsmacked to see the devastation through the city. As we made our way down Trower and Bagot Roads I realised it wasn't just our neighbourhood that had taken a hit, it was the whole city. Everyone was affected.

We flew to Brisbane first and finally onto a migrant hostel in Nunawading, Melbourne where we spent much of the next year before finally settling in Adelaide, where I have lived ever since. I returned to Darwin in 1999 for a couple of weeks to visit a friend and it was lovely to see Darwin again and how much it had changed. I went past everywhere that we had lived including the house where we survived Tracy. Darwin's a beautiful city now. Some of my happiest childhood memories are growing up in the 'frontier town' of Darwin.

I hope to make it back again one day.

John Howard

John Howard and Lynda Burke met in August 1974, when Lynda joined one of the many prawn trawlers operating out of Darwin Harbour as crew. They soon became inseparable, and they rode out the cyclone together on a 73-foot prawn trawler. They married in February 1975. They currently live in Victoria and have four children and nine grandchildren.

Lynda and I were working as deckhands on the N.R. *Buckingham*, one of the many prawn trawlers owned by Northern Research in Darwin Harbour in the early 1970s. The *Buckingham* had a new crew of six: the skipper Greg, and his girlfriend; Geronimo the engineer; Lynda, me, and another deckhand named Tony, who left to help the skipper of N.R. *Anson*.

Some time on December 24 1974, the harbourmaster ordered all boats to leave the wharf to seek shelter – a standard practice to protect both wharf and boats from damage should the harbour become rough.

Unfortunately, the *Buckingham* was in port for a crew refit and not prepared for sea. Lynda and I were staying at a residence near the corner of Cavenagh and Daly Street. Like most people in Darwin, we weren't overly concerned about the threat of a cyclone actually hitting. It would more likely miss us, as Cyclone Selma had a few weeks before.

Being Christmas Eve, we planned to celebrate and went into town to purchase fish and chips, roast chicken, beer, and wine.

We both called our parents from the pay phone on the wharf

to let them know what we were doing and to wish them a merry Christmas. The weather was overcast, and it began to rain while we were on the phone.

We rejoined Greg on the *Buckingham* and headed out to find a safe anchorage dropping anchor somewhere off Lameroo Beach, between Elliott Point and the western end of Fort Hill Wharf. Then, once we were secure, it was time to eat and a have a few drinks.

As the wind began to strengthen so too did the size of the waves and it wasn't long before the anchor began to drag. When this happens, you need to drive the boat forward against the wind and waves to hold position. I drew the first watch and made my way, via the outside stairs on the rear deck, to the wheelhouse. During the watch the wind and waves continued to intensify, and this required more and more effort to hold the boat in position. I had the radio on for company, one of those 'fire and brimstone' American evangelist preachers was in full swing. "Repent now sinners for the day of judgment is at hand" he was screaming.

Then nothing but static from the radio: shhhhhhhhhhhhhh.

"That's strange", I thought and looked over to the radio. It was still on but something else caught my attention. The lights of Darwin, visible a short time ago through the starboard wheelhouse window, had gone. My first thought was the boat had changed direction, but after looking around I soon realised there were no lights to be seen anywhere.

Then the wind and waves began to multiply in intensity so quickly that Greg and Geronimo joined me the wheelhouse. They were then trapped there with me as the sea became so rough we were unable to hold the boat in position. When the main engine went out we lost all control of the steering, but by now we had also lost all reference to our location. The only thing we could do was hang on.

The waves crashed into and over us and smashed onto the rear deck. The wheelhouse creaked in protest as the wind threatened to blow it off the top deck. The pressure in our ears was intense as the wind came in shrieking gusts. The life raft, one of those square orange foam filled fibreglass types that was secured on the top deck in front of the wheelhouse, was ripped from its mount. It flipped over the wheelhouse and smashed into one of the three rear windows and became wedged between the sorting trays on the rear deck. Then the batteries under the wheelhouse dashboard broke free and this started an electrical fire.

Buckingham was a 73-foot, 200-ton seagoing prawn trawler and it was being tossed around like a rag doll with its anchor down. Below us, in the accommodation area, sloshing with water and spilled paint left over from the recent refit, Lynda and Greg's girlfriend were trying to hang on in total darkness. The girls became trapped when the fridge was ripped from the wall and wedged against the door. They had no idea if we were still onboard or alive.

Tracy took us on the ride of our lives and the pounding continued through the night. Eventually the wind and waves eased enough so we could leave the wheelhouse and check on the girls. With relief, we found them alive and well.

Now it was time to check the damage: engine room – flooded and useless; accommodation – unliveable due to no power, fumes and ankle-deep water mixed with paint; food – none; water – plenty in the boat's water tank.

And then we had to find out where the hell we were. We could see a sandy beach with a bush backdrop, not the sandstone cliffs off Darwin that were there when we dropped the anchor the night before. We sorted out the batteries in the wheelhouse and powered up the radio but there was no signal. There was plenty of debris in the water, a shack on the beach with a vehicle we saw moving, but nothing else to give a clue to our location. We fired some distress flares when a RAAF DC3 flew over our position on Christmas Day, and this gave us hope that our position was known, and help would soon be on its way.

By this time, we had worked out where we thought we were

– Shoal Bay at Gunn Point. Tracy had dragged us all the way with the anchor down, missing Elliot Point, Emery Point, East Point, Nightcliff, and Lee Point. Luck was certainly with us that night.

After two hot, wet nights on the front deck with no help arriving, I suggested to Greg that we go ashore; he was happy for Lynda and me to go, but as skipper, he would stay onboard until help arrived. In our minds, Darwin was as we had left it on Christmas Eve, we had no idea of the destruction Tracy had caused. The penny was still to drop.

We grabbed some essentials like water and my rifle and freed the life raft from the rear deck. We allowed the wind and waves to take us in to the shore and then beached the raft and followed the vehicle tracks to the shack we had seen from the boat. We were met by an older couple who confirmed we were in Shoal Bay. They kindly offered us some food and directed us to Gunn Point Prison Farm, a short walk away, where we would be able get a lift back to Darwin.

We were certainly the centre of attention when we walked into the farm: a girl and a guy, with a rifle over his shoulder, walking through prison grounds. A guard took us to the warden's office, and I was asked to surrender my rifle for safe keeping, while a car was organised to take us to Darwin.

The realisation of what had happened to the city began to set in the closer we got to it. No leaves on the trees, no bird life, and the destruction of buildings was shocking. We were dropped at Stokes Hill Wharf and, after making inquiries, found out that a plan was already in place to recover the *Buckingham*. Our love affair with the sea had come to an abrupt and lucky ending.

A day or two later we self-evacuated by car to South Australia. We returned in March 1975 with a caravan and Lynda found work with the City Mutual Life Insurance Agency in Cavenagh Street as their receptionist, while I became the first and last whitefella to be employed under the Black Trackers Award with the NT Police Department because they needed someone to clean up the Casuarina Police Station in a hurry. I next joined the Northern Territory Port

Authority as a storeman, and then joined the Australian Defence Force. We left Darwin in September 1975 to begin a new adventure that would take us around the world.

We are grateful that Cyclone Tracy left no long-lasting negative effects on us, other than a dislike of strong winds. We were lucky that night; particularly because we did not lose any family or friends. But to all the wonderful people who went out of their way to help the people of Darwin recover, rebuild and prosper, *thank you*.

Jen Howson

Jen Howson was thirteen at the time of Tracy and living with her family in an elevated house at 11 Symes Street, Nakara. She and her two siblings were excited for the Christmas that never came.

When Christmas Eve 1974 dawned, the air was heavy and it was hot, humid, and oppressive, but no different from most Darwin wet season days. I was 13 years old, my brother 15, and my sister 11. There was excitement in the air, as we knew there was only one more sleep until *The Big Day*.

Preparations were well under way by mid-morning. Mum was busy in the kitchen. The traditional Christmas pudding had been made weeks prior and was sitting proudly in its cloth in one corner. The ham and turkey were prepared and ready to go in the oven. Bing Crosby was singing *White Christmas* on the tranny, and Dad was bringing extra chairs and tables upstairs for the visitors we would have the next day.

We had an upstairs house on stilts. All that was underneath was a small laundry that doubled as a storage shed and cyclone shelter if needed. Life was good, as we kids played happily, without a care in the world.

We had heard, over the previous couple of days, on the radio and telly that a cyclone was tracking its way in Darwin's direction but thought little of it. Cyclones had come and gone in previous years with no major dramas, and this cyclone was to the northeast and was tracking west so most likely would miss us.

Anyway, there were more important things to think about that day.

About midafternoon, Mum was having a nanna nap while the turkey was cooking, and Dad asked us kids to give him a hand. He had heard a warning on the radio that Cyclone Tracy was getting closer. He still wasn't too concerned, but there was a house being built behind ours, and there were a few sheets of corrugated iron lying around the block. Just as a precaution, we put a few bricks on the sheets of iron to hold them down. "There, that should do the trick," he said.

By this time the sky had turned quite dark and foreboding, but that was ok. A little bit of a cyclone wasn't going to get in the way of a good Christmas. Dad and us kids made sure there was nothing in our yard left out that could cause damage and we went back to playing and enjoying our day. There was an unusual quietness to the afternoon, but other than that, all seemed normal.

After dinner, we helped with the washing up, and we kids were in bed by 7 pm, as we usually were on Christmas Eve. But of course, I couldn't sleep for thinking about the exciting day ahead.

I could hear the wind starting to whistle and the curtains began billowing into the room. I was grateful for the coolness after the hot day.

By about 8pm the wind was starting to howl, and I was scared. Dad came into our rooms and told us to get out of bed, get dressed, including our sandshoes, and bring a coat or jumper. The wind started to scream, and rain was now pelting down. I heard banging noises. Dad thought it was too late and too dangerous to make our way down the external stairs to the shelter, so he took us to the bathroom (supposedly the strongest room in the house due to all the plumbing).

Mum was already there, along with our cat, Molly and our budgie, Lucky, in his cage. The bath was full of water, as the man on the tranny had told us to do in case the water supply was cut off. To my surprise, the cooked turkey was bobbing around in the bath in its baking dish, and the pudding, still in its cloth, was in the basin.

Mum said she had put too much time and effort into them, and they were coming with us. The bathroom was only small, and it was a bit of a squeeze, but at least we were all together and would be safe.

The next ten hours or so are a bit of a blur. We all huddled together on the floor, as the wind got stronger. It was not too long before we heard the first big crash and the sound of iron being ripped from the roof along with the terrible roar of the wind. The noise was incredible. We clung to each other, each of us terrified. Our world was crashing around us.

Through the small window, and with the flashes of lightning, we could see trees and sheets of metal flying through the air. We saw our neighbours house break apart, and the four of them (including a baby and toddler) just make it down the stairs before their house blew over the top of them.

I don't know what time it was when something big slammed into the bathroom. The roof ripped off but incredibly the walls still stood. We gazed skyward in horror at the swirling blackness. It was filled with objects of all kinds whizzing over our heads. The door was threatening to give way, so Dad and Mum stood with their backs to the door, and we three kids leant back into them. How we ever held it shut I don't know.

After what seemed like many hours, the wind suddenly stopped, the flying objects fell to the ground and there was an eerie silence. We knew it was the eye of the cyclone and we had to stay put. Fifteen minutes later we could hear a roar as Tracy resumed from the opposite direction and with an even more ferocious intensity. I really thought we were all going to die that night. Christmas was long forgotten.

As the first light of dawn came, the wind started to ease, and by about 6.30 it had dropped enough for us to believe that the danger was over, and we could get out. The door was buckled and twisted so much it wouldn't open, so we all helped each other climb up over the walls, to a scene of utter devastation. Our home and surroundings were unrecognizable.

We had to climb over and through all the debris. Our whole house was gone, except for the bathroom. The steel power poles in our street were twisted like corkscrews then bent in half.

Neighbours slowly emerged from beneath rubble with varying degrees of injuries, thankfully none too major. Everyone was numb with shock. As the day went on people gathered under the floorboards of our house, to tell their stories, give each other a hug, and wonder in amazement that we were all still alive. There were many tears spilled that day, under the floorboards, amid the rubble, and everyone sharing Mum's turkey, ham, and pudding.

The official death toll was recorded as 66 people. How we ever survived I will never know. Someone had been watching over us that night. I later realised that the quietness of Christmas Eve was due to the lack of birds. They had all left Darwin, flown to safer places. They knew the danger that was coming. I'm pleased to say that they returned a few days later.

Matthew James

Matthew James was 12 years old in 1974. One of four sons of Earl and Wendy James, the family lived in Verbena Street in Nightcliff. A lesson from Matt's story is to not store pool chemicals in the cyclone shelter.

At 2.00 am Mum woke me yelling over the noise "time to come into the loungeroom and stick together." Our elevated house was shaking and banging. I swung my legs off the bed and stood in ankle deep water on the timber floor. The old louvre bays were no match for the horizontal rain.

Earlier in the night, two of my brothers, Alan and Peter, went to Nana's house in Millner to look after her. My brother John and I stayed with Mum and Dad at the family home in Verbena St, overlooking the Nightcliff Oval.

I was 12 years old, and the threat of a cyclone had conjured up a good deal of excitement and adventure. Now, as I followed Mum into the loungeroom a slight trepidation started to seep in.

As we were busy stashing our Christmas presents under rugs on the couch, a six-metre timber beam speared through the kitchen roof and jammed the kitchen door shut. It wasn't from our house. I could hear something on the roof above the loungeroom constantly banging.

To calm her nerves, Mum poured herself a whisky and went for water at the bathroom basin. Instantly, she came running out backwards, just as the louvre bay above the basin exploded, shattering glass, and embedding in the wall. She explained an overwhelming feeling had come upon her to run from the bathroom. She placed the whiskey glass on the piano in the loungeroom.

I caught a glimpse of the sky outside and always remember the tinge of green through the darkness. The banging above the loungeroom grew louder.

As we huddled together, the ceiling suddenly started to collapse, sparking Dad to yell "let's get out here". Considering the bathroom was not safe, we decided to run for the small storage shed downstairs under the house. On opening the front door, the wind pressure hit us with a force. Our cat bolted out the door and we never saw it again. As we descended the stairs, the strength of the wind was immense, taking all our effort to hold onto the handrail.

At the bottom, it seemed that everything that was loose was hurled at us at great velocity. A big wooden barrel struck Mum in the legs but luckily she suffered little more than a few grazes. As Dad opened the door to the shed we piled in, but in the crush, I ended on the floor with everyone standing on me. There was hardly any room, and it was pitch-black inside.

The wind was furious. Powdered pool chlorine and filter sand exploded from their containers and filled the air. It was a toxic mess where we could not remain for long, so we worked our way to the protected side of the shed and dashed to the car. I lay on the floor in the back, feeling ill from the chlorine. There was not much more we could do but wait.

After 5 minutes or so, it suddenly became silent, the eye of the cyclone had arrived. It is quite eerie when a roaring storm becomes silent in seconds. Dad knew it would only last a few minute and when he heard the screams of a woman across the road, he ran over to help. She had been trapped under a wall but he managed to free her.

When he returned, he decided to risk driving us to Nana's place, as he and Mum were concerned for their safety.

The route for the car down Verbena Street was littered with power poles and lines, trees, and house debris. It was a mission to negotiate. We made it to the Nightcliff shops, turned left onto Pavonia Place and onto Oleander Street, trying to get to Progress Drive. We soon found that that was impossible. So, we turned left and headed up Oleander Street and turned right into Camphor Street. We were at the intersection of Camphor Street and Nightcliff Road opposite the Carpentaria College (now the Hellenic Centre) when the cyclone returned.

We had managed our fears quite well to this point. Practical thinking and minimal panicking had got us through. That all changed when the tranquillity of the eye left us and the inside wall of the cyclone was again upon us. The car lifted onto two wheels. The fear rose dramatically in the car.

A torch flickered at us through the storm from a doorway of a small caretaker's flat attached to the college. Dad drove the car up to the door, and a lady led us into her spare room. There was a double mattress leaning on a wall facing a wall of glass louvres, and the four of us crouched down behind the mattress. Once or twice, Dad left us to check on things, but we didn't move for next few hours. The louvres rattled fiercely, threating us the entire time, but somehow held.

The little flat was our haven, and when the storm had subsided, John and I opened the louvres to view a very grey scene. Looking down Nightcliff Road, we could see steel power poles bent to ground level over the road, and a few people emerging from the ruins, climbing over debris here and there.

Mum and Dad's concern for the others took precedence. We thanked our host and climbed into the car, which now looked sand blasted. We bumped our way to Robinson Road and found Nana and brother Peter all ok, but brother Alan was not there. In his concern for our safety, he had walked to Nightcliff in search for us. He was quite distraught on having walked through such devastation to discover our family home ruined and us missing, but eventually we were all reunited.

Nana's house sustained minimal damage – apart from three

tin louvres. During the height of the storm, she was sitting in her rocking chair enjoying several sherries. She was asked to come into the hallway for better safety and just as she stood up a timber beam crashed through the tin louvres and smashed into the chair she had left just seconds before. Fortunately, she was unhurt.

Nana's house became the base for all family members in Darwin. All that was left of the elevated house next door were its floorboards. Underneath it we built an external kitchen with a big fireplace. There was no running water, electricity, or sewerage. There were daily food hunts, and supermarkets opened their doors for the taking. We collected rainwater in a 44-gallon drum via Nana's roof. Looting became an issue, and some people were protecting property with firearms.

The day after the cyclone, Boxing Day, we visited our wrecked home. The loungeroom and bedrooms had disappeared, and our belongings were everywhere or lost on the wind, but amazingly, Mum's whisky glass still sat on the piano in the loungeroom, and our Christmas presents were still under the rugs on the couch.

After hours of searching over debris for our belongings, Dad found his harmonica. He sat on the handrail of the upstairs fire escape where the back wall used to be, and silhouetted against the setting sun, he played a sorrowful song. It was a poignant moment that drew emotions from us all.

Besides the fear of howling winds and flying wreckage, a lasting memory is the smell of a demolished city gone putrid in the tropical heat. The pungent odour of mould, rotting food, decaying buildings, dead animals etc, has stayed with me. It is a smell I will never forget.

Dad, Alan, and Uncle Geoff stayed to assist the clean-up crews as they were able-bodied men. Women and children were evacuated as quickly as possible. It took seven days for us to leave.

On New Years Day, Mum, John, Peter, and I flew on an RAAF Hercules to Adelaide, then TAA to Perth, to stay with Mum's brother. We were a part of the largest civil air evacuation in Australian history.

Keith Kroger

Keith, an insurance agent arrived in Darwin in April 1973, having transferred from Geelong with Commercial Union Insurance for a two-year term. He settled in quickly and became involved in Darwin sporting activities including football and cricket. His memories, upon which this chapter is based, were recorded at the time in the pages of a street directory. This is now in the Museum and Art Gallery of the Northern Territory.

Christmas, for those of us in the Darwin office of Commercial Union Insurance was progressing as in previous years with agents' and clients' Christmas parties and copious quantities of the chilled article being consumed.

On the 24th, we had a few agents join us for a drink after work, not for one minute expecting what was to come. We had heard there was a cyclone in the vicinity, but as previous warnings had proved fruitless, few people thought twice about it and were content to continue with the season's festivities.

After an early close to the office proceedings, each of us went our own way. Branch manager, Bill Bottrell, invited the three single male staff around to his house for a bite to eat and a spirited game of 500 resulted.

With each beer consumed, the wind gathered force and the rain intensified. Much debate over whether to go to the office or not followed but Mrs Bottrell said at 11.30 pm, "we can't go yet, I haven't finished making the salad dressing for tomorrow".

At 11.45, those of us living at the staff quarters decided to go home and sit on the balcony to watch the storm, a favourite pastime of our predecessors. At this stage we didn't realise the danger.

So, with a radio, gas lanterns (as the power had gone off) and packets of peanuts we watched the might of Tracy develop. The radio was silenced, halfway through the broadcast of midnight mass, by a bolt of lightning and it was then things began to happen.

When a 30-foot mango tree crashed onto the side of the house, smashing louvres, someone ran a book on the chances of our biggest tree going over.

The wind was steadily increasing its velocity and soon rooves began to lift. We heard a neighbour's roof fly off and crash into another house. All of a sudden there was the deafening sounds of roofing iron, steel girders and timber being ripped from its place and thrown through the air before demolishing yet another house.

By this stage we had acknowledged that Tracy was getting a bit fair dinkum, so we decided to go downstairs. We heard a window in an upstairs room blow out and saw more large trees being uprooted. We tried the phone to see if the Bottrells were ok, but the phone was out. It was agony not knowing.

By this stage every louvre on the windward side of the house had been broken, glass was flying everywhere. The pressure was so low that our ears began to 'pop' and the winds grew fiercer. The wind then changed direction from east to south and the fury was then aimed at the less-protected front of the house.

Sheets of roofing iron were being slammed up against our windows and doors. In an attempt to keep the front door closed we barricaded every chair in the room up against it. The door was subsequently blown from its hinges.

Water gushed in under the doors of the house and through the broken windows. By then the kitchen area was the only protected area. We chose a corner of the room and swung the two fridges around to make a small square. The three of us huddled into the corner.

Glass and debris were blown everywhere and one of the others took the shelves from the fridge and sat in it for protection, while the fridge defrosted around him.

About two hours passed with the wind coming from two directions, but the worst was yet to come. The eye of the cyclone missed where we were, and therefore we received no lull midway like many people in Darwin, but the velocity of the storm reached its maximum in the next two or so hours before 5 am. The might of the elements was so enormously powerful that it is very difficult to describe on paper and unless one has lived through it one cannot comprehend just how terrifying it was. There were stages during this period when we were prepared to see the house tumble around us and have death stare us in the face.

Fortunately, at around 6 am, things slowed down and it started to get light. We did not know how lucky we were until we saw the utter and total devastation before our eyes when we summoned enough guts to step outside.

Our immediate concern was for the Bottrells, so with the wind still blowing we started around to their place, just 200 yards away.

The debris was astonishing. Rooves, walls, cars, and everything. The severity of the situation suddenly hit home, and we knew there must have been fatalities. Dodging the flattened power poles and wires, as we didn't know whether they were dead or alive, we finally arrived to see the Bottrell's bedrooms on the front lawn, without a roof. We sprinted up the back stairs to a dead end, then round the front. We knocked, and the door flew open in the wind and there they were. Mr and Mrs Bottrell and the three kiddies had huddled under a mattress on the bottom three steps of the staircase leading to the front door.

Relief. Hurriedly we got everyone, including several neighbours, around to the staff quarters where we knew it to be safe. Once everyone had settled down, we decided to see how the office had fared in order that it may be used as a temporary home.

Picking our way through the streets it was subsequently found that the CU Building was nearly cyclone-proof up to 210 mph. Three windows were broken, and a couple of bricks were missing, but that was all. Everyone was shunted up to the office where the security of the double-brick walls and the warmth of the carpeted surrounds diverted us all from the trauma we had survived.

Many events happened after this due to the efforts of Mr Bottrell. The Insurance fraternity, as a whole, rose to the occasion and it was a credit to the industry. We opened a bureau for insurance claims just a day-and-a-half after the disaster.

The staff received a great morale-booster when our GM flew in on the following Saturday. Team spirit was high and there was an enormous challenge ahead, but we were determined to keep faith with the insuring public.

The only way to appreciate our unwelcome Christmas guest was to live through her fury. However, the best way to convey the feeling of the majority of Darwin's people is to quote what we heard from many of our clients "I'll take what I can get through my insurance – all I am thankful for is that I've got my life".

In 1975, when my two-year term ended, I signed on for a further two years but was compulsorily transferred to the Head Office Internal Audit Team. I lasted there for 18 months but the lure of Darwin became too strong, I wanted to be back with my Darwin mates and a young person in the 70s couldn't beat the Darwin lifestyle. Then several years later, after various sports-related experiences, I moved south. I still have children and grandchildren living in Darwin, so visit regularly.

Diana Kupke

Diana arrived in Darwin in 1971 with her then husband, interrupting an intended round-Australia road trip to visit a former Melbourne journalist colleague. A journalist herself, in 1974 Diana became the first public relations officer for the newly opened Darwin Community College, which later became Charles Darwin University.

'Twas the day before Christmas 1974, and in Darwin the air was still. My partner Nick and I were enjoying a day off from our jobs with the Darwin Community College and I had done my latest opinion piece for the Commercial radio station, 8DN. As the DCC's first journalist I had completed the second handbook which included photographs from the official opening.

I pushed my 15-month-old son, Nicholas to the house we were looking after in Fannie Bay, not realising the peacefulness was about to be shattered.

The general feeling was to ignore the latest cyclone warning as the previous one had not eventuated. I don't think we were in denial and, as a journalist, I thought a major cyclone would be an interesting story. Little did I know, it was the one story which, almost fifty years later, I find very difficult to write about.

We were house-sitting a two-storey home, owned by friends who had gone south for the holiday period. I have no idea how we heard about the latest warnings; I have no recollection of listening to a radio. What I do remember is that as it became obvious a cyclone was heading our way, we looked at sheltering in an upstairs bedroom.

For some reason we changed our minds and dragged two armchairs into the downstairs kitchen with the fridge in front of us and the freezer next to me and my son.

We had barely got settled and the cyclone was upon us. The noise was so horrendous it was impossible to think. We sat, not speaking. I clutched my son tightly who, amazingly slept in spite of the noise. During the eye we checked the bedroom where we originally planned to stay and discovered the room, and the bed, were covered with metal louvres. We had had a lucky escape.

During those few minutes of peace, we tried to find somewhere else. The stairs had been built-in, which resulted in a small, but to our way of thinking, safe space. We dragged down a mattress from upstairs to the little room but again, for some reason, decided to return to the kitchen.

The night seemed endless. Our time in the kitchen was horrendous. It sounded as if a train was coming through the house. Years later I heard a recording of the sound and was violently ill. The other sound which haunts me to this day is that of scraping iron roofing.

The cyclone seemed to go on for many hours. I sat and held my son who apparently slept but he had nightmares for years afterwards. We were right next to water, food, and alcohol but it never occurred to us to eat or drink. We sat, frozen, in terror.

When the cyclone finally moved away we checked the room under the stairs and a roof beam had crashed through the wall and lay across the mattress. A second lucky escape.

We had made some good decisions, and we are probably all alive because of them but, like so many others, we suffered emotionally and mentally.

When the cyclone moved away we went outside, thinking we were the only ones who had gone through this, and discovered Fannie Bay was now filled with wrecked homes.

The house we were supposed to be caring for was now roofless with smashed walls and windows. An entire roof, from somewhere else, had landed in the back yard.

Because of the holiday period we were looking after seven cars. Amazingly, none of them were damaged. I wanted to check on my ex-husband, but it took us a long time to find even one set of car keys. Driving through the streets, lined with demolished houses, bent electricity poles, and trees denuded of leaves and wrapped around with sheets of roofing iron, was an experience that remains in my mind forever.

My ex-husband was not at his almost demolished ABC house in Jingili and somehow it was suggested I check the temporary morgue at the Casuarina Post Office. A very young policeman was standing outside, obviously in shock.

I went in and saw many bodies on benches amongst Christmas parcels which had not been delivered. Another sight I can never forget. But my husband was not there. I later learned he had been hit by roofing iron and had been evacuated to a hospital in Melbourne.

We drove to the Darwin Community College, only recently officially opened, and the chaos continued. The two-storey administration block was now one storey, the double walls of Besser blocks had not resisted the cyclone. All the buildings were damaged in some way.

We returned to the demolished house but after a visit from a policeman, who said looting was underway and things could become dangerous, we moved back to the DCC.

The remains of the college became a centre for employees with the caretaker running a kitchen. A policeman remained on site with his radio, and we heard, over and over, voices saying another family had been found, all dead. Somehow I had collected my tabby, Kat Stephens. I have no idea where she had been, but she was housed in an indoor courtyard.

With the situation being grim, I somehow arranged with a complete stranger to take my son with her on an evacuation flight to

Melbourne where he would be met by my family.

Over and over, writing this, I am faced with large blocks of memory loss. This was in the days before mobile phones, only a few telephones had been connected in the city heart, so how did I make all these arrangements?

One of the things we did was to join a queue for a telephone in the city, and I was able to speak briefly with my family to let them know we were all right.

We remained at the college doing clean-up work and later we were housed in student residences, also previously two-storey, now down to one. Once we had housing, my mother flew to Darwin with my son. I met her plane as she had to fly straight back to Melbourne, because she was not allowed out of the airport.

Later we moved to Queensland and following the break-up of my marriage, I moved to Mackay where I have now lived for more than 40 years, cowering in terror every time there is even the faintest threat of a cyclone.

Figure 10: Cyclone Tracy damage in the northern suburbs of Darwin
(Coburg Collection, LANT ph0377-0113)

Michael Lo

Michael (Mickey) Lo was born in Sydney but arrived in Darwin as a child when his father, a Methodist Pastor, was posted to the Northern Territory to provide services to Methodist congregations in Darwin and some remote communities. At the time of Cyclone Tracy, he was married to Roberta (nee Yuen), known as Bobbie, and they had three children.

Bobbie and I were living in a former Housing Commission house on the corner of Margaret Street and Westralia Street, Stuart Park. It was a standard brick home, but I had built on a carport at one end. I don't remember much about the lead-up to the cyclone or the warnings, but on Christmas Eve afternoon we closed my mechanical business, Progress Motors in Finniss Street, and we went shopping for Christmas presents at Cashmans, the newsagency in Smith Street.

Returning home, I cleared up any objects around the house that could become missiles, but otherwise life went on as normal. Gradually the wind picked up, the rain got heavier, and it started to blow through the louvres. My mother tried to mop up the water, but it was coming in too quickly and was soon covering the floor. The noise got louder, sounding like there was a train in the house and we could hear debris blowing around outside.

At that time there were seven of us in the house: my mother and father, me, Bobbie and our three young children, Michael junior, who was almost four years old, Melisa aged six and the baby, Katrina who was six weeks old. I knew we had to stay away from windows so while the two older children huddled under a set of steel double bunks I had made, the rest of us moved into the smallest room on the side of the house away from the wind and huddled there listening as the storm got worse.

I have no memory of the times of events but when the eye arrived, and everything went still, we ventured out to see what we could see. In the lightning flashes we saw that the elevated house across the road was cleared to the floorboards.

When the cyclone returned, with stronger winds and even more noise, we moved to another room, again away from the wind direction where I put a mattress against the windows in case of breakage and sat it out. I think the two children under the bunks slept through it all while Bobby nursed Katrina.

When dawn came and the winds and rain eased, we went outside and were amazed at what we saw. With every tree stripped of leaves and branches and so many houses damaged or destroyed, we could see right down to Frances Bay for the first time.

The only damage to our house was the loss of the carport roof.

As soon as I could, I went to check on my workshop in Finniss Street. The only damage was that the sliding door had blown off. I was able to replace it and secure the workshop though without power there was no work to do.

Bobbie and I drove out to Wagaman to check on her sister, Dawn Chong Fong, whose elevated house had also been cleared to the floorboards. Luckily, the family had survived uninjured.

We also checked on other relatives, and over the following days helped collect their belongings from their destroyed houses and take them to various sheds, and places like Ray Yee's carport and under Doug Yuen's house, where they would be secure.

I remember visiting a friend in Millner who also lived in one of the ground-level Housing Commission houses. He showed me where, at the height of the cyclone, the roof had lifted the concrete bond beam that sat on top of the brick wall and the curtains had blown through the gap. When the roof and beam settled back it looked like the curtains were hanging off the outside wall.

Without power or water, we joined the many others who were washing or collecting water from the pipeline along the Stuart Highway and kept food cool with ice from Carba Ice Works, which re-opened quickly. It always had long queues of people wanting ice. Sometime later we got a generator from the government and were able to get our refrigerator working.

Like many others we got meals at the café arrangement set up at Darwin High School and some of Bobbie's sisters, who had owned takeaway food shops, helped with the cooking there. Rather than eat at the school, we took food home to my parents.

Although there was a huge evacuation of women and children in the week after the disaster, we chose to stay because we had an undamaged house, and we took part in the clean-up, salvaging various belongings. About a month after the cyclone, with mains power restored to town, I re-opened Progress Motors, my motor repairs and speed equipment business.

I was in the workshop watching the big clean-up by the navy outside when I saw the navy helicopter's tail rotor clip the side of the Telford Hotel. It had to make a forced landing in the gardens of what is now the golf course, a lucky escape for those onboard.

When asked to think about the Cyclone Tracy experience I am thankful my family and I all survived. Our house was undamaged, perhaps due to the mature mango trees that surrounded it. Now, if there's a cyclone warning, I make sure I do everything that is advised and if I build or repair anything, I make sure the work is cyclone-proof. And, like many others, when I remember the extent of the devastation I am amazed that there was not a much greater loss of life.

Figure 11: Cyclone Tracy destroyed houses (Ken Doust Collection, 1975, LANT, PH0821-0017).

Geoff Loveday

Geoff arrived in Darwin as an 18-year-old in 1960, after a transfer from South Australia to the Shell Depot in McMinn Street. Returning to Adelaide he sat the Public Service entry examinations and was promptly returned to Darwin where he was put in charge of providing furniture for government housing. At the time of Cyclone Tracy, he was Executive Assistant to the Head of the Department of the Northern Territory, Alan O'Brien.

Between my arrival in Darwin in 1960, and Tracy in 1974, several cyclones visited the NT. Warnings created tension, and the cyclones dumped torrential rain, uprooted trees, and damaged property. While always concerned by cyclone warnings I never imagined that anything on the scale of Tracy was possible.

When I was single, I played cards through one of the storms, and at Gove Peninsula one Easter about 1970, I went fishing and was marooned for three days on an island in the Gulf of Carpentaria. That was nothing we couldn't handle as our boat was loaded with beer, we caught fish, and were able to radio home that we were safe, albeit a little wet.

Tracy was different. The warnings were foreboding, and I checked the tide times, concerned a tidal surge might race up Rapid Creek near where we lived, if the cyclone coincided with high tide. Luckily Tracy hit at low tide.

I had serious concerns for the safety of my wife, Margaret, and my children, Llara and Mark as well as relatives who had flown in from

Nhulunbuy to share Christmas. As it transpired it was a Christmas they would never forget.

Christmas Eve had always been a time for merriment for me but not in 1974. For the first time in my adult life there were no Christmas drinks. I spent Christmas Eve preparing our ground-level brick home at Coconut Grove for the storm by securing loose objects and taping windows. The roof was held down by screws and I was confident it was secure.

As evening fell, a Boeing airliner flew low over our home looking for the runway at Darwin Airport. The aircraft was so low I could see the faces of passengers framed in the windows. When I guessed the pilot had lined up with McMillans Road thinking it was the runway, I realised how quickly conditions were deteriorating.

I phoned my parents in Adelaide to wish them a Happy Christmas and told them I expected it to be a long night. That was something of an understatement and they spent the following days listening to news broadcasts and searching for information. Eventually a friend travelling south called them from Katherine with the (good) news that we were alive, but homeless.

As Tracy approached, two neighbouring above-ground homes were destroyed. Part of one of them landed on our roof and a timber beam speared through the ceiling and into our dining table. Debris from the second filled our back yard and piled against our back wall. Margaret tried to console the children above the shrieking sound of the wind.

As the eye of the cyclone passed over, we had about 20 minutes of calm and set about finding our neighbours and moved them to our bathroom. Among the 20 refugees we collected was a young man with a broken leg. He sat on the bathroom floor with a bottle of rum to relieve his pain. I told him that if I was still alive in the morning, I would take him to hospital.

Following the eye, the storm intensified in the reverse direction and a floor beam from another home speared through our outside sliding doors and knocked me into the next room, inflicting a deep cut on my left leg before demolishing an internal wall. Then, with a roar the whole roof, including the ceilings and roof trusses, lifted off and disappeared into the night. Windows were smashed and parts of the walls collapsed. That was game, set and match.

When dawn broke, I could see the carnage of wrecked homes and the skeletons of stripped trees for hundreds of metres. Luckily, one nearby house had miraculously withstood the storm and the whole neighbourhood moved into it. We sourced three small generators to run refrigerators and all our Christmas food and drinks were pooled. While the women dealt with domestic issues, the guys cleared the neighbourhood of rotting food and cleaned rubbish out of the pool so the children could swim. We all slept on the floor. The bar from my home was moved to the carport.

During Christmas morning I was worried that Tracy could retrace her course and against that possibility I established another "safe bathroom" in a building across the road that had lost its roof. It wasn't needed.

After untangling one of my two cars, the other one having had the roof flattened, I managed to keep my promise and deliver the young man with the broken leg to the Darwin Hospital. The scene in the hospital emergency department is one I will never forget of people injured and bleeding being tended by staff working against all odds.

Between Christmas and New Year, Margaret and I had to make many decisions that would determine our future. After eight years of marriage, we had two children, a block of land, and two damaged motor cars to show for our hard work.

The list went something like this:

- We needed to be inoculated as soon as possible against tetanus and malaria etc.
- I needed medical treatment for the deep cut across my upper left leg that I had stitched together with electrical tape and sterilized with whisky.

- As Executive Assistant to the head of the Department of NT, I needed to return to work.
- We decided to demolish what was left of the house and give away anything of use such as air conditioners, stoves etc. and sell the land at a later date.
- We inspected, and decided to write off, our two bookshops and a real estate business located at Nightcliff and Moil which were operated by Margaret.
- In line with the Government direction to downsize the Darwin population, Margaret and the children would move to Adelaide to live with her parents and enroll the children in school.
- I would remain in Darwin until my future employment became clear and the family could be reunited.
- We decided we would not invest again in a home in Darwin.

In the New Year, Margaret and the children travelled to Alice Springs by bus and I instructed the driver to drop them (unannounced); at Bernie Kilgariff's house. I knew they would be looked after and indeed Bernie arranged a flight to Adelaide for them. I returned to work which included helping run the Tracy Relief Fund, until February 1975, when I drove to Adelaide to see my family and generally recuperate.

I had a stomach ulcer during this period and acting on my doctor's advice stopped smoking cigarettes. When I look back 50 years later that was a small bonus.

Around March 1975, the Commonwealth Government decided to appoint a Regional Coordinator to Alice Springs to provide some local autonomy while the massive task of rebuilding Darwin got under way. I was offered this position and moved to Alice Springs. This changed the course of my career, and the lives of my family, who joined me from Adelaide. We became 'locals' and made many new friends.

In 1976, Natasha was born to make it three children, Margaret opened a book exchange and then the Newsagent's in the new Coles

Shopping Centre.

On the handover to self-government, in 1978, I transferred to the newly created N.T. Electricity Commission and two years later to the Yulara Development Office.

At last, in 1984 we decided it was time to 'return home" to Adelaide.

Peter Lyster

Peter, who now lives in Maryland in the United States, was taking a summer break from university studies in Adelaide and was in Darwin working as an Intern Engineer on the Radio Australia transmitters on the Cox Peninsula.

On the morning of December 24, 1974, I boarded a ferry at the wharf in Darwin harbor for the trip to Cox Peninsula. At breakfast I had heard an announcement on the radio about a cyclone off the coast, but no one on the boat seemed to pay any attention, so I didn't. I thought a cyclone was a brand of washing machine, or a kind of fence.

The bay was extremely rough that morning compared with the usual trip, and I spent an anxious half hour checking out the reactions of my fellow travellers who were all engineers and staff at the radio transmitter. On the bus ride across the Peninsula one of the guys pointed out a quarter mile wide swath of forest where trees had been wiped out by a cyclone a few years before.

He told me a cyclone was like a giant tornado that spins onto the land from the ocean, bringing extreme winds that can destroy structures and sometimes brings high water and floods. He said none had *ever* struck a big city, but one had cut through here not so long ago and taken out the forest. I had seen television footage of death and destruction from tornados in America, and this gave me visions of a giant whirlwind, which later turned out to be a pretty close to the real thing.

Since it was Christmas Eve, we were let off early in the afternoon. The bus ride from west to east back to Mandorah took us along the same trajectory that Tracy would take eight hours later.

The weather had freshened and this time the ferry across Darwin harbor rode serious waves, at times the nose pointed directly down into the sea and then up at the increasingly overcast sky.

None of the staff was particularly calm but they got their swagger back when we disembarked and went to the annual Christmas party at a local hotel.

Back then Darwin was an old tropical city. I had been told that the only people in Darwin were government workers and those who were escaping the law or their wives. Like a lot of isolated places in Australia it was a man's town. Teams of men lived their lives on the perimeters of Darwin bars.

But it was also a family town, not particularly sophisticated in terms of urban living, but it was relatively safe and full of activities for a family with young children, especially if you owned a four-wheel drive. During my brief stay there I fraternized mostly with government engineers and many of them had stable families, homes, and long-term lives in Darwin.

The senior engineer, and my mentor, Mr. Shaw, was happily married with children. He moved there for promotion within Radio Australia, whose facilities were administered by the Postmaster General's Department (PMG) but liked the place enough to stay.

Mr. Shaw told me the government wanted people in Darwin to secure a base in the wilderness of northern Australia. A lot of people looked back on that Darwin as a place of adventure.

During the party I leaned out of the window a few times to assess the weather. It was windier than I was used to in Adelaide but once again no one paid attention, so I had another beer and enjoyed the conversation of these tight-knit expatriates from the big cities.

When I arrived, my impression was of isolation and too much quiet. Quite frankly, I was depressed at first, but now my impression of Darwin improved. Radio Australia was an exciting place to work. They had recently installed a world-class log antenna with an array of thirty-meter-high towers that filled a space the size of a football field. Workers were required to shut down radio operations for their safety before they could venture out to the antenna. The main capacitor was the size of a storeroom and I flinched at the sight of workers casually going about their business surrounded by intense microwave energy. Tropical paradise it was, but I was glad my tenure there was to be only two months over the Christmas holidays.

Mr. Shaw drove me to my room at the Asti Motel at about 9 pm. The radio played regular warnings along with an eerie cyclone alarm that would become part of people's nightmares in years to come. Around 10 pm I noticed that wires on the high-voltage line were sparking as they swayed to and fro in the wind. I made a mental note to alert the Electricity Trust about this design flaw the next day, and a couple of hours later had a rueful laugh when I realized how absurd that was—the wires were flying around like a spider's web in a storm.

As I looked out of the window, I peered sideways and realized to my shock that fifty square feet of glass was bowed-in five inches and about to shatter over me.

There was an accelerating, nerve-wracking noise as the early morning wore on. I decided the bathroom in my third-floor apartment was the safest place because a small room would collapse less when the building fell down, but when I sat down in the tub, I hit the tap with my elbow and got drenched in the shower.

I stood on a stool to peer out of the skylight and saw to my horror houses exploding, their roofs lifting off and spinning up like frisbees and shattering against the side of the Asti Motel. On the northern side of the building a large water tower hung over me all night. Besides the potential of being crushed like a bug by the tower, I was in great danger of a projectile such as a wooden beam spearing through my room, so I sandwiched myself in bed between the mattresses where

I huddled and shook the rest of the night out, waiting for the place to come down, my hands over my ears, eventually to fall asleep from fright and exhaustion.

I was woken in the morning by a man checking the rooms of the motel. He said that sleeping between the mattresses had been a bad move because several people had been found crushed to death in that position.

I made my way downstairs and joined a group of people listening to a transmission from an out-of-state radio station on a car radio. It became clear from the bland news and Christmas Carols that the rest of the country did not know what had happened the night before – so began our Christmas Day of abandonment.

We must have been quite a sight – a group of worn-out traumatized people standing around in silence. Of course, food, water and sanitation were out of the question, and I had to crawl over wreckage to make my way down the road. The Asti Motel was badly damaged but to my surprise the building was standing and none of the rooms had caved in.

I was on the top floor. The roof only partially came off, but all the windows were shattered. Somehow, I was spared the shower of glass. The rest of Darwin was in complete ruins. I walked around the neighbourhood in a daze but was aware enough to notice the absence of people. I saw women weeping on the steps of their levelled homes.

I wondered how high the casualty rate could go and was reluctant to look too closely at some of the collapsed houses. Others would do that, other 'rescue workers'… but not me.

The city was almost silent and as the day wore on, I became bored, depressed, and thirsty. I don't have much memory after that, and I holed up on my own in my room in a state of ennui. When a road was cleared to the airport a car made its way back with the first disaster relief – beer and eggs. It was months before I could take the taste of beer and eggs.

About the middle of the week someone said that a telephone

line was available downtown for short calls to family. When I called, I heard my mother cry on the other end of the line and regretted that I caused her three days of grief thinking she'd lost a son.

During the week after Christmas there was no substantial food, water, or sanitation at our Asti Motel site. I don't think I spoke with anyone. I was younger than most (20 at the time) and felt like an outsider. From my damaged apartment window, I watched the army patrol along roads past houses that I had seen explode days before.

The Government announced a compulsory evacuation of the city by air with no exceptions, starting with women and children and after five days I decided it must be time for the men to go. I hitched a ride to a busing point to the airport. The bus travelled through a suburb that had been flattened, and we stared in silence at even greater destruction than we'd witnessed downtown. Later, we entered the airport where aircraft lay mangled and upended among scattered sheet metal and destroyed hangars – this was starting to look normal.

We were asked to wait, a lot of us sitting on the ground, in what was left of the passenger terminal at Darwin Airport. This being late December it was nearing the peak of the humid rainy season, and I was grumpy and thirsty. Throughout the evening, every fifteen minutes or so buses arrived and unloaded more men, women and children.

Every hour one or two regular-sized passenger jets arrived and departed with a plane load of refugees for a random state capital city, from where, we were assured, the airlines would continue transportation to a city of choice. The women and children were a first priority, and the remaining seats were assigned to a waiting list of an increasingly motley crew of men. It became obvious that we were in a delicate equilibrium phase of operations where the number of women and children arriving equalled the rate of extraction on the aircraft.

I sat on the floor in the first open spot I could find, and pretty soon the guy next to me in fishnet T-shirt and tattoos, showed me how to play Gin. I don't think we exchanged words other than what was necessary for me to understand the rules and exchange cards.

About 10 pm a USAF Starlifter transport jet arrived from Guam on a humanitarian mission – the cavalry had arrived. I have no idea how I know the origin of the plane other than the instantaneous communication network that formed. I watched the giant land. It appeared to flap its wings. A massive sight of mechanical beauty, it was a show of American power and largesse. Army security assured us that we would all fit in the plane, so like an idiot I dawdled and found myself at the end of the long line that snaked out from the plane's main doorway.

After some time, I got close enough to see that the large crowd sitting on the floor was at capacity. The line slowed to a crawl and finally one of the crew waved us off. It must have been an uncomfortable flight sitting on the floor of a cargo plane, but it was a jet, and the worst-case scenario was a flight to Perth of about 8 hours.

The remaining fifty or so of us were sent back to the broken hanger, hang dog, and were told that operations had ceased and that we might as well settle down for the night.

An airport counter doubled as makeshift security desk for soldiers doing security. I wandered over and chatted with the young soldier. I thought I was being friendly with the soldier, just to pass the time. He picked up a knife that was on the desk and said, "Is this your switch blade?"

To be honest, the knife looked very much at home in that crowd, and I hadn't noticed it. Needless to say, it was not mine, which I told the soldier. Nothing more was said, and I took a walk. Sometime later I saw the soldier return with two of his colleagues, and they asked if I would step behind the counter into one of their white rooms.

Still thinking that I was in for a friendly conversation with the guys I went in and was thrown against the wall and 'roughed up'. I considered fighting back and gave myself a pretty good chance – I don't know why, I guess I was young and pretty strong, and I decided that they just wouldn't expect it.

Luckily, I thought about the big picture, which included the fact that they wore side arms. They were frustrated and couldn't get a story out of me that matched with the knife. They didn't ask for any ID (did anyone in the airport that night have ID?), or even ask who I was, or what I was doing in Darwin. I think they had already made up their mind, and there was definitely not enough conversation space for me to tell them my story. I just had enough room to repeat that I had never even seen a switch-blade knife in my life.

Eventually the senior guy pushed me against the wall and, from behind my ear said "Listen mate, there are only a couple of us who are responsible for security overnight. The crowd out there is dangerous, and anything can happen. If I get a peep out of you, I will put a bullet in your head, do you get what I mean?" I told him I understood, and they let me go. After that, the night was quiet. I considered some sort of revenge, or at least formal protest, but decided that, aside from their crude tactics, they had a point.

I have vague memories of anxiety about newly arriving refugees and whether there would be enough aircraft. The next day, December 31, 1974, I got a seat on an RAAF C130 Hercules military transport headed to Brisbane. We were placed in paratrooper configuration on webbed seating, shoulder to shoulder, and with another person seated immediately opposite with his knees almost between mine.

Three weeks earlier I had flown to Darwin from Adelaide, which is way down south, and I had a mental picture of Brisbane as being Darwin's nearest neighbour to the east. I had badly underestimated the length of this miserable flight. In the propellor aircraft it took ten hours.

The only relief from the boredom was to crawl over people and sit on the rear doorway and fantasize how many people sitting there would cause the floor to give way and spill us all out. On the flight they gave us chocolate bars, which thus got added to beer and eggs as problem foods for me for some time to come.

We arrived in Brisbane late in the day and stumbled out of the rear door to bright lights, reporters, and TV cameras. Their looks of concern didn't fit with the bad mood of the passengers. I felt foolish squinting into the lights of the cameras, hoping none of my college friends would be watching, and having to change my attitude to look like a sorry refugee rather than a grumpy one.

A man handed me a hundred dollars or so and said it was a gift from the government for refugees. I told him I had lost nothing, and no thank you, but he said everyone *had* to take it, a very Australian assertion, so I took the money. We arrived on New Year's Eve and were housed in the Enoggera Army Barracks outside of Brisbane. The place seemed like a tropical paradise compare with where we had come from.

The airlines were extremely good about ferrying refugees to their city of choice, although it took until January 2, 1975, before I got a domestic flight to Adelaide.

I arrived home to a welcome that I have seen again and again over the years when I returned from America – it is the welcome of optimism, that everything is and maybe always will be alright.

A surprise was my dislocation about the shape of the well-ordered city of Adelaide. Only one week among a tangled mess of buildings had made the normal vertical and horizontal shapes of big cities seem too organized. I spaced out in front of a TV set watching John Newcombe win an exhibition match against a new rising star from America named Jimmy Connors. At least I think I did – I recently searched the Internet and found no record of the match. I swear I was aware that the match, which exhibited Connor's brash ways, was the end of the period of the dominant Australian tennis players. I spaced out for a second day.

Remembering that I was an employee of Telecom Australia, I showed up for work on the third day. It wasn't a survivor's or even a hero's welcome, and I think most people hadn't noticed I'd been gone. The senior engineer motioned me into his office and asked why

I hadn't showed up at work the day before since I was not officially on holidays.

I looked at him blankly, and for a while we had a standoff. It wasn't that I didn't care, but I didn't even think of showing up for work – people had lost everything! I couldn't form any kind of answer.

He then wanted to know the status of the Long Line equipment. I told him I did not know what Long Line equipment was. There was a longer silence while he looked at me. I'd had a shower and some food by then. I started to wake up from the dream. He looked at me sympathetically and explained. Staff in Telecom actually cared about the status of the equipment, and Long Line is the specific communication infrastructure to get communications in and out of Darwin. He gave up on getting any useful information out of me.

I didn't speak with people much at all about Darwin in the days and years to come. I was welcomed back at university the next semester in another very Australian way when a fellow student said, "I thought you got blown away", and walked off, not waiting for an answer.

Occasional nightmares subsided in a year, and I can now listen to thunder like any other person.

The following Christmas I bumped into Mr. Shaw in a lift at work. I felt bad for him because he and his family had a settled life in Darwin before Tracy, and he clearly liked his job there. After Tracy he had resettled in Adelaide. We traded stories about how we got out of Darwin. I shook hands with Mr. Shaw and that was the end of my direct association with Tracy.

Harry Maschke

Harry emigrated from Germany after the Second World War, settling in Melbourne where he worked for a major air-conditioning firm as a sheet metal worker. In 1966 he and his wife, Lyn, moved to Darwin but the unsuccessful treatment of a medical condition prompted him to return to Germany for corrective surgery. After touring Europe, he and Lyn returned to Australia overland, arriving back in Darwin in 1969 where he worked for a firm in the city before starting Action Sheet Metal in 1972. They lived in an elevated home in Rapid Creek.

My wife, Lyn, was the librarian at the recently opened Wagaman Open School and at Christmas 1974 was on holiday in Bali with a fellow teacher.

On Christmas Eve I was doing some last-minute shopping in one of the northern suburbs supermarkets when I started to talk with a couple of young backpackers. They were on their way to Bali and were looking for accommodation, so, having a big, empty house in Rapid Creek all to myself, I offered them a room.

That evening, I left them at home while I went to dinner at a friend's place. I left there early as conditions were getting worse. On the way home to Rapid Creek the wind was getting stronger and power lines were flashing sparks.

When I got back to my above-ground house I looked out of the window and saw the house across the road, occupied by a Catholic priest, disintegrate and its debris hit my house. I told the travellers to get into the bathroom. I had filled the bath with water as instructed in the cyclone warnings.

I held the door closed until all of the bathroom walls blew away, together with the rest of the house. The three of us were left clinging to the edge of the bath and were battered by flying debris. In the lightning flashes I could see the ground level brick house next door seemed to be standing so I jumped down to the ground, calling to the couple to jump too. The girl was wearing only panties and being wet, slipped through my arms as I tried to catch her. I tried to catch the young man, but he also slipped. He badly hurt his foot, but we were all able to run to the neighbour's house.

It was then that I was hit on the head by some flying debris.

I remember nothing until I woke up in Adelaide River with blood all over my head.

I don't remember how we got my Peugeot ute out from under the debris of the house, or how I got to Adelaide River, but we must have been the first to evacuate by road because it was early morning and no-one there knew there had been a cyclone.

We checked into the motel. People were suspicious because of the blood on my head. They thought I must have been in a fight.

I slept for more than a day before I regained my senses and asked the backpackers what we were doing in Adelaide River? They said I was driving south. I said that couldn't be right, I wasn't leaving Darwin. I don't know how long I was in Adelaide River, but I abandoned the travellers, turned around and drove back to Darwin.

By the time I got back to the Arnhem Highway intersection police had set up a roadblock and were stopping people from driving into the city, so I went bush, drove around the roadblock, and got back to my Berrimah factory.

My two partners, Don and Atse were there with their wives, Val and Carol, and their children. The workshop doors had been blown out and part of the roof was missing, but it had mostly withstood the Cyclone's ferocity.

At some stage I returned to my house to find it had been looted.

I found a pair of shoes in the bottom of a cupboard and although they were full of water, they still contained the wages for my workers that I had hidden in them.

With the city and suburbs incredibly damaged and plenty of repair work needed, my sheet metal business was declared an emergency industry. The army installed a huge diesel generator to keep my machines working and we had enough stocks of metal.

They were good days. We had power, a refrigerator and plenty of cold beer because a 'carton' became a more common currency than money.

I never moved back to Rapid Creek. Instead, I built on a block of land I bought at Humpty Doo. When Lyn returned to Darwin, sometime later, she started the business known as Weavers Workshop and eventually moved to a shop in Parap. Lyn and her sister became a part of starting the popular Parap Market.

Darwin has a great future under the right leadership, but we must never under-estimate the potential for another devastating cyclone.

Therese McCubbin

Terri first came to Darwin in 1956 as a girl of 9, the sixth of seven children of John and Rebecca (Becky) McCubbin. Her father was an air traffic controller who had been appointed to Darwin for a two-year term but rather than leave at the end of his time, he began his own Chartered Accounting business. Terri and her older sister Janis went back to Melbourne for several years of schooling before returning in 1962 where, after a brief period at St. Mary's, and aged 15, she began work at a childcare centre in the city. Married at 17 she was 26 years old and a mother of four children at the time of Cyclone Tracy. A registered childcare provider by then, she operated the Donald Duck Childcare Centre from her home on Bagot Road and looked after 32 children.

It is often said that the people of Darwin weren't prepared for Cyclone Tracy, but my husband Tony and I certainly were. By late morning on Christmas Eve, I was calling parents telling them to collect their children at lunchtime. Some were reluctant because they had Christmas parties they wanted to attend but I had my own four children – Leah 8, Clifford 7, Jason 6, and Simon 5 – to consider.

Tony – a fireman at Darwin Airport – was due to begin a 12-hour shift at 6 pm, so he spent the afternoon clearing the yard of any potential missiles and taking great care to ensure our ski-boat was half-filled with water and securely lashed in a web of ropes tied to the piers of the house. Tony and I were keen water skiers and I had set a couple of distance records. For even more protection Tony made sure his four-wheel-drive was parked close to shelter the boat.

He took my car to work telling me I would be alright, though when I got it back, the car had been sandblasted back to bare metal. During the evening, as the weather deteriorated, I was talking on the phone to my mother in Chrisp Street, Rapid Creek. She lived in a ground-level Housing Commission house with my sister Janis, brother Richard and two children, Patrick and Maree from her second marriage (to Josef). She wanted me to go to her house while Richard wanted to come to my house to look after us, but by then conditions prohibited travel.

As we were talking, I saw the roof of a neighbour's house fly away. Then the phone went dead, and I knew it was time to seek shelter. I gathered my four children, and we hid under our big heavy dining room table. But the table collapsed when my roof took off and the ceiling fell in. Luckily, with just one leg left, it formed a sort of cave. But the wind was so strong it threatened to take Clifford out of my arms. I held his arm so tightly it was a month before my finger marks faded from his arm.

I had invited Dawn, my neighbour, who was recently widowed with a one-year-old baby and a daughter about seven, to come to our house. She had refused, suggesting we went there instead, so when the eye came, the five of us managed to scramble downstairs and over to her house.

She suggested we shelter behind her piano, but instead we chose to get under her dining room table, then watched in amazement as first a wall took off and flew over the top of us, followed by the piano. The eight of us were left totally exposed to the elements, wet, freezing cold and would have been colder if not for the constant flow of warm pee.

As dawn broke and the wind eased we managed to get downstairs to the storeroom and were there when another neighbour, Reg Lowry, called out asking if anyone was alive. I left the children and emerged to see the unbelievable devastation. Dawn's car had been blown from under her house, across Bagot Road and had ended up against the brick wall of a house on the RAAF Base across the road.

Sometime during Christmas morning my brother Richard arrived and took us all back to my mother's house in Rapid Creek. It had a hole in its roof where a big beam had speared through the ceiling, but otherwise it was virtually undamaged. The beam had speared through a bed and into the concrete floor. The house didn't even lose any windows and soon provided a haven for a number of people. My stepfather, Josef, cooked for large numbers and went on to cook at the Nightcliff High School canteen until it closed.

Meanwhile Tony, relieved of his duties, found us at Mum's house and after a day or two took me and the children back to the Air Traffic Control Tower where about 100 men, women and children had gathered. It was from there that we were evacuated a few days later, as one of the last families to leave, on a Fokker Friendship flight to Brisbane. It stopped many times and took all day and into the evening to arrive. It was a horrendous flight.

My mother, in the meantime had also been evacuated. She went to Perth and took not only her two youngest children, but a gaggle of other children as well.

My brother George and Tony stayed on to help with the clean-up but after a few weeks, Tony drove his four-wheel-drive down to Brisbane, towing the undamaged ski-boat. Much later George told the story of his friend Brian who had interstate visitors staying. The visitors, convinced they were going to die, appealed to God to 'take us quickly'. A voice answered: 'don't listen to him God, there's nothing wrong with us'.

My sister Judith and her husband Phil, having been unable to return to Darwin because of the permit system, also came to Brisbane and we rented a big house right on the river. In February 1975, the ABC Television program *Today Tonight* did a story on our family of four adults and eight children, all Darwin evacuees, living in this one house.

Tony joined the Brisbane Fire Service and had been adamant

that he was never going back to Darwin, but I very much wanted to return. Then suddenly and unexpectedly, during the television interview he said we were all going back. It was a promise I told him he had to keep because he'd announced it on national television.

In March, Tony and Phil returned to Darwin to collect their cars, drove them to Brisbane and we all returned to Darwin in three vehicles towing the boat and two caravans. We had bought the vans to give us the accommodations we required to get the permits to return.

Both Tony and Phil built in under the floorboards of our elevated houses, while we lived in the caravan. We later sold the caravan but when the government offered caravans as emergency accommodation we got one and put it next to the house, while Tony rebuilt the upper storey. The renovated bottom half of the house was occupied by my brother Richard, a racehorse owner and trainer, and his jockey and strapper. They stayed for several years.

When I returned to Darwin in March, it was to discover that there was a huge demand for childcare from government workers, so Tony fixed the fences, cleaned up the downstairs area and I soon had nearly as many in childcare as I had before the cyclone.

There was an unusual postscript to my story. At the time of the cyclone, we had two large dogs, a Labrador and a Red Setter. The Labrador survived and was waiting at the bottom of the stairs when I emerged, but the Red Setter disappeared. Some months later, we were visiting friends at Berry Springs when a big red Setter rushed up, put her paws on my shoulders and began licking my face. Her carers, who couldn't explain how she had come to them, said 'it must be your dog'.

Leonie McNally

Leonie and her husband Jim had been in Darwin for 12 months following Jim's appointment as Manager of Darwin's only Commercial radio station, 8DN owned at that time by Darwin Broadcasters, a subsidiary of Perth-based Swan Breweries. Leonie was working in various administrative roles.

We were living in a small ground level house on Beagle Street, off Smith Street and within walking distance of Peary Street, where 8DN was located. As Darwin had been our home for only twelve months the cyclone season was very new to us. The experience of Selma earlier in December, and the 'cyclone preparation segments' regularly presented by 8DN provided us with a good overview of steps to take: opening and closing of louvres; filling the bath with water; and more.

The bathroom of our house had been very basic but the final stages of its renovation and upgrade had finished on December 23. The old bath was outside waiting for removal in the new year, and this proved to be a life saver in the days following.

Jim's parents had arrived from Sydney on Christmas Eve, on the last flight allowed to land at Darwin airport. As it was the first flight anywhere for Jim's mother, she arrived in an anxious state, and we did our best to play down the seriousness of what was happening.

On that night, 8DN was broadcasting Midnight Mass from Saint Mary's Cathedral. The technician had set up all the equipment and because the Cathedral was close to the station, Jim was to pack up after the broadcast.

By 10 pm the wind gusts prevented opening doors and despite our best-efforts, water was seeping through the louvres and into the living area. By then 8DN was off the air and it wasn't worth risking anything to investigate the state of play at the Cathedral or station premises.

We huddled into the newly renovated bathroom, under the manhole cover, with refreshments and a torch, hoping what was happening would blow over soon. Water began swirling around the Christmas tree, so gifts were retrieved and opened in our bunker.

There was a lot of noise, howling winds followed by periods of stillness, repeat and repeat. Later we realised that the eerie stillness might have been the eye, but we didn't register how long it lasted. The manhole cover above us stayed in place for the duration of the storm. It was reassuring until daylight showed that the bathroom roof was the only piece of roof remaining anywhere in the house. All the walls were intact but there was no roof.

The 8DN premises suffered only minimal damage, with a small window broken. As there were adequate kitchen facilities and bathrooms there, including a shower, we quickly gathered basic household and bedding items that were still usable and relocated to 8DN. This became our temporary home for some time. The planned Christmas dinner ingredients were soon transferred to a barbeque for anyone who was in the Peary Street area. The barbequed turkey and trimmings were most enjoyable in fact.

While walking around the house block inspecting the devastation we came across the unwanted but now overflowing, discarded bath. The bucket brigade of neighbours using that water was a welcome and happy sight in following days.

The station's transmitter tower was badly damaged so, to enable broadcasting to recommence within days, a Hills hoist, located at Charlton Place, off Bishop Street, became a temporary transmitter.

Of the twenty-six permanent staff members at 8DN, only six

remained, and they immediately became on-air presenters along with their other duties. I joined them as a volunteer, keeping track of daily schedules and rosters.

The station's most key role became dissemination of information – the who, where, and what, of daily happenings such as food availability, evacuation flights and Street clean-ups. Also important was playing music as light relief in the evenings.

To that end, Naval Officer Chris "Timber" Mills was released from his duties aboard his ship, HMAS *Hobart*, to assist with the evening announcing roster.

A new transmitter finally arrived by Hercules from Richmond Air Base and once installed, our daily life became less stressful. With very few telephones still working it was some time before we could contact interstate family members to let them know we were safe and uninjured.

As soon as practicable the chairman, and a couple of directors of Swan Breweries, who owned 8DN, flew to Darwin in the company's Lear Jet to assess damage and decide the future of their Darwin assets. They also operated a broadcasting network in northern WA, and Port Hedland was their first port of call on the return journey. From there, they made phone calls to our families.

A few days later, Jim's parents evacuated to their home city of Sydney. Life became very busy for us, assisting where possible, and ensuring 8DN was providing the best possible service to the community. One of the overwhelming memories of those post cyclone days was the caring and sharing for others.

At weekends we often drove to Berry Springs for a swim and during one of those visits I had a chance meeting with a long-lost cousin who was on HMAS *Melbourne*, one of the first Navy ships to arrive and provide repair crews.

Within days the boys had cleared the Beagle Street house for us and several weeks later we had a temporary roof and were able to return home. It was several months before necessary repairs were completed and even longer before electricity was reinstated to our street and individual dwellings. Until then we shared a generator with the next-door neighbour, and ran a fridge and a light each, if one household wanted to do a load of washing or use a big appliance the other would turn off everything for that period of time. These experiences certainly reminded us of what was important and what we could live without.

Jim had initially signed a two-year contract with thoughts that he would pursue further opportunities with the Swan Brewery regional WA network, however those thoughts went out the window. There was so much happening with the rebuilding of Darwin, resurrecting and/or forming community associations and grass roots engagement with the broader Darwin population, we never thought of leaving.

With his love for horse racing, Jim became involved with the Darwin Turf Club when it brought racing back to the Top End. It was a passion for the rest of his life. During Jim's time as chairman of the club, we worked together to establish the Darwin Cup Gala Ball and I developed the 'Ladies Day' initiative. Both events are now highlights of the Darwin racing calendar.

In June 1975, I joined the management team of Casuarina Shopping Centre during its rebuild and became its first marketing manager. I went on to be the inaugural manager for the Casuarina Village Shopping Centre. In 1988, I was appointed executive officer of the Crafts Council of the NT, formerly known as Territory Craft, overseeing the development, and showcasing of, contemporary crafts throughout the NT and more widely. It was a wonderful journey that lasted 20 years.

Darwin has continued to be home, probably because of the "Girl". It was an experience that shaped and changed our lives.

I don't ever want to experience another devastating blow; however, I am thankful for the life-long lessons provided by Tracy and her aftermath.

Perry Matthews

As a young unmarried Air Force officer based at Richmond NSW, Perry spent a week on leave in Darwin in 1971, returning briefly in 1972 after taking part in exercises at Tindal. After undergoing civilian air traffic control training in Queensland in 1973, he was posted to RAAF Air Traffic Control in Darwin for two years with the rank of Flying Officer. He ended up staying for six years.

On Christmas Eve 1974, my hospitable Air Traffic Control (ATC) colleague, Flying Officer David Collins and his wife Jan invited me and the other unmarried controller, Flying Officer Tom Doran, to join their young family in their on-base married quarters for some Christmas cheer.

Tom and I were the rostered controllers for the morning shift in the control tower from 06.00 to 13.00. There were also Department of Civil Aviation (DCA) civilian air traffic controllers on duty. Although the ATC unit had 32 officers it was normal at Christmas to reduce staff because air traffic was usually low.

We were to relieve the RAAF night shift controller, Flying Officer Maurice Kneen, freeing him to rejoin his wife Madeleine and their new-born child around dawn.

We were aware of Tracy nearby because Maurice had been tracking its centre over the previous week on a somewhat ancient ground-controlled approach radar. By about 10 pm the wind was extremely strong, so Tom and I chose to remain with the Collins rather than return to our single quarters.

As the night progressed the situation became somewhat fraught, as all those in Darwin at the time well know. About 3 am the wind eased a bit as the eye began to cross the coast and, I later discovered, effectively followed runway 11, the main runway that was 200 ft wide and 11,000 ft long.

I had the keys to the crew van – a yellow VW Kombi – and as we would be the 'morning' shift but with roads impassable, I drove cross country over debris towards the tarmac which took us past the WRAAF (women's) barracks where we found two WRAAFs – wet, cold and like us frightened holding on to a palm tree.

We continued with the wind making steering difficult. The plan was to replace Maurice with Tom while I would take the WRAAFs to the cyclone-secure base operations centre where operations and communications staff were on duty.

At the Tower it became obvious that it was uninhabitable, with windows blown in and essential operational equipment destroyed. Maurice and three or four DCA controllers were huddled inside the entrance. They all got in the Kombi, and I drove to DCA's operations building.

By now, RAAF Service Police could be heard shouting over a megaphone to take cover as the eye was passing, with wind speed and direction increasing. At DCA Operations, the DCA controllers got out with the WRAAFs, and I told Tom to stay with the young women; no time to argue.

I then took Maurice to his married quarters before parking nearby at the Collins' house and I scuttled upstairs. I joined the family in the bathroom and briefly outlined the outside situation. The two children were in the bathtub with towels covering their heads. Shortly after, the roof blew off.

We spent a couple of miserable hours, saying that 'it will be ok and not to worry, it will pass soon' and so on.

Around dawn, the wind and rain seemed to ease a bit, so I left the Collins and their heartbroken Christmas morning and drove to

Base Operations, where I briefed the duty operations officer on the situation as I knew it, while the response started gearing up.

Throughout Christmas Day I was involved in a variety of communication, liaison, transportation, and local recovery duties. I presumed my shared apartment in The Mansions in Sabine Road, Milner had been blown out, so gave it little further thought especially as I had a room in the officers' mess with meals entitlements at my own expense.

An ATC radio in the crew vehicle had a single channel set up for surface movement on the runways and taxiways. It was the only ATC channel operating at Darwin for some days, until a Hercules delivered a Transportable Telecommunications Unit, which reestablished (or resurrected) a tactical air navigation beacon on the airport.

Throughout Christmas Day, I made irregular "All stations, this is …" transmissions in case there were flights in the area, and when possible listened for any incoming contacts.

About 4pm, I heard the unmistakable sound of Rolls Royce Dart turbo prop engines which powered Fokker Friendships. Looking up I saw an Ansett aircraft overhead and immediately tried to make contact but was unsuccessful.

I reported this to the operations officer in Base Operations, who told me that a group of airmen had cleared debris from the first 6000 feet (almost two kilometres) of runway 29 sufficient for a Friendship to land.

A short time later I saw another Friendship approaching, and knew this would be TAA's VH-TQT, I called the aircraft and got an immediate loud and clear response.

There was no known traffic in the circuit, no meteorological information and no instrument approach beacons but conditions were adequate for the "visual approach" then underway. I relayed the recent information about runway debris and informed the crew that I would meet them near the intersection of the main runway from where I led the aircraft to the normal Friendship parking position on the apron in front of the old civil air terminal.

When the crew disembarked I was surprised and pleased to hear captain Ray Vuillermin introduce himself, with FO Tony Burgess. Ray and his family used to live a few hundred metres from us in Macleod and Ray and I both attended the local high school, and the school Air Training Corps flight. We both graduated as Cadet Under Officers.

As the first turbo-prop airliner to arrive post cyclone, with normal apron services disrupted, the pilots and I walked across the apron to RAAF Base Operations, where I introduced them to Group Captain David Hitchins, Officer Commanding the Top End. That was the last I saw of them, as I returned to my radio duties as I was expecting other aircraft to follow.

Although they didn't leave until the next day they were among the earliest aircraft to take part in what would become Australia's greatest peacetime evacuation involving dozens of different aircraft from not only the RAAF and domestic and regional airlines but international services as well. It was truly a monumental operation.

Ian Miller

Ian and his wife, Maritza, were living in a flat in Grevillea Circuit, Nightcliff. Ian was employed as a plant introduction officer with the Animal Industry and Agriculture Branch of the Department of the Northern Territory. Maritza had moved with Ian from Venezuela where they met, to Darwin in late 1973 and was studying English.

On the evening of December 24, 1974, we went for Christmas drinks at a friend's house in Wagaman, however with all of the warnings on the radio about the approaching cyclone we decided to go home early. The impending cyclone was the second cyclone warning for the month, the first being Cyclone Selma which threatened Darwin over December 3 and 4, but which dissipated without any impact.

Our accommodation at the time was in a two-storey grey brick building of six flats, three at ground level and three flats on the upper level. Our flat was the upper middle one. Each upper flat had a separate external stairway on the eastern side to enable access, while on the western side each flat had a balcony overlooking Grevillea Circuit.

At home we followed the recommended pre-cyclone procedure of filling the bathtub with water and putting important documents in a metal filing cabinet in a cupboard. All our personal possessions were inside the flat except for our Ford Cortina station wagon which was parked in front of the flats close to Grevillea Circuit.

During the evening the wind speed and driving rain gradually increased and water started to come under the door. The rain was accompanied by loud whistling and high-pitched howling winds, and the noise of buildings breaking up.

The very loud noise of the whistling and howling is the most memorable part of the night.

Because of uncertainty about the situation, we decided to go downstairs during the cyclone, but the external stairway was blocked with debris from neighbouring buildings. We therefore went to the other side of the building and descended by climbing over the balcony, then using the holes in breeze blocks on the side of the flat below as steps to get down to ground level. We were then able to enter one of the ground level flats where other tenants were present.

Later the roof of our flat blew off but the vertical brick walls of the lower flats remained intact.

The "eye" of the cyclone, where the wind speed was reduced, was very distinct so a few of us from the flats walked across the road to check on the well-being of neighbours. Everyone seemed to be safe.

We knew that it was the "eye" and that the cyclone would come back with the winds blowing in the other direction so we walked back to the flats. Everyone from the six flats then collected in Flat 2 which was the middle of the three downstairs flats.

This flat was protected by the brick walls of Flat 1 on one side, by the walls of Flat 3 on the other side, and by the concrete floor of the upper storey. This concrete upper floor then became a substitute roof for the building. As a result, the ground level flats remained virtually intact, and all occupants were protected within a concrete structure.

All 12 persons who had gathered in Flat 2 were adults. During the rest of the cyclone, we just sat in the flat without any power waiting for the cyclone to pass, and wondering what was happening outside as we couldn't see clearly through the driving rain, the lightning, and the darkness.

After the eye had passed the winds seemed to be more destructive. Perhaps this was because the first part of the cyclone had pre-loosened buildings for the second onslaught. In this regard a cyclone is "well designed" for destruction, with winds firstly coming in one direction then the other in order to complete the destructive process.

Our Ford Cortina which was parked outside the flats was protected by the lower-level flats, so it received only minor damage except that the duco had been "sand-blasted" by particles carried by the cyclonic winds. Later the entire vehicle required re-painting.

During the clean-up we found some of our possessions elsewhere in Grevillea Circuit. They had been sucked out of cupboards through the open roof.

On Christmas morning we realised that we had witnessed and survived an incident of gross natural destruction. Also, in the morning we watched as a QANTAS Boeing 747 Jumbo Jet appeared in the skies over Darwin and did a low altitude aerial survey of the city. Apparently the authorities elsewhere had heard that something had happened in Darwin and the plane had been diverted from its normal international route to report on what could be seen.

Because of debris on the runway the plane could not land, and it soon disappeared, however its appearance was our first indication that someone else knew about the situation in Darwin. I heard later that the pilot radioed that it looked like an atomic bomb had hit Darwin.

For three days after the cyclone the weather turned to bright sunshine, being hot and humid but with no rain and little wind. Roads were blocked with debris such as twisted power poles, power lines and corrugated iron, but the fine weather enabled us to take stock of what had happened and look for friends.

The upper level of our friends' elevated house in Wagaman, where we had Christmas drinks, was completely destroyed. This house was typical of many such elevated houses in Casuarina, Nakara, and Wagaman where only floorboards remained, with a metal stair frame and concrete steps leading to the bare-boarded upper level. Later these structures were called "dance floors".

Without telephone contact it took about a week for one of the other occupants of our flats to relay a message to my family in Sydney that we were OK.

Being Christmas there was plenty of perishable food that was still suitable for consumption for a short time after the Cyclone. We therefore shared barbecues with other tenants in the car park until the Defence Forces established kitchens at some of the schools.

In Nightcliff there was no electricity for about one month after the cyclone and drinking water came from taps that were installed in the main Darwin water pipeline beside the Stuart Highway. Water for other purposes such as washing came from a home swimming pool across the road from our flats.

In the aftermath of the cyclone, regular aerial spraying of the city and suburbs with insecticide took place to control flies and mosquitoes.

Maritza was evacuated to Sydney in early January 1975 and stayed there for some months where she continued studies in English. Upon leaving she was vaccinated, probably for tetanus.

I remained in Darwin to help with the clean-up, firstly in the immediate Nightcliff area then at Berrimah Farm cleaning up the plant quarantine facility and ensuring that plants in quarantine during the cyclone were retrieved, accounted for, and their culture continued.

Not long after the evacuation, when there were only about 10,000 people left in Darwin, Rolf Harris came to Darwin to entertain the population. It is said that virtually all remaining persons in Darwin were present at the concert which was held at the amphitheatre in Darwin Botanic Gardens. During the concert I saw Rolf Harris fall from the stage when he tripped while performing the song "Jake the Peg" (with an extra leg).

I was granted "R & R" leave in Sydney from January 17, returning to work in Darwin on 3 February 1975.

On my return I took part in a vegetation survey into the effects of the cyclone. Some trees protected buildings and infrastructure from wind damage by forming a physical barrier against flying debris. On the other hand, certain tree species were more prone to dislodgement by the winds and soaking rains, becoming part of the general devastation scene. Virtually all trees beside the Stuart Highway from Darwin out to the Arnhem Highway were completely defoliated, forming a very stark landscape.

The head office of the Animal Industry and Agriculture Branch of the Department of the Northern Territory was in Government Block 1 in Mitchell Street. A memorable moment during the clean-up of this building was being told to throw water-damaged Government files from a third-floor window into a tip truck parked below for transport to the dump.

The fact that the lower level of our flats was not substantially damaged, and that the other occupants had left Darwin, allowed us to negotiate a move to live in Flat 2 for about two years after the cyclone. This gave us time to build a house on a block of land we had purchased in Howard Springs.

In February 1975, the Darwin Reconstruction Commission was established to rebuild the city. The flats at 18 Grevillea Circuit were eventually rebuilt.

A few years after Cyclone Tracy there was a "back to Darwin" celebration to encourage people to return to the city.

David Molesworth

David was a journalist with ABC Radio and TV News. He and his then wife, Diana Kupke, had arrived in Darwin in late 1971, as part of an intended round-Australia road trip. They had called in to visit a former colleague from The Age in Melbourne, Mike Hayes. With the arrival of ABC TV, only a few months earlier, several journalist's positions were available, and David was offered a job. Diana's story also appears in this book. David lived in Rothdale Road, Jingili.

In the grey dawn of Christmas morning 1974, I stood outside my house in Darwin and thought of Hiroshima. As far as I could see in every direction there was total devastation. The homes of my neighbours destroyed or severely damaged, the contents, corrugated roofing iron, sheets of cladding, strewn over the landscape.

I had just lived through hours of howling winds, teeming rain, thumping, banging, and crashing, had come close to death, yet could not comprehend what had happened.

Just a week earlier, I had been in England, on leave from my job as an ABC journalist. Now, I was facing the biggest news story of my 13-year career but was unable to function as a reporter.

I had known for several days that a cyclone was heading for Darwin, but no-one seemed particularly concerned. Several weeks earlier one had veered away from the city.

After preparing news bulletins at work on Christmas Eve, several of us attended a Christmas drinks party. By then it was drizzling and a little breezy but nothing too alarming. Some hours, and several cans of beer later, I managed to put my elbow though a louvre window and decided it was time to head for home.

Driving to Rothdale Road in Jingili, the wind was building up and it was raining steadily. There were four of us in the house. Kathy, a former ABC news typist and her two daughters had just moved back to Darwin from England and were staying with me. There was also Kat Stephens, a tabby kitten belonging to my ex-wife, then house-sitting in Fannie Bay with our fifteen months old son, and her partner.

My account of what followed includes long forgotten details and times, courtesy of a recently rediscovered interview given to the ABC's *Radio Active* publication in a Sydney hospital, just days after the cyclone.

I was woken at 1 am on Christmas morning with rain coming through the window louvres. A high wind was raging, and the power was off. When the light fittings crashed to the floor, it was time to move. I stooped to collect my shoes just as a sheet of corrugated iron sliced through the window. It struck me just below the ribs on my right side.

I am told I screamed but I have no recollection of that. I was dazed, but knew I had to get out of the side of the house where the storm was coming from. The roof blew off, and the ceiling was collapsing, and windows were breaking. It was dangerous to move because pieces of wood and crockery from the kitchen were flying around.

I found a T-shirt my mother had sent me for Christmas, emblazoned with Ballarat Bertie, the logo of a brewery near where I grew up in Victoria. I crawled under a coffee table in the lounge room.

The others, including the kitten, were under a couch and chairs. I had managed to collect a torch, another Christmas present, and a bottle of duty-free French brandy from the kitchen. I needed that brandy as I lay in two inches of water for the rest of the night.

No-one moved or spoke much – one of the girls cried out that Kat Stephens had urinated on her. It was freezing cold. From time to time, I flashed my torch and saw cracks appearing, the ceiling collapsing and louvres shattering.

The wind increased until it sounded to me like an express train but much louder; there was intense weird green lightning and continual thunder, the noise of objects hitting, the scraping of tin, the plaster ceiling falling, and then, a lull. The eye had arrived. We stayed put.

Around 4.30 the express train returned in earnest. Bookshelves in the lounge room broke up and their contents scattered. The house shook. I was afraid it would be blown down on us. We lay cocooned by the fallen plaster ceiling until the wind finally eased around dawn. The house still stood. We had survived.

A quick check revealed the front bedroom wall on the lawn below, but all the other walls were intact, though holed in many places. In the main bedroom the air-conditioner was lying on the bed where I had been sleeping. We moved downstairs and huddled in a minivan parked underneath the bedroom wing. I thought that we were the only people alive, but someone, I believe from emergency services, eventually came by and soon I was on my way to hospital.

That journey, which normally took about 15 minutes lasted considerably longer with the roads littered with debris and fallen power lines. At Bagot Road I remember police directing traffic, identified as cops only by their uniform caps.

At the hospital, the floor of the reception area was flooded with blood-stained water and mud, and I saw people with injuries I considered much worse than my own, so I walked out and headed for the ABC. One of our casual news typists driving past picked me up and drove me to her nearby flat where she was somehow able to provide hot coffee and toast and vegemite. Then she delivered me to the office, and I joined staff gathered in front of the TV building.

I was shocked and suffering from post-trauma stress, yet I

attended a press conference with disaster officials still wearing my blood-stained Ballarat Bertie T-shirt. I accompanied some newsroom colleagues on a tour of the city in the ABC Landcruiser to check on staff houses. We came across my ex-wife, Diana. She told me she had already been to Rothdale Road looking for me, and to the temporary morgue in Casuarina – an experience seared into her memory to this day. My son had slept through the cyclone.

Early on Christmas night, exhausted, sore, and feeling unwell, I lay down on a mattress in the television studio. The manager came by and remarked "Who's the sleeping beauty?" A colleague's wife, a nurse, told him plainly that I was injured. The next day, when I noticed I was passing blood in my urine she insisted on driving me to hospital. This time I was admitted.

Late that night, I was loaded onto an RAAF Hercules transport at Darwin Airport and flown to Sydney. I was on my back on a stretcher throughout the 10-hour flight and in considerable discomfort.

From Sydney airport I was transferred in a convoy of ambulances to the Royal Prince Alfred Hospital in Camperdown where I was diagnosed with a lacerated kidney and damaged vertebrae, the cause of my in-flight discomfort.

I know to this day that I was extremely lucky – I shudder to think what would have happened to me if the deadly sharp corner of that sheet of corrugated iron had not bent back as it came through the window. A month later, back in Darwin, I found it in the garden, identifiable from the strands of pyjama cloth attached to the bent corner.

Figure 11: David Molesworth holds the sheet of corrugated iron that injured him (Molesworth, 1975).

Figure 13: The suburb of Moil after Cyclone Tracy (Joe Karlhuber Collection, LANT ph0026-0022)

Susannah O'Brien

Susie's father, John Francis O'Brien, had come to Darwin a few years earlier to join the NT Police force. He had been in the Australian Army since a teenager and had not long returned from the Vietnam War, still a young man. Her mother Elaine, originally from Roma, Queensland, had followed John to Darwin, and in 1974 was a happy mum to three young daughters: Elizabeth, Catherine, and Susie 6. They lived in an elevated government house at 57 Dripstone Road, Alawa.

In 1974, I was a cheeky six-year-old. A barefoot, white-haired, ratbag, roaming the streets of Alawa. It was a childhood I am grateful for: no mobile phones, social media, or computer games, and many freedoms. I was in Year 2 at Alawa Primary School.

What is now Charles Darwin University was Darwin Community College, and Casuarina Square consisted of just Coles and maybe six to eight other small speciality shops, including Picasso's Cafe, my favourite for a milkshake. Happiness was heading to Alawa Shops with my sister with 50 cents each to buy a packet of chips and a can of coke.

In December 1974, I was looking forward to Christmas, and knew the gift under the tree was the Teddy-bear I had been harassing my mum for over many months. We were a very typical family of the time. Unlike many families, however, we intended to remain in Darwin over Christmas and not visit the relatives down south.

Dad was working shifts at the new Mitchell Street Police Station (across from where the Darwin Hotel is today). It was a time of BBQs, drinks with neighbours, and even a visit from Santa at Casuarina Police station.

My mum tells me that Cyclone Selma had brought much rain already that December, but it veered off and missed Darwin. People were ready to forget about that and focus on Christmas and having fun.

My parents, especially Dad, loved to socialise and partied well. We were quite close to our neighbours, John and Bev Conway, and their three children, Vicki, Darren and Bradley, who lived next door at 55 Dripstone Road. John Conway was a barge master, a strong, hard-working man and Bev was his straight-talking, kind, and generous wife.

I was only six, so my memories are not extensive, however what I do recall is clear. Many talk of the horrendous howl of the wind, but I remember the rain, so much, never-ending, torrential rain. Sometime late on Christmas Eve, my older sister went into Mum and Dad's room, "Mummy, my walls are shaking" she said.

By that stage, the wind had picked up so much it was driving the rain through the louvres and directly onto her bed. Soon the rain would start coming into other areas of the house, quickly soaking our brand-new carpet, and running down the walls.

This might have been the first sign for Mum and Dad that things could get rough that night. Previously, there had been no sign of worry or concern from them, with Dad returning from a party that night in a jolly mood.

A decision was made – we would all go downstairs and shelter in the little brick shed built under the house. However, just before that, John Conway appeared at the back door inviting us over, as he also must have thought things were turning nasty.

My night began when I was woken and guided out of the house with my sisters. We pushed out into, and then through very strong winds down the back stairs, over the back fence and into the Conway's house. That was the last time I saw my bedroom with all my favourite toys, or indeed the house again.

Once at the Conway's before midnight, the adults sat in the dining room, and all the children and teenagers (five in total) sat together playing board games, and admiring Darren Conway's Christmas gift – a brand new, shiny drum set.

I dare say Darren had been instructed to watch over the smaller kids, which he did brilliantly and bravely, as I remained totally oblivious to the impending danger. I'm still not sure anyone really knew what was in store for us at this stage. The adults did a marvellous job at hiding, or containing, what would have surely been fear, and for that I give my greatest thanks and admiration, as I have no trauma from Tracy, unlike many others, who were older and more aware, and suffer to this day.

At some point before midnight, water began dribbling down the walls from the ceiling, bringing dirt and black sludge with it. Like a slow building nightmare, the dribbles became stronger and stronger, turning into streams on the floor as the house began to flood.

Water was everywhere, and it was no longer possible to remain where we were. We all moved into the Conway's bathroom. In total, 6 adults, 5 children and two german shepherds, in a cramped, rapidly flooding space, with no power.

The two dogs sat in the bathtub, which was filling with water, hunched over, but completely quiet. My six-year-old brain did not understand that my Dad and John Conway were taking out the glass louvers above the toilet, knowing that as the wind became stronger and stronger they would explode over us all.

In the early hours of the morning, I just wanted to sleep, and my head kept drifting lower toward the water. My sisters and I were still in our pyjamas, and I was also wearing a long, thick terry-towelling dressing gown that was popular for girls at the time. But the robe acted like a sponge and filled up with water. It felt like a lead weight all over pushing me down further and further toward the water. I wanted to fall asleep under the water, but adult hands kept lifting my head up. Hours and hours in the dark, sitting in water, drenched and cold.

Only at one point do I ever remember being scared. I saw a look on my Dad's face I'd never seen before, as he stretched out his big arms and enveloped us in a circle. His arms wrapped around Mum, with myself and my sisters sort of tucked in below. Dad's head was down, and the top of his back faced the ceiling. I think Mum started praying.

Years later, I learned that after the eye of Tracy had passed, and the wind was coming back the other way stronger and more ferocious than ever, Dad was certain the roof was going to fail, and the ceiling fall in on us all.

Now, as a parent, I can't image what Mum and Dad were feeling, or what they thought when shapes and debris as big as washing machines could be seen through the completely open toilet window flash-flying through the sky. It is truly absurd to think they saw their own furniture and bits of our house fly past the Conway's window like they were nothing but bits of paper.

We made it through that night and morning and zombie-walked out of the bathroom, saturated, and freezing at 6 or 7 am. It was an implausible scene. Most of the Conway's roof had blown off, and our house was gone! Cars were upturned, trees uprooted, everything from an everyday life – pots/pan, books, carpets, chairs, refrigerators, clothes, photos, money, toys, bikes – anything and everything all jumbled up and flung away – a huge, wet, flattened rubbish dump.

I remember little of Christmas day, except that we were let into a battered, but still standing and well-stocked Coles at Casuarina to get food and anything else we wanted, to my absolute six-year-old amazement. Like a kid in a lolly store, I wanted the sweets. Mum took milk, I think.

Our fridge had been blown down into the front garden and Dad found a roast chicken Mum had cooked the day before; that was Christmas lunch. That night all five of us tried to sleep in our car among the ruins.

Mum and we girls were flown out the next day, to family in Brisbane. Mum tells me Dad drove a bus of police families to the airport. There are no records of us on the evacuation lists at the Darwin Museum.

My dad remained in Darwin as a policeman, and I remember crying when we left him standing alone on the tarmac as the QANTAS plane pulled away. I can't imagine what he was thinking, or what he experienced in the days and weeks after Tracy.

The Salvation Army, *God bless them*, met us at Brisbane airport and I got my Teddy bear. A lovely older man, who my sister Liz said "was just as nice as Santa" appeared like an angel telling me that my Teddy bear had floated down from Darwin in a river of chocolate milk, and that was why he was brown. I still have that bear.

We returned to Darwin in 1975 and lived in a caravan parked next to the only bit left of the house – the floor on stilts. We would go up the stairs to sit under the stars, sometimes watching a small TV attached to a very long extension cord. This is where I first watched TV in colour! In 1977, we moved into a house in Wulagi, a brand-new suburb back then, and I started Year 5 in 1978, at the newly opened Wulagi Primary School.

It's now December 2023, and I'm back in Darwin after about 20 years in Sydney. My big, strong, larger-than-life dad, who I always thought was indestructible, was ravaged by kidney cancer and passed away in December 2018. My beautiful Mum is defying all expectations of old age and is definitely still alive.

Surprisingly perhaps, I still love the spectacular and dramatic storms of the Wet. In the back of my mind, I know it could all happen again, and am struck by the absolute transience of things.

Tracy taught me many lessons, which I've taken consciously or subconsciously through my life: people can go through harrowing and dire experiences in life over which they have no control, where every possession is lost, and the world seems irrevocably altered, and yet life is still there, there are laughs to have, joy and love to experience. Possessions are meaningless, but life and loved ones are precious. We just have to keep going and never give up.

Richard O'Sullivan

Richard arrived in the wild city of Darwin in November 1974, expecting to stay and work for a few months and then continue on the hippie trail via Asia onto London, the mecca for all adventurous Aussies at that time. Cyclone Tracy certainly put paid to those plans. He spent the night in Jingili, at the home of Wally and Carlien Mauger. He then ended up staying through the tumultuous and exhilarating post Cyclone rebuild of the city.

After arriving in Darwin in the early wet of November 1974, I set out looking for work to tide me over until my expected departure north. I ended up in the office of Verity Montgomery, a very efficient and sprightly lady in charge of recruitment for the Federal Department of the NT. On learning I had a University Degree in Economics she was keen to find me a placement and ultimately offered me a temporary, if not entirely suitable, position as Secretary to the NT Building and Planning Boards. I worked at Moonta House in Mitchell Street alongside town planning doyen, June D'Rozario.

I was blissfully ignorant of all matters relating to area zoning, town planning and building code requirements but no one appeared aware or concerned with my shortcomings. Things went swimmingly and one afternoon I was invited to the RSL by senior bureaucrats Terry Brooks of Urban Development and Town Planning and Tom Lawler, husband of the soon to be Mayor, Ella Stack and then the head of Lands Branch. The convivial and very liquid lunch must have left my hosts with a positive impression for reasons that will soon become apparent.

Then on December 24, Cyclone Tracy launched its devastation on Darwin. I was living in a caravan owned by ABC cameraman Keith Bushnell, but at the time was also house-sitting Wally and Carlien Mauger's house in Jingili.

While the cyclone gathered steam during the afternoon, I was blithely enjoying pre-Christmas drinks with colleagues at the Darwin Hotel before moving on to the Don. I put my indifference to the storm down to having been through the non-event of Cyclone Selma a few weeks prior.

Drinks were flowing at the Don until a manageress told us the bar was closing due to imminent cyclonic winds. Lights flickered and then the hotel was in complete darkness. It was being lashed by howling wind and rain.

I headed for the Maugers' Jingili house with a stranger from the Don who needed somewhere to sleep for the night. On the way, we pulled into the Kentucky Fried Chicken outlet on Bagot Road. It had its own generator, and the staff were handing out fried chicken before shutting up.

Once home, I recall sitting on the bed alongside the dog, chicken in hand, when the roof blew off. Guided by the light of lightning strikes the house guest came into my room petrified and asked where he could relieve himself. Before I could answer, the walls collapsed, the floor lifted and we all went sailing out into the abyss, holding onto the mattress and bedding. We (minus the dog) landed in a park adjoining the Maugers' house and crawled into a car under the house where we spent the remainder of the cyclone.

The next day we walked to the badly damaged, partly roofless Darwin Hospital for medical attention. I needed stitches to a hand cut from protecting myself during the fall into the park while my house guest had a severe head injury and was medically evacuated out of Darwin. I never saw him, or the dog, again.

Back at Jingili there was nothing of the house remaining, other than the columns and the bathroom floor.

In return for helping cover an area of my neighbour Bruce's house, I was offered shelter and food that was sourced from help-yourself nearby supermarket shelves.

Bruce was a technical contractor to the PMG, the forerunner to Telstra, and was able to arrange a phone call to the Maugers in Adelaide. Not one word of concern was expressed for their demolished house, all they were concerned about was the whereabouts and wellbeing of their dog, for which I had no answer.

Bruce's wife was heavily pregnant and was evacuated to family in Adelaide. A plan was devised for Bruce and me to drive to Adelaide, Bruce in the family car laden up with salvaged household effects and me driving his wife's Mini Wagon with all the new baby gear. On arrival we were met by a very relieved wife and family and celebrated excessively.

Still tired and emotional, the next day I boarded a plane to Melbourne and then had a commonwealth driver take me to my parents' home in Wangaratta, Victoria – all arranged by cyclone relief agencies. There, I was engrossed in retelling cyclone survival stories when a telegram arrived instructing me to return to Darwin to assist with its rebuilding.

I was dumbfounded. Who knew of my existence or my former Victorian address? And what the heck could I offer in the rebuilding of Darwin? Then I remembered the RSL lunch with Terry Brooks and Tom Lawler back in Darwin, who must have assumed that I had some planning or building background.

So, I returned to Darwin, and I resumed my supposedly temporary roles as Secretary of both the Planning and Building Boards. I was even delegated roles with what became the all-powerful Darwin Reconstruction Commission (DRC).

One event from this period is typical of the early confusion: about twenty building inspectors had been recruited to oversee adherence to the new Building Code and related standards. When one of these

Inspectors put a 'stop order' on unauthorized unit building in Stuart Park, the DRC publicly overrode his action claiming new housing was desperately needed even if it didn't conform to code.

On another occasion I was required to submit some documents to a meeting of the DRC. Entering the room, I was met by the famously florid-complexioned Clem Jones (Chairman), Arch Jones (GM) and Ella Stack (Darwin mayor/member). Arch Jones efficiently carried out the required business, while the other two, scotches in hand, continued drinking. There were so many empty bottles and glasses in the room that at the time I (incorrectly) thought that was how the chairman's florid complexion came about.

I was ultimately caught out when the chairman of the NT Planning Board, George Redmond, threw me a slide rule with a request to calculate an area or zoning distance, or something similar. He saw the blank look on my face and realized I didn't have a clue, couldn't use a slide rule and wasn't a town planner or anything equivalent. The penny had finally dropped!

I was subsequently moved on to another position in that mammoth bureaucracy that was the Department of the Northern Territory.

Post cyclone life continued at a frenetic, albeit chaotic, pace both socially and with the rebuild. It was characterized by living in demountables, caravans or improvised structures beneath former elevated houses; sharing and helping friends and neighbours rebuild; endless barbecues and drinking sessions, and a level of lawlessness and chaos to a degree accepted or even welcomed by the Darwin population.

In 1977, I finally took that trip to London and returned to Australia two years later. I ended up back in Darwin where I still live with wife Maureen. We raised our three children in this vibrant multi-cultural city.

Linda Parker

Lin first came to Darwin in 1970 as a 'Ten pound Pom' catching up with her brother George, who was an agronomist with the Federal Government's Primary Industry Branch at Tortilla Flats Research Station on the Adelaide River. After two years living all over Australia she returned to England. When George returned to England to introduce Madeline, his new wife, in 1974, he persuaded Lin's boyfriend, Tony, to come to Australia. Tony, staying with George and Madeline, was missing Lin and invited her to join him in Darwin and get married. She accepted both the invitation and proposal, and they were married in Christ Church Anglican Cathedral on December 21, 1974.

On December 24 we were made aware that a cyclone was imminent, the warnings were frequently on the radio. It was decided that the four of us should be together at my brother's house in Henbury Avenue, as it might be difficult to travel after the cyclone. My brother, George, collected us in his white VW.

That night, as the rain was pushing the louvres open and the wind was systematically ripping the tin off the roof, we knew the house was unsafe and went to the back door to escape. However, as the back steps were metal and live electricity cables were all over them, there was no way we could go down them.

George decided we had to get to the bathroom, and the four of us crouched in the bath: Tony, my new husband, by the taps and me, Madeline and George perched up on the end. The roof had been ripped off, the ceiling and fluorescent light were dangling above our heads. I pulled the shower curtain over our heads to keep dry.

The last thing I remember that night is George telling Madeline he loved her. The bath was ripped out of the house and George, Madeline and Tony landed over by the boundary fence. Unfortunately, my leg got stuck in the banister of the stairs. It broke my flight and I landed under the house.

I remember Tony trying to lift me away from the house during the eye of the cyclone but because I was so badly injured he couldn't move me. He went and laid back where Madeline and George were and kept shouting to me to get away from the house. Somehow, I managed to crawl to where they were, although I had several broken ribs. I have no memory of how I did it.

The winds returned, I fell unconscious but Tony recalls the rainwater building up around us and being frightened of drowning. We couldn't lift our heads as there were flying objects hitting us and we could have had our heads cut off.

When dawn came and the wind had calmed down, there was an eerie white light. The only sound was the creaking of corrugated iron. A man came over and stood looking at us for a minute or so then went away. A woman came and I think she must have been a nurse. Madeline asked her to look at George who was behind us. We couldn't see him but could hear him groaning. She came straight back and said there was nothing she could do for him. She covered me with a tartan blanket that stayed with me for years.

I was in excruciating pain. My right leg had been wrenched at the knee and stuck out at a 90-degree angle. Both arms were smashed, and I later discovered I had terrible internal injuries having had my legs torn apart.

I remember looking at Madeline, half her hair had been ripped off her skull and was hanging down onto her shoulder which itself was badly dislocated. Her skull was bare, white, no blood, she had been scalped, missing death by a fraction.

Her hair was later sewn back on in a Sydney hospital and grew back but for years afterwards she could pick small particles of grit out of her scalp. Rescuers eventually came and helped Madeline and Tony to a rescue centre across the road. I was picked up by a lot of men, laid on a door and taken to the rescue centre. I spent a few hours laid on a vegetable rack from a supermarket and it was there a doctor gave me my first pain injection. Eventually I made it to hospital.

All this time I had no idea where George was. Upon my arrival in hospital, I was given a blood transfusion in the reception area of the hospital then a doctor, seeing my foot sticking out at right angles instructed the chap pushing the stretcher to take me to surgery so he could straighten my leg.

Soon after that my husband found me and told me not to worry as we were being flown out to Sydney. I was put on the first Hercules aircraft to leave Darwin with lots of other injured people on stretchers. I overheard a nurse saying the plane was going to Brisbane. I shouted in a panic that I was supposed to go to Sydney. That is the last I recall of the flight as the nurse stuck a needle in my arm and I was out for the count.

The day after Boxing Day, after I had undergone two major operations, my husband appeared at the Brisbane Hospital. As one of the 'walking wounded' he had been evacuated on a different plane but luckily we both ended up at the Brisbane Hospital.

He was brought to my bedside and had to tell me my dearest brother George had been killed almost straight away. He then used the ward phone to ring my parents back in Hampshire to tell them that George had been killed. My parents' neighbour later told me she could hear my mum wailing for a week afterwards.

Tony and I lost everything we owned in Australia. I spent three months in hospital in Brisbane. When I was allowed out I had a full plaster on my right leg, a full plaster on my right arm and an iron clamp on my hand to try to get it to work (try using crutches with that lot).

I managed to find work on the hospital switchboard for a few months using my left hand to work the plugs and cords. My husband, who was a plumber, went back up to Darwin to help with the rebuild.

During those months I lived with the wonderful Smith family from Paddington, with whom I have remained in close contact ever since. They say that out of something bad, something good happens and it certainly did when I met them. Patrick and Joan have now passed but their four daughters, Robyn, Margaret, Sandy and Karen are my Australian sisters. It was through their son Ian, that they heard about us. He was a student working as a porter in the hospital the day I was brought in.

I have often wondered who those men were who carefully put me on the door and who encouraged me to 'swear away the pain' when they lifted me and the lady who came to help. I would thank them from the bottom of my heart.

I would also like to thank the wonderful Salvation Army who provided me with clothes for months after; the Red Cross who bought my husband a whole new set of tools and the Lions Club who found and paid rent for our first flat when we were eventually able to be independent.

Although I was told I would never have children, I went on to have four and I managed to run and have a very active life. I now have an artificial knee and hip and have two long screws in both my ankles but apart from that I am pretty fit. Tony and I divorced more than 20 years ago.

Madeline was evacuated to Sydney to be near her family and eventually did find love again.

Every Christmas my head is full of memories of that terrible night. I try to fill my head with other things but it's no good, it will be with me forever.

Figure 14: Looking across Lyons Street towards Henbury Avenue in the distance, Wanguri (Steve Andrews).

Tom Pauling

Tom came to Darwin in March 1970 to work as a lawyer for Cridland and Bauer. There had been no real "Wet Season" and what vegetation was still alive was barely hanging on. The Darwin Sailing Club was the centre of activity every night of the week often with the ebullient and magnificently bearded director of the Museum and Art Gallery, Dr Colin Jack-Hinton, rousing the rabble when not hiding from his wife.

After a customary bout at the Sailing Club on Christmas Eve, Ian Barker, the newly minted QC, took me home for dinner to a none too enthusiastic family of Nel and six children plus Father Pye from the Catholic community on Bathurst Island.

About 11.30 with Ian snoring loudly, I was driven home to Leichhardt Crescent. Carpentaria palms thrashed about in the powerful winds, but the streets were spookily quiet. My housemates included Terence Coulehan, with whom I owned the house, his partner Kerin and our friend Chris Rooney and his dog. Downstairs was Terry's mother, Sheila.

Many accounts will relate the slow and then rapid build-up of the wind and I won't repeat this common experience.

Our house faced the sea, but the wind came steady from behind us. Two recovering alcoholic brick-makers, who were our clients, had dropped off a large and varied supply of spirits and the top-notch Brandy was the drop of choice when, after each 'whump' shook us to the core, Chris would announce "that was the worst of them!".

The intensity built up as we huddled in front of the kitchen island bench. And then it stopped. Or so it seemed. A dash down the central stairs to see how Shiela was, ended abruptly when a sheet of corrugated iron whistled through the passageway.

The "eye" lasted quite a while. "Well, that's the worst of it!" said Chris until an immense roar as of three or four jumbo jets came up from the seaside and peeled off our tin roof.

This was quickly followed by the ceiling being sucked out to reveal a green tinged wet sky with the occasional flying fridge or washing machine cartwheeling through the suddenly very cold night. More Courvoisier helped to warm us.

In the morning calm, Sheila was found shaken but otherwise calm. Terry and I set off to see if there were people in need of help. Gregory Street was a giant water mattress bouncing up and down. We went down Clancy Street.

There in the early morning light was a standard elevated house with the lounge at the front connected to the rest of the house by a corridor. The side and front walls were missing as was the roof and ceiling, but standing in elegant loneliness was a decorated Christmas tree. Dramatically the door to the rest of the house opened, the occupant unplugged the decorative tree and advanced to the front where, without anger or bitterness, he dispatched it saying only, "Hooray, Fuck!"

Returning to Ian Barker's House in Wells Street we could see no damage. It was an elevated house large enough to accommodate his family. At the rear was a fire-escape exit with small stairs. Barker appeared at that door.

"How come your house isn't damaged?" I timorously enquired.

"I am a catholic!" he boomed and slammed the door shut.

When the door reopened the cry was "What do you want now?" "Brandy? We drank it all last night!"

Terry and I shuffled home past the now wall-less Fannie Bay Gaol, only to be warned off by prison staff who seemed quite scared of us!

We still had Christmas lunch with all the trimmings, and the only guest of fifteen who didn't attend had lost her car keys.

The following day I foolishly applied myself to roofing and nearly lost a finger to corrugated iron. Somehow, I ended up at the evacuation centre in Cavenagh Street and, armed with a list of persons heading for the same city 'down south', I was directed to a bus going to the airport. There was a lot of confusion. The RAAF, although knowing where the aircraft, (including civilian planes) were going, did not have a clear flow plan.

At the RAAF control, I made a few suggestions only to be recognised as an RAAF Reserve Officer (legal), by the head of the RAAF in Darwin, Group Captain Hitchins. He 'called me up' on the spot and I became one of a number of dedicated liaison officers – a full-time task indeed. This task was made easier when the Sallies (Salvation Army) gave me some boots and the airport manager lent me (for a few days) his son's Christmas present, a bicycle.

One incident stands out. A team of us were helping to load a United States Air Force Starlifter, one of the largest planes in the sky. The loadmaster, Top Sergeant Abney from New York, calmed an elderly lady when she saw its giant interior "Won't we float around in there?" she cried out in fear.

Abney's reply: "No ma'am we gonna pack you in tight as sardines You ain't goin' nowhere!" And boy did they.

And who could forget the 697 passengers and crew on the QANTAS 747 safely arriving in Sydney.

Things calmed down pretty quickly, and Hitchins was very grateful for my strong support. To my surprise, sometime later, he invited me to go to Dum-In-Mirrie Island in Bynoe Harbour to see if the local resident Maxie Baumber was OK, although it turned out the real reason was the superb fishing and crabbing on offer.

I asked if my mate Ian could come. Is he a reserve officer? No. A plumbing inspector? Quite possibly. Not long afterwards an Iroquois Huey Series Helicopter dumped us on a glorious beach.

The plumbing pretence was soon discarded and out came the wine. On the return voyage Ian was facing out of the open doorway with no communications and a large (I mean huge) box of live mud crabs on his lap when the pilot executed a Vietnam-style turn which had Ian looking straight down at the ground below.

When we landed Ian swore I said it, though I believe it was *him*: "Headline in the NT News: *QC with Crabs falls from helicopter.*" We thought it was hilarious.

Marie-Louise Pearson

Marie-Louise Pearson (nee Quong) is the second child of well-known members of Darwin's Chinese community, the late Eddie and Greta Quong. She, and her three siblings, Terry, Rodney and Donna were all born in Darwin as were her father, Eddie Chin Hong Wing Quong and his mother, Ethel Low Sue Oy Quong. In December 1974 Marie-Louise was 16 years old and had recently returned from 10 months in Singapore as a Rotary Exchange student from Darwin High School.

On Christmas Eve I was a casual worker in a dress shop on Knuckey Street and had plans that night to help Mum and Dad prepare for Christmas day, before going to midnight mass at Saint Mary's Cathedral. The increasingly strong wind and rain changed our plans. The shop closed early and because I couldn't walk home safely, I rang Dad from the work phone, and he picked me up.

As it was likely there would be no electricity – blackouts being common in a storm in Darwin – Dad and Mum prepared by roasting the turkey because we could always eat it cold if we had no power on Christmas Day. We spent that evening putting Christmas presents under the tree and arranging the house in readiness for the family Christmas.

We went to bed 'early' as the winds and rain were getting stronger. Dad made us go to bed dressed and with shoes near our bed. I remember looking out of my bedroom window and seeing trees and things being blown around, but when I saw part of the roof of the house next door being blown off, I jumped out of bed.

Dad and Mum gathered my sister Donna and I up under a 'tent' of mattresses in our hallway.

By now our roof was also moving and windows were breaking. My two brothers, Terry, and Rodney, were in their bedroom, built in underneath our elevated house, and Dad was calling out to them, but couldn't get out of the house to see them. We just held on to each other and waited.

When all went 'quiet', I thought we had survived. But my father was much wiser and told us after looking up at the sky, that this was the eye of the cyclone. I had no idea there was such a thing. Dad quickly raced downstairs, found my brothers were ok, and he told them to stay inside their room. They couldn't get out anyway due to debris. Dad came back upstairs to us as the cyclone returned, stronger and louder. I'll never forget the noise of the wind.

My first memory on Christmas Day was a neighbour walking down the street waving a hurricane lantern calling out:

"Is everyone ok, does anyone need help?'

We helped Dad to get the two boys out of their room. A plastic container had lodged in their door about head height and tree branches and debris had blocked them in. They were fine. We were all fine.

The house was mostly intact though part of the roof and ceiling and one wall had gone but we still had most of a home, unlike others.

Dad immediately retrieved some large containers and put them out to collect rainwater. He had us all help to lift the fallen ceiling off the kitchen table very gently as we knew that the cooked turkey and ham were there. Thankfully the food had been well covered in foil and towels and was able to be rescued.

We also cleared access to the fridge and managed to get vegetables and bottles of drink out of it. Mum and Dad set up a camp underneath our house and for days we ate the very best turkey, ham, and vegetable stew one could ever imagine.

We were encouraged to drink bottled soft drinks, and we washed and rinsed our teeth in Dad's good whiskey: the bottle had survived even though the wall behind it didn't. We had enough to get by, but to this day I still put toilet paper into plastic bags on any cyclone watch or warning being issued and today we still eat the baked ham for Christmas breakfast just as soon as it's cooked, we never wait, just in case.

I am so grateful that my dad was so experienced in "making do" and "living rough." I remember being in awe that he just knew what to do. The family stayed together for four days in our rubble then, while Dad and my older brother Terry stayed to help clean up and rebuild Darwin, the rest of us were bused out to the airport and lined up to get onto a plane. We children sat on the floor in the aisle of the plane.

In Brisbane, The Salvation Army identified us, vaccinated us, and fed us (I remember getting a fresh bread sandwich and thought it was wonderful). They gave Mum some money, and we were allowed to pick through the mountains of donated clothes and goods as we had landed with only what we were wearing – and they weren't exactly clean.

Mum rang her parents who lived in West End, and they came to collect us. We stayed with them for about 3 months before we were allowed a return permit and flight back to Darwin. We were very grateful that we had grandparents to go to. We found out later that many of our friends didn't have such luck and we lost contact with so many of them.

While I was away, I collected newspapers and anything I could find on the cyclone, studying every printed word looking for any mention of our friends and extended family. I still have a wonderful scrap book of the collected items.

Dad and Terry had managed to get a blue tarpaulin put on the house, cleaned up the water damage, and fixed the holes in the walls. We had water, electricity, and beds, so we could return. It was very basic, and all of our possessions were gone, cleared out because of the water damage. We had no photos of us prior to 1974 for example. But we were back together.

The whole family got on to help with the return of Darwin to life. Dad was on the reconstruction committee. Mum was involved with Red Cross. We all helped with the soup kitchen that was set up at Darwin High School. Mum and I helped with events for ladies to give them something to do, and to help each other including ladies' lunches with fashion parades held at the Travelodge Hotel. At one stage, Dad got a very bad case of shingles from the stress, and we very nearly lost him.

Terry and I were sent away to University in Adelaide as soon as we could get in. Our family was split up again, but this time we knew we would have a home to come back to.

Dad and Mum, Eddie, and Greta Quong were always community-minded and gave so much of their lives to helping wherever they could to make Darwin a better place. All our family still love Darwin. Many of us still live in Darwin. Darwin will always be home.

Barbara Pottle

Barbara was acting supervisor of casualty and outpatients at Darwin Hospital at the time of Cyclone Tracy. Recently returned from an overseas holiday she was house-sitting for fellow staff members Pat and Jim Parker, who had gone south on holidays. This reunited her with her beloved dachshund, Rufus, who the Parkers had been looking after in her absence. The house was a well-built older-style design in Larrakeyah.

Three weeks earlier Darwin had been subjected to Cyclone Selma which knocked over a few trees and made a bit of a mess around the gardens, so not too many people were fazed by another one, even though it could have chosen a better time to visit us – being Christmas Eve and all.

My shift ended at 4pm and I immediately went to pick up my pre-ordered turkey and leg ham from the supermarket at Stuart Park. I was planning to enjoy these on Boxing Day when my mother was due to arrive from Brisbane for a short holiday. It was during that shopping expedition that I began to feel very uneasy about the approaching cyclone because the sky over the city towards the west was something I had never seen before (or since!) ink black, dense like oil and unbelievably threatening.

Having grown up in Brisbane I was used to cyclones. The radio was reminding us to prepare property and surrounding areas to lessen the risk of flying debris, so I spent the rest of the daylight hours moving garden furniture, pot plants and other things into the shed beneath the house.

To while away the evening, I was sewing the final touches to a new dress to wear to midnight mass at Christ Church Anglican Cathedral as I was rostered to work the following day, so unable to attend morning mass. The cathedral disappeared in the early hours of the morning after the Bishop had cut the service short and sent his parishioners home. I wasn't one of them – having been too anxious about the wind and rain and my little car being blown or washed away to attend.

The wind increased in intensity quite quickly after about 7.30 pm, but I kept at that sewing machine until around 9.00 pm when the power went off. I then resorted to hand-sewing by candlelight determined as I was, to finish the task. That resolve soon evaporated when an almighty crash into the kitchen and lounge room walls sent the wall tiles in the kitchen flying off and I fled for the safety of the middle small bedroom at the end of the hallway.

The recommendation that one move to the bathroom with smaller walls didn't appeal to me as they were moving in and out like the walls of a tent, so the little dog and I cowered under the bed, shaking uncontrollably together.

As the house moved up and down on its piers I realised I was in an awfully dangerous situation and tried to get down the stairs to the storeroom. However, my passage was completely blocked by trees that had come crashing down at both front and back of the house. In hindsight that proved valuable, as all the dangerous debris piled up against those trees and prevented further damage to the house.

The noise of the roaring, screaming wind, crashing of debris, roofing iron being hurled around and scraped down roads at high speed was quite unbelievable – as if there was a fighter jet at full throttle just above the roof. Had I had company, conversation would have been impossible.

Rufus and I spent the rest of the night in that middle bedroom with a mattress over a table to form a cave in case the roof blew away. It didn't, fortunately and around first light I decided to peek outside.

That sight was more than one could take in – the street and its buildings had disappeared; my neighbour across the road, who had worried about me being alone and had invited me to join him, his very pregnant wife, Keena, and two small children, no longer had a house. It was just a pile of rubble but, fortunately, the shed where they had managed to find shelter, was still intact.

They joined me shortly after with the most terrified Siamese cat I have ever seen draped around the little boy's neck like a scarf. I remember having difficulty getting the door open to let them in, but I was glad to see them and they were glad to be in a safe place.

Keena had been experiencing labour contractions all night and her husband had begged her not to deliver. As a midwife I know the dangers of alcohol in pregnancy, but I didn't hesitate to give Keena a good swig of the Johnny Walker Black Label I had bought for a Christmas treat. I figured the baby was big enough to handle it and as we were all wet through from the rain and so cold, I thought a heart starter was well and truly in order.

That family left on one of the first evacuation flights on Boxing Day and the baby was born very soon after.

Knowing I had to go to work, I had kept my white uniform in a plastic bag to keep it dry. I changed out of my wet clothes and left for work, leaving the family of four plus cat and unborn baby to shelter in the house.

Somehow I was able to get my little car out from under the trees and rubble and negotiate the short drive to work around piles of debris: fridges, smashed furniture, overturned cars, roofing iron, bits of houses, trees and power poles, and arrived at the Darwin Hospital to more shocking and unbelievable sights.

The laboratory, a small sturdy stone building near the main entrance, had completely disappeared. The front of the administration building was intact. A maintenance crew had placed cyclone wire over the plate glass the afternoon before. This had preserved the entrance but entering the building was difficult. It was about 7.30 am and the crowds of people inside that building were enough to give me heart failure.

Arriving at the non-functioning electronic doors in a white uniform, I was greeted with a path being cleared so I could reach the casualty room. Here, the night staff and the doctors who had turned up as soon as they could get out of their wrecked quarters, were frantically attending to injured people. Ambulances were mobilising and people were arriving in any form of conveyance they could find.

I had never before and never since felt such a feeling of overwhelming shock and horror at the sight which greeted me, but soon realised I needed to get busy.

My best friend and second-in-charge, Nesta Cubis turned up shortly after in the most un-uniform getup imaginable. They were the only dry clothes she could find in the chest of drawers in her garden, where all her furniture ended up when their house was demolished – pale blue Bermuda shorts and her husband's old khaki shirt about 4 sizes too big. She had managed to dig her nursing badges out of the mud and had them lined up on her collar so people would know she was qualified. The flip-flops completed the picture of elegance.

The night staff were almost at collapsing point, so I sent them off duty around mid-morning as staff were coming through the door to work after they placed their children into safe hands.

The roads were already being cleared, as much as possible, by emergency crews, the police, and the fire brigade, to allow ambulances and vehicles to bring the injured to hospital, and the emergency treatment centres set up in schools and shopping centres.

Miraculously, we had a huge quantity of first aid materials available because an over-zealous staff member had ordered monumental amounts of bandages, dressings and suture material in error, and I had decided not to return it to stores until 'after Christmas'.

That allowed us to supply the first aid stations set up in the suburbs where local GPs, nurses and volunteers attended to the 'walking wounded'. This saved the hospital for the major trauma victims, and the people who had made their way to the casualty independently.

The police, once mobilised, brought in lists of requirements. We filled dozens of large garbags and they were then taken to the first aid posts.

Many people volunteered their services and they were a tremendous help. With all phones out, communication within the hospital could only happen by foot couriers. It was essential that we knew when beds were available as the ward staff got control of their situations and these volunteers kept us well informed and allowed us to clear the emergency room as soon as a bed was available.

The operating theatre suite had lost its roof but, as it was necessary to start surgery urgently, the surgeons used spare Mayo tables (extendable height wheeled trays usually used to hold instruments) to cover the patient on the operating table while the maintenance crew put the roof back on. These wonderful maintenance crews also got the emergency generator going, so that by mid-morning we had a functional, though damaged, hospital.

Cheryl Shelley, the dietician, found some urns and heated up soup and hot water for tea and coffee for people waiting to be attended to, or just as comfort food for grieving folk, lost or scared people, and those with nowhere to go. Bishop Mason turned up in stubbies and singlet, (his house was gone) with his cross around his neck and spent hours talking and comforting the crush of people huddled in the building or waiting to see if a missing relative or friend turned up.

The building was in semi-darkness, and as a building designed for air-conditioning and modern lighting, seeing was not easy but, with the aid of torches and whatever light came in through the windows, and the openings where windows had been, staff managed to function at a furious pace and cope with the constant stream of people.

The floors were covered in water which was quickly bloodstained from the wounds caused by the flying debris, broken glass and, in some horrible cases, lethal roofing iron. Brooms and mops were soon employed pushing as much of the water out of the building as could be managed by staff and volunteers, but it was a long time before that floor took on its very highly polished look again.

The pharmacy and laboratory staffs were kept very busy as not only had the laboratory been demolished but the Red Cross blood transfusion service building was also demolished. It was obvious that grouping, cross-matching, and collection of blood would be essential for the severely injured and emergency fluids, drugs, pain relief, tetanus toxoid, antibiotics, and other medications would be needed. People had lost their prescription medicine, and that needed replacing too.

To cope with the walking wounded who needed first aid, their wounds cleaned, suturing where necessary and attending to other injuries, wherever there was light, a doctor and a nurse worked. As fast as one was treated, another would arrive and this kept up until early evening.

Dr. Margaret James, a local GP, was busy in the annex near the temporary mortuary storeroom at the end of the corridor we had set up for the DOA's (Dead on Arrivals). She told me that one of the corpses had sat up when she entered the room and as the sheet covering him fell away, asked in a polite English accent would she mind getting him a nice hot cup of tea. This old man had arrived cold, blue and apparently lifeless, at a particularly frantic time in the emergency room and the doctor, unable to discern a heartbeat, had sent him through to the 'end room'. Having warmed up and regained his senses he made his wishes known. We quickly got him through to a ward, and hope he never knew where we had placed him.

Towards mid-afternoon our matron, Miss Brennan, sent word we were to down tools in relay and present to the staff dining room for something hot to eat. She had spent the day pushing the equivalent of Darwin Harbour out of the ground floor of Lambell House (the nurses' quarters), had found a portable gas ring and was heating mountains of baked beans to sustain us. They tasted good, I can tell you.

The most terrible loss of life in the staff was that of Dr. Paul Macklin, a senior anaesthetist, who was killed by flying roofing iron when trying to reach the hospital in the early hours of the morning – 'in case he was needed'.

The most amazing feats were performed that day by all the staff, and the selfless efforts from the volunteers, who often stayed on to help after their own wounds were bandaged, filled us with gratitude. Every person that day had been through the most terrifying night, most lost their home and possessions, and yet the hospital staff and emergency service personnel, our NT police, local GPs as well as hospital doctors, worked all day and well into the night until every injured person had been treated – either in the hospital, or in the first aid stations in the suburbs.

Mr. Bromwich the senior surgeon was a tower of strength to the staff and the young doctors in particular who were faced with awful decision making. If an ambulance wasn't available, neighbours ferried the injured to hospital using doors as stretchers, wheelbarrows, anything with support or wheels to get them to safety.

A friend of mine, Rob McBryde, who had scurried into his VW for shelter as his new home at Wanguri was being demolished around him, brought in a man from the next street with an horrific wound from flying roofing iron. Rob ferried him across the yard in a wheelbarrow, as the man was very tall and solidly built (which saved him from being killed) to his VW, somehow got him into it and for the next two hours struggled to get him to the hospital with two flat tyres along the way. The tin had missed his renal artery by a few millimetres and he almost succumbed to the ensuing infection from lying in filthy water all night, but months later he returned to Darwin and came to the casualty department to thank us for giving him the confidence not to give in to his terrible injury, when he himself thought he had no chance of survival.

As darkness settled over the wrecked city and suburbs and with light rain still falling those people remaining in 'outpatients' asked to stay the night as they had nowhere to go. We gave out blankets and pillows and bedded them down on the waiting room bench seating. The sobbing and despairing murmuring of the day was replaced by sounds of sleeping and snoring.

Nesta and I were sitting at our desk in the midst of these people with a candle burning around 1.00 a.m. having been on duty for 18 hours, quietly discussing future plans – we both decided that no matter what happened to Darwin in the next few months NOTHING would induce us to leave, a very different feeling from the morning before when all we wanted to do was get as far away as possible from such a place of wreckage and fear.

Sadness surrounded us from the loss of life and terrible injuries we had witnessed passing through the emergency department but, against all the odds, the hospital, town, and people had managed to do what had to be done.

When the relief medical and nursing teams turned up the following day as word *had* got through to the rest of Australia, to their amazement they had nothing much to do. The hospital was purring along efficiently with all staff present as required, but nevertheless looking forward to a few hours off to assess their own home situations and check on friends and neighbours. We gladly handed over to them.

Special mention must go the staff of Katherine Hospital. They knew something big had happened to Darwin as people fled south in their cars and passed on the news and they turned up just after lunch to lend a hand. Dr. Scattini and his staff were a sight for exhausted eyes. They worked tirelessly with their Darwin compatriots. The Territory is like that.

Figure 15: Christ Church Anglican Cathedral (LANT, ph0091-0126).

Nerelee Scanlan

Figure 16: Kipper, a corgi who was lucky to survive (Nerelee Scanlan).

KIPPY'S STORY: I have few memories of Tracy as I was only five. However, I'm writing because I want to say a big thank you to an unknown vet and their assistant. I don't know who you were but thank you for saving our Corgi.

Kippy was the only member of our family who was hurt in the cyclone. A piece of wood came through the bathroom wall and into his leg, shattering the bone. Through the evacuation centre, my dad got a hold of a vet. There was no power, but the vet gave our boy a local and his assistant and dad held Kippy down while the vet attached a steel bar to the damaged bone, saving Kippy and his leg. Our boy lived until the age of eight. He always hated storms and vets, but we always wished we could say thank you to these beautiful people.

Growing up, Kippy was my best friend. The vet and his assistant did a fantastic job with his leg, and he only ever limped in cold weather. We moved to south-east Queensland, and the winters there bothered him, so we had to be careful. He led a very active life, following us as we wandered over the 600-acre cattle farm that neighboured our home.

Kerry Sharp

Kerry Sharp was a journalist on Western Australia's Albany Advertiser newspaper when she and a girlfriend set off on what was to be a round-Australia trip. They worked at a Port Hedland iron ore facility then in 1972 travelled by coastal cargo ship to Darwin, where Kerry soon found work as a journalist at the ABC – and met the man she would marry.

We were happily entrenched Darwinites by 1974, but counted ourselves among the lucky locals who were far from home when Cyclone Tracy slammed into our vibrant tropical city on Christmas morning, leaving little in its path unscathed, including the lives of thousands of deeply traumatized Darwin families.

At sunset on Christmas Eve, our little family – Col, baby Marnie and I – were 4000 km away at beachside Broulee on the glorious NSW south coast, toasting the start of an overdue family festive gathering, when a neighbour shouted across the fence, "Hey, did you hear there's a cyclone heading for Darwin?"

We'd heard rumblings of a potential blow but weren't alarmed. "We often get Cyclone warnings at this time of the year, but they usually fizzle out," we reassured him, recalling historic data that just five cyclones had hit Darwin in the past 100 years. Just a few weeks earlier, Cyclone Selma had been tracking towards Darwin before veering away before having an impact.

By Boxing Day, we were shell-shocked as news filtered through about the enormity of Cyclone Tracy's impact, including an inconceivable loss of life. Any thoughts of festive celebration faded fast as we turned our attention to what we should do now, how we could get home quickly, how we could check the fate of our neighbours, mates, and personal property without phone communications.

Our first direct word came a few days after Tracy, when our house-sitters, then Darwin ABC colleague Mary Fraser and husband Jim, sent a Telex message via the ABC's Canberra newsroom team who tracked us down. Mary and Jim were safe and in remarkably good spirits after surviving a pitch-black night huddled in the bathroom terrorised by Tracy's screeching winds ripping off roofing iron, wooden beams, windows, and other house parts and turning them into lethal missiles.

In what seemed unimaginable to us at the time, they told us they'd watched our fridge move from the kitchen and take out a full-length triple-bay louvre bank as it catapulted out of the living room window.

An unopened 4.5-litre bottle of Scotch, won in a pre-Christmas raffle, smashed on the floor spilling an immense pool of alcohol that they feared might ignite in a lightning strike and set the house on fire! Crucially, Mary and Jim were able to confirm that while the roof and two-thirds of our house were gone the rest was 'habitable'. As word of neighbours and mates filtered through, we quickly realized that our own 'unimaginables' were woefully insignificant alongside the extreme trauma that Darwinites endured and survived in those terrifying pre-daybreak hours.

We were desperate to get back to Darwin, but it wasn't going to happen quickly. Emergency services had begun evacuating 25,000 devastated women and children and bringing in huge clean-up crews who occupied all available safe accommodation. Able-bodied Darwin locals keen to get home were stopped at highway roadblocks unless they had safe accommodation.

Many did get back in the days after Tracy, driving in from holidays cut short or travelling by train to Alice Springs then plane to Darwin.

While Marnie and I headed to Perth to stay with my wonderful comforting dad, Col flew to Alice and was booked on the first commercial flight back into Darwin – but the airport crew couldn't find him come departure time, so he caught the next day's flight instead.

He talked about his extreme shock when coming in to land, witnessing destruction far worse than he'd imagined. Across the entire city landscape almost every building was flattened, or severely damaged, and roads and open spaces buried in debris.

He can't recall how he got to our northern suburbs house but thinks he must have walked the few kilometres from the airport. There were certainly no taxis waiting.

Our wrecked Wagaman house became temporary headquarters for some homeless close mates who rigged up makeshift quarters downstairs or found dry sleeping spots among the rubble upstairs. Interspersed with the shock of Tracy's impact, there seemed no shortage of hilarity and good-natured mischief – sometimes at others' expense.

One short-sighted mate had his 'coke-bottle' spectacles whipped from his head when he opened his front door to look outside mid-cyclone. Later, he found himself opening multiple cans of dog food in his search for baked beans – because the sodden paper labels had fallen off.

With a generator onsite but no receptacle for keeping food and drinks cold, the fellas laid claim to an intact fridge one night from the floorboards of a wrecked house three doors down. They were hauling it home by wheelbarrow when a police car, siren howling, screamed up behind them.

There was side-splitting relief when it turned out the policeman was a good mate coming to check on them and share a cold beer. At one stage, they found out the city's upmarket Travelodge Hotel was serving hot meals for in-house clean-up crews and, keen for a change from the sameness of the Darwin High School's canteen stews and brussels sprouts, lined up and gave required room numbers.

A few bluffed their way through and dined in style, but one was sent packing because his quoted room number didn't exist. One highlight for male workers was Nightcliff Drive-In's screening of the X-rated 'The Erotic Adventures of Zorro' – though apparently lots of raunchy bits got lost in the gaping black holes left where Tracy had ripped giant panels off the screen.

Meanwhile in Perth, Marnie and I spent lots of time with evacuated friends listening to their harrowing stories of trying to protect themselves and their kids against the onslaught, and of much-loved unattended family dogs having to be shot because there was no food or shelter for pets. Still emotionally raw from their terrifying ordeal, they vowed they'd never go back to Darwin. Thankfully, they did return and resumed happy, fulfilling lives in the city they loved.

The Perth community, like those nationwide, embraced Darwin's cyclone survivors with an overwhelming outpouring of kindness and generosity. Immediate support came in the form of emergency cash handouts from government agencies, donations of household goods, food, clothing, toys, and other essentials via charity groups, and offers of accommodation or other help from a caring public.

People worked overtime to embrace the immediate needs of Tracy survivors and in the face of their warm generosity, I cringed with shame the day an ungracious evacuee griped on radio that she'd prefer a bigger fridge than the one she'd been given!

With our house deemed 'fit for habitation', Marnie and I were able to fly back a few weeks later and once overcoming the numbing shock of such widespread destruction to our beautiful city, and home, we mustered the means to start reclaiming our disrupted lives.

Despite the desolate backdrop of our suburban street lined with abandoned wrecked houses, it was good to be home. Spirits were high, the camaraderie among mates was infectious and every tiny makeshift step forward felt like a vast improvement in our living conditions – a tarpaulin dropped off to cover the gaping hole where the roof used to be, a generator delivered to power lights and a fan found somewhere – and the sheer excitement when bags of precious ice came back on line at a Winnellie factory.

Slowly but surely, the mud and slush and broken pieces were cleared away, family heirlooms and treasures were unearthed from the rubble, and we all got on with life that became more normal as each day passed.

We felt truly blessed to be 4000 kilometres away from Darwin when Cyclone Tracy hit – albeit with an occasional strange twinge of regret that being absent meant we could never accurately grasp the enormity of what happened or empathize with survivors of that terrifying 1974 Christmas Morning.

Some short-lived traumas hit us in the aftermath – when we landed back home and were left shell-shocked by the severity of the devastation. The shock was soon overtaken by an urgency to clear away dangerous rubble and start putting our lives back together.

There were frustrations, difficulties, safety concerns and emotional flare-ups at times over the perceived slow pace of change, but we were young and indestructible and buoyed by the positive company of close Darwin mates who were all in the same boat.

We thank Cyclone Tracy for instilling a resilience to cope with difficult situations and to get life's priorities in order. We'd lost a new house full of precious possessions that we thought we could never do without – but suddenly the material trappings and comforts of life, including power and fans and running water, all became less critical.

One of Tracy's most important messages was to never second-guess the potential strength and harm of a forecast tropical cyclone developing off the coast. We've snapped to attention a number of times since Tracy and feel far less ill-at-ease these days about alerts on low pressure systems. Preparedness is the catchcry! They're our early signal to make a beeline for the fuel bowser and to replenish the baked beans and other long-life essentials before supermarket shelves are later stripped bare by a panicked public.

We love the charming vibrant city that Darwin has become since Cyclone Tracy.

Admittedly, there was a special charm to Darwin's dishevelled, laid-back frontier persona of the early 1970s, with its mishmash of rusty tin sheds and shacks and long grass choking footpaths and vacant urban land, but civic standards demanded change and Cyclone Tracy was the catalyst for making that happen.

Derelict eyesores gave way to modern, structurally sound buildings, thousands of shady buffer zone trees were planted, and judicious landscaping created exquisite green spaces for outdoor recreation. In the wash-up, we've inherited a beautiful and appealing tropical city that we're proud to call home.

Lyn Serventy

Lyn and her husband Peter came to Darwin in 1967. Peter was developing a tin prospect at Wandi Creek, about forty kilometres from Pine Creek, while Lyn taught at Darwin High School and became increasingly involved in directing and acting with Darwin Theatre Group. She started Mobs, a children's activity group, and led a project to save an old stone building from demolition and convert it into a small theatre known as Brown's Mart. The Serventy's lived in Coconut Grove.

Two days before Christmas Eve, 1974 I returned from Darwin Hospital with my first-born baby, Astrid, to the beautiful new home we had built in Coconut Grove.

With a newly arrived baby to fuss and wonder over, there was no question of going out that evening. The ABC Radio relayed the warnings of an approaching cyclone and I remember feeling a twinge of excitement. Perhaps this time it would hit Darwin. There had been several cyclones that had approached but not passed anywhere near to Darwin.

Pete had said that Darwin was overdue for a cyclone when you considered its history. He had built our house from Besser blocks and I felt very safe.

But as the night wore on and the winds increased, the adrenalin kicked in and fear began. From the radio broadcasts, Pete marked the location readings of the approaching cyclone onto a map and finally joined the dots. The pencilled line of the cyclone path went right through where we were.

The sliding glass doors began to curve inward and then the sky filled with apple green light as the power blew up. But our house held and by the early hours of the morning, the winds suddenly stopped as the eye arrived, and we inspected our small home to find that there was only a leak in one of the bedrooms. We stepped outside and could hear voices from the damaged houses and small block of apartments behind us.

Our neighbour's house was still intact, and the occupants of the damaged buildings were quickly assigned to the surviving homes. Quickly. Quickly, the eye won't last. And just as we were deciding where everyone would shelter we heard a huge noise as the cyclone hit the mangroves fringing the coast. Grabbing the sponge cushions from the couch we all dashed into a very small space at the centre of the house where four doorways formed a small corridor. And there we remained for hours, the couch cushions over our heads; Pete, six strangers, a dog and me clutching a very small baby Astrid.

The roof peeled off almost immediately, one sheet after another with roars like the departing underground trains I remembered in London. That was the last time I remembered feeling fear and adrenaline. The roof, that protective covering, vanished, and from then on we stood, soaked through, in the middle of dense noise. No waves could be distinguished, just solid and huge noise. Fear as I knew it had gone. No-one could survive this force that enveloped us. We would die. I felt a numb, calm certainty of death.

Pete had assigned a man to hold each of the four doors closed so we were separated by other people. I had my back hard up against the brick wall.

After some time, I could feel the wall shuddering behind me. Pete asked how the baby was and shone the torch over to my side and as I twisted to look up behind me I could see a large slab of brickwork swaying above my head.

We were so crowded together that I couldn't move, so I calmly asked him to turn off the torch. For some time after that I pondered what I would do when the slab of bricks fell on me. I was a mother so I knew I should throw my body over my baby, but I didn't feel like a mother. Perhaps I would just react by dropping the baby and putting my hands over my head. Numbness filled my being but luckily, when it fell, the slab of bricks fell outwards.

Then after hours of standing I started to think I could distinguish some pulsing in the wall of sound. Perhaps the cyclone was passing. Perhaps we might survive. Normal fear returned, mingled with hope. Perhaps we would live… but then perhaps, we would not.

Gradually the wind eased and eventually we walked outside to a world that seemed stripped of colour – like the photos of France in World War One, and I knew that I would never feel the same again about our world. I had been allowed an insight into the vastness of the natural world.

On Christmas Eve our home had been destroyed, but we were alive and uninjured. We were alive! As I surveyed the wreckage on Christmas morning and our possessions strewn in bare tree branches and scattered about, I felt an overpowering feeling of awe, an awareness of the vastness and power of the natural world, transcending our everyday life, so much larger than us and the things that fill our days. And for that awareness I will always be grateful, despite the hours of numbing terror that filled that night. My focus had shifted from inward concern to an outward sense of universality and connectedness.

Several days later, I flew in a RAAF Hercules with a small group of women who had premature babies because of the cyclone. Their babies were wrapped in alfoil. Two of the women spoke almost no English. I tried sign language to interpret the directions to protect your ears (and your baby's ears) as we took off in the unpressurised plane to Sydney. I felt, in comparison, that I was already a very experienced mother.

We rebuilt our home in Darwin then later settled on a small farm in Margaret River, Western Australia, a place of amazing beauty.

For the past forty years I have enjoyed championing the environment and attempting to do something to stop our rush into climate change. I thank that terrifying cyclone for the vital insight it provided.

Figure 17: Brown's Mart after the cyclone (LANT, ph0238-0589, Peter Spillett Collection).

Lex Silvester

Lex was working as a lawyer in Melbourne when the lure of the north became too strong, and he headed to Darwin in late 1970, joining John McCormack's practice and spending his free time perfecting the art of saltwater fly-fishing. In that same year, Chrissie returned from a year's working holiday overseas and came to Darwin with a lawyer boyfriend and work as a pre-school teacher. She and Lex met soon after they arrived and were married in 1973. They rode out the cyclone in their home in Macartney Street, Fannie Bay.

Chrissie and I had bought our house in Macartney Street a few months before Christmas 1974. Cyclone Selma had turned away from Darwin three weeks earlier, but we didn't assume that Cyclone Tracy would do the same. We were new parents and our daughter Sophie was just four months old, so I didn't want to take any chances.

I went down to the chandlery and bought a huge roll of good rope. I then spent the afternoon tying the roof down, using my sailor's knots and a lot of strong truckie's hitches. I also went to my office in town and taped up the filing cabinets containing all my legal files.

It was extremely hot and humid the day Tracy struck, with short squalls and showers. The weather began to get more blustery as evening came. We were to host Christmas Day lunch for friends at our house, so we had a huge amount of food in the fridge including ham, turkey, and Christmas pudding, plus plenty of food for the forthcoming holiday period.

For the first part of the cyclone, we sheltered upstairs in the hallway. Towards midnight it began to get more frightening, with the wind getting stronger and the noise louder and louder. We could hear the corrugated iron roofing coming loose and flapping, and buildings breaking up all around us.

When the eye came it was much quieter for about half an hour, and very eerie. We were able to go downstairs and into the street and spoke with neighbours.

None of us knew what to expect next and were just glad that our houses seemed, at that time, to be standing up to the forces of the weather without too much damage.

However, after the eye passed, the winds strengthened, and the noise was incredible. Parts of the house began to break up and we very slowly crawled downstairs with Sophie in our arms. We got into a car where we spent the next few hours terrified by the deafening, unbearable noise and the force of the wind shaking the car.

When it became light, I looked up at our house. The rope was still in place, but the roof was somewhere else. I said to Chrissie, "Well, we can't stay here – we're going to have to stay with the neighbours tonight." And then I looked at the neighbours' houses.

Going upstairs that morning was unbelievable. As well as the roof, the whole main front wall had blown away – we were standing on a deck looking across the neighbourhood, all the way down to the sea, about five streets away. There were no leaves left on trees and shrubs, it was like a moonscape, grey and quiet. It was incredibly eerie.

Inside, what remained of the house was a complete mess. Everything was soaking wet with so much leaf and branch debris everywhere. At that stage, little did we realise that, living in one of the older more established suburbs with hills and large trees, we were in a relatively good situation compared to the Northern suburbs.

Later that day we managed to find our friends who were okay. We then moved into a room in what was a new dress shop, meant to be opening soon, in a large building in the old Woolworths site on the corner of Knuckey Street and Austin Lane. We slept there for several nights along with our friends and another family with a new baby.

I went into my office at Withnall and Barker, Solicitors in Cavenagh Street. The office was in a very old building and had been completely destroyed. I was politely told I no longer had a job, as the future of working in legal practice in Darwin was uncertain in those early days. I retrieved my files – the taping had worked.

Chrissie and baby Sophie flew south a day or two later. I tried to salvage what I could from the wreckage of our house and joined in the clean-up. On New Year's Day I drove a friend's Mini Moke, with the family dog, to Sydney. All the way down, wherever I stopped for fuel, locals were handing out money and supplies. The community response was absolutely incredible.

During the period after Cyclone Tracy, we travelled around in the southern states, visiting family and friends, which was fun as it was summer and the holiday season. We visited friends in Singapore for a fortnight and began to contemplate living elsewhere.

While we were with my parents in Melbourne I applied for several jobs, but I think we knew that, at that stage of our lives we did not want to live in a southern Australian capital city!

I was really keen to return to Darwin and get involved in rebuilding the house and our lives. I returned about March 1975, with Chrissie and Sophie following in late April. It was extremely difficult to get a permit to return and we had to prove we had suitable accommodation. We spent a few weeks with friends in their damaged home in McKinlay Street, Fannie Bay, while I worked on our house in Macartney Street to make it habitable.

This proved to be the right decision for both of us. That following period, rebuilding our own home and being involved in the reconstruction of Darwin is another story in itself. There were many challenges, but we as a family were up for it and it was a fantastic time in our lives.

Barry Spencer

Barry was the Petty Officer Coxswain posted to HMAS Arrow based in Sydney where it was being re-commissioned after a period of service with the Naval Reserves. In August 1974, the boat, and its crew of 19 under its captain, Lieutenant Bob Dagworthy, sailed north to join the other three patrol boats based in Darwin. Their work in the north was mainly patrols to intercept illegal fishermen fishing within Australian territorial waters. Barry's wife, Carolyn, joined Barry in Darwin and became secretary to the Executive Officer of HMAS Coonawarra.

Early in the afternoon of Christmas Eve the crew had been advised that with a cyclone imminent we would be proceeding to the cyclone buoys in Darwin Harbour later that afternoon.

At 1pm the boat's Commanding Officer, Lieutenant Bob Dagworthy, Chief Boatswain's Mate (Buffer) Les Catton and I went to a Xmas party being held by the Fisheries Department with whom we worked regularly. We restricted our drinking to orange juice knowing we would be at sea later in the day.

My wife, Carolyn, picked up the three of us and drove us down to Stokes Hill Wharf where we joined the crew already onboard and proceeded to our designated cyclone buoy, intending to sit out the cyclone. The rest of the evening was spent playing cards and I retired around 10.30pm.

I was preparing to take over the Watch at 0250, when I heard the mooring cable snaking across the upper deck, the cable had parted from the ship. I proceeded to the Bridge with three other senior sailors, told the CO what we had heard and at the same time the chief engineer started both engines which were on standby. The conditions were quite rough, and we tried to keep the ship heading into the wind. At this stage the Ship's Company mustered in the Galley and put on life jackets.

The radar was being continually stopped due to the force of the wind. That meant the ship was blind, with zero visibility. The Radio Operator sent a signal to Naval Officer Commanding Northern Australia (NOCNA) informing him that we had broken our mooring and were underway. This was the last message we could send or receive due to the conditions.

About 0340, we did two very heavy rolls of about 80 degrees, one to starboard and one to port, which brought the cooling water inlet ports out of the water. This caused the engines to start to overheat and alarms to go off.

The CO decided we would try to beach *Arrow* on the mudflats at Frances Bay, however due to the strength of the wind as we were turning, the ship was blown into Stokes Hill Wharf.

The CO ordered abandon ship. At this time Petty Officer Danny Grose and leading seaman 'Flash' Jordan scrambled onto the wharf and grabbed the rest of the sailors by their lifejackets to pull them onto the wharf.

Meanwhile, I was on the quarterdeck with Sub Lieutenant Andrew Birchnell and the Buffer, Catton. Catton went to secure the after hatch leading to the sailor's Mess Deck, which was the last I saw of him. Birchnell suggested we should go over the side and try to make shore.

I told him to go but I had work to do onboard. Andrew went over the side, and I released the 20-man life raft behind him. I then went to the portside where I helped get the crew off the boat and mustered on the wharf.

When AB McLeod told me everyone was off the ship, I told the ship's company to stay together, and we headed for the boom gate keeper's office at the end of the wharf. At this time the CO appeared from under the wharf, having been last to abandon ship.

At the boom gate office, Seaman Doug Cousins and I smashed a window to gain shelter but immediately the whole building disintegrated so we went on to a carpark with four cars where we broke windows to get in and take shelter. One of the crew found a carton of cigarettes and even the CO who had never smoked before enjoyed it!

About 0600 the CO said we should seek help from Naval Headquarters (NHQ) but as he was unable to go due to cuts on his feet, Seaman Peter Sargeant and I walked up the hill to Naval Headquarters to report to NOCNA, at that time Commodore Eric Johnston (later to be the NT Administrator).

I told him what had happened, and that *Arrow* had blown up against the wharf and sunk. While there, we helped free one of his staff who was trapped under a desk with some of the building on top of him but was unhurt.

When a 4-wheel-drive arrived outside with a cameraman and driver filming the damage (almost certainly Keith Bushnell and his companion) Commodore Johnson commandeered use of the vehicle and with the two civilians I went down to Stokes Hill Wharf where I could see our life raft. That was when I found Jack Rennie, who had drowned.

I then saw someone who said there was another person lying in the inner harbour so I went there and found Sub Lieutenant Andrew Birchnell. He was alive but not in very good shape, so we put him in the 4-wheel-drive and went to Darwin Hospital. There I ran into Petty Officer Payne who was Buffer on our sister ship, HMAS *Attack*.

He told me that the *Attack* was aground at Larrakeyah Barracks where they were tied to a tree. I then returned to NOCNA's office and reported to him what I had found, then went to the Darwin Police Station to report Rennie's death.

Transport was arranged to take the crew to Larrakeyah Barracks and then NOCNA instructed his secretary to take me to HMAS *Coonawarra* where the first person I saw was my wife, Carolyn. She had been told by one of the senior officers at *Coonawarra* that "HMAS *Arrow* had sunk with the loss of all lives".

The following day Carolyn and I went out to our house at the 11 Mile Transmitting Station to find all that was left standing was the floor, although our bed remained completely untouched as if ready for us to sleep in it.

We then returned to Coonawarra, where we were accommodated while I was employed by NOCNA to assist naval personnel on flights out of Darwin.

On December 30 the remaining *Arrow* crew members were directed to leave Darwin so, in a convoy of cars, together with our old english sheepdog Mandy, we arrived at Alice Springs, were accommodated overnight, and then flown out the next morning, New Year's Eve, to Melbourne.

There, my brother picked us up and took us to my parents' home at Benalla. Three days later, Carolyn and I boarded a train to Sydney, and I reported to HMAS Penguin to resume work. Carolyn got work with the navy in Sydney until, a few months later, I was promoted to Chief Petty Officer and found myself posted back to HMAS *Coonawarra* as Chief Coxswain.

Once again Carolyn and I were living in Darwin. But this time, we were in a caravan, which was cosy, before being allocated the comparative luxury of a demountable.

Figure 18: Wreck of HMAS *Arrow* on Francis Beach (Alison Cheater, LANT, ph0070-0003).

Lloyd Stumer

Lloyd was a duty meteorologist in Darwin the night Tracy destroyed the city. He spent the night in his office in the MLC building. He and his wife, Debbi, had been married in April and were looking forward to moving into their new house. They had met while both were working for the Australian Bureau of Meteorology in Port Moresby.

Early in December meteorological observations were indicating a strong possibility that a developing tropical low could cause serious damage to Darwin, and to the new house, nearing completion and the contents recently acquired by my wife Debbi and I.

A colleague from the bureau and I took a few minutes off work and increased our contents insurances by several thousands of dollars, the friendly insurance clerk assuring us that our contents would be immediately covered for storm and tempest and cyclones.

An hour later the first warnings were issued that the newly formed Tropical Cyclone Selma posed a threat to Darwin, but after several days of warnings it passed within about 50 km of Darwin. It was a very near miss indeed.

Thanks to Cyclone Selma, our contents insurance was now adequate. Our home builder had been selected because he was the only one who had offered cyclone rods to tie the roof down to the floor joists and the floor bearers to the posts. The elevated home was near completion and should have been ready for occupation by Christmas, but it still needed minor painting work.

The only thing left for us to do was to ensure there were adequate stocks of barramundi and freshwater crayfish in the new freezer, a job happily completed in the Top End creeks, rivers and billabongs with Bureau of Met mates and fishermen Vin Shuey and Jordi Maas

Meanwhile a new tropical depression was developing and went on to form Severe Tropical Cyclone Tracy. The Bureau of Meteorology operational team was at battle stations, even on Christmas Eve.

As we had not yet moved into the new house, I took a quick trip to personally tighten up all the cyclone rods and check that the builder had removed all rubbish before doing a last few hours of Christmas shopping.

The warnings on Cyclone Tracy were being discussed by the friendly shoppers. One woman falsely believed that Darwin was safe because the Tiwi Islands would always protect it. Another said she hoped the cyclone *would* hit Darwin because it was a long time since she had experienced a cyclone – she had previously enjoyed slightly windy and wet weather on the fringes of cyclones and mistakenly believed that was all a cyclone was about.

General optimism and high spirits abounded everywhere on Christmas Eve. The recent Cyclone Selma was not a good role model to educate the Darwin public to the real dangers of tropical cyclones.

A late afternoon check at the Regional Forecasting Office of the Bureau reinforced my belief in the potential seriousness of the situation. I reported several hours early for my rostered midnight to dawn shift, known as the *doggo shift* on Christmas morning, because I knew the weather just before midnight would make driving dangerous.

In a decision that probably saved their lives, Debbi and my newly arrived brother Glen wisely resolved to stay the night with Debbi's parents and sisters in their robust-looking brick house in Rothdale Road, Jingili rather than in our rented flimsy fibro-clad commonwealth elevated house in Trower Road.

Technical Assistant Jordi and Observer and Radar Operator Vin were also due to do the doggo shift. Jordi stopped on his way to work for about 10 minutes in blinding rain at the flashing lights of the Salonika Railway Crossing waiting for the train to cross.

Then thinking that the lights were malfunctioning, with great trepidation he quickly but blindly drove over the crossing. There was no train.

Vin meanwhile drove to the lonely meteorological radar at the airport and parked his car on the downwind side of the building to protect it from expected flying debris. Vin was an unsung hero of that night. He provided frequent radar images via photo and facsimile which were essential to the forecasting staff for assessing the latest location, plus direction and speed of movement, of the cyclone.

When the eye was over the radar hut, Vin quickly ran outside and parked his car on the other side of the building to avoid the change in direction of flying debris.

Fellow forecaster Graeme Crooks was to write the public and marine forecasts, I was to write the aviation forecasts and Din Siregar was to draw the weather charts routinely transmitted from Darwin to the world. Judy Kroll handled communications. Several other technicians and observers were responsible for the collation and presentation of all the observations from various sources.

Responsibility for the writing of the actual cyclone warnings belonged to the two most senior meteorologists, Regional Director Ray Wilkie, and Geoff Crane.

The eighth floor of the MLC Building in Smith Street, where the Regional Forecasting Office was located, began to shake, rattle, and almost roll as the howling wind steadily increased. This was particularly so after 1.00 am when wind gusts started to exceed 130 kph.

When the town power supply dropped out, the bureau's emergency diesel generator cut in to help maintain our operations. Our lights were blazing brightly inside the office, while outside Darwin was blacked out, though eerily illuminated by constant lightning flashes in the driving rain.

As the building's precast concrete walls started to flex inwards and outwards by a couple of inches and some windows broke, staff began to position themselves and their work behind internal concrete pillars for safety in case the walls collapsed.

At various stages of the night, we all lost local telephone communications with our loved ones in Darwin as their homes were being destroyed, but ironically for some time we maintained contact with the outside world.

At 2.30 am, the last warning issued by the Darwin Office said "Tropical Cyclone Tracy, at 2.00 am, was 18 km west-northwest of Darwin moving east-southeast at 6 kph with the eye expected to move over Darwin soon. Winds should become lighter to calm for a period up to 1.5 hours before rapidly increasing to its previous intensity from the opposite direction."

Very few of the local Darwin population were then in any position to receive or respond to this latest warning, but other recipients outside of Darwin were.

It appeared likely there would soon be loss of communications from the Darwin office and as meteorological services needed to be maintained, particularly for aviation, shipping and emergency services, responsibilities for forecasts and warnings throughout the Darwin region were formally passed to the Perth Regional Forecasting Office, until further notice. Darwin, Perth, and Brisbane were the only offices equipped and skilled to handle tropical cyclones.

We then all bunkered down to survive the night on the eighth floor.

The wind anemometer broke at 3.00 am so there is no record of the wind strengths after that, but as the cyclone eye approached, we anxiously watched the steepening fall of the barometer readings.

The scale on the recording chart paper of the aneroid barometer used to continuously record atmospheric pressure ranged from 950 to 1040 hectopascal. About 4.30 am everyone in the Office stared quietly in disbelief as the pen trace dropped below 950 hpa and continued to drop to the bottom edge of the chart, below the set recording range of the instrumentation.

The orchestra of Tracy was by now playing a deafening and frightening deadly crescendo as the wind shrieked and howled and the building shook and bucked in response.

Between 5.30 and 6.30 am, despite the now faltering and intermittent state of telephone communications from the office, I managed to ring my mother in Kingaroy, Queensland. I told her Darwin was seriously damaged by Tropical Cyclone Tracy but said not to worry and I would contact her again if anyone in the family was harmed. She wished us Merry Christmas!

We unlocked the ground floor doors to the MLC Building and let in a very frightened group of people we discovered cowering outside the building for shelter. At this stage it was very obvious that security of residents from the elements was of much higher priority than mere security of materials and information on the various floors of the building.

However, Meteorologist Bill Manchur was in a Katherine hotel a week or so later when by coincidence he spotted a young man displaying the Bureau of Meteorology barometric chart recording he had 'souvenired' from the Darwin Office, while taking advantage of the shelter offered. Bill politely retrieved the irreplaceable chart.

When the winds had abated to a level where we thought there would be no danger from flying debris, I drove home with Jordi in my ute. We weaved and dodged between, or drove over, the mangled and twisted remnants of houses, electricity poles and cables and other debris scattered randomly over the roads.

There was no one to be seen. Only rubble seemed to exist. It was like driving into a city that had just been flattened by an atomic bomb. Our thoughts and conversation during this slow bumpy trip to the northern suburbs were that everyone nearby must be either lying trapped under all the wreckage or have been killed.

We managed to eventually reach Rothdale Road and then, with

a cold shiver, I saw in the distance that Debbi's parents' house had been flattened like most of the rest. But when we got to the house there was no one there.

We hurried to Casuarina High School, the nearest and most substantial public building but still there were no signs of Debbi, her family or Glen. Frantically, we sprinted back to the Rothdale ruins and were just beginning to drive away when we were spotted by Debbi who had just emerged from a less damaged house across the road, where she had been sheltering with her family.

They had spent a horrifying night under a bed and a table as the house was being completely destroyed around them. They survived with minor cuts and bruising from the blasting by the wind and debris.

Our own new house had disappeared apart from the leaning posts, the bearers, and the stairs. All the floorboards were missing as the floor joists had not been fastened strongly enough to the floor bearers, so that when the roof went, so did the attached joists and floor.

The Commonwealth house we lived in was also destroyed, with only the toilet left standing. The next few days were spent collecting rainwater in buckets by funnelling it from sheets of iron, eating the tinned food which had been stockpiled for the wet, scrounging through the yard under the remnants of our houses for personal belongings, and deciding our options for the future.

We were overjoyed to be alive. Six days later we drove to Mount Isa, where we loaded our vehicles with our salvaged possessions onto an emergency relief train to Brisbane, supplied by the Queensland Government for Darwin evacuees. We returned to Darwin about a month later to resume work, but then left Darwin permanently in December of 1975 to go back to Brisbane.

Figure 19: 64 Rothdale Road Moil (Lloyd Stumer)

Jim Toomey

Jim was the production manager for Darwin's commercial television station, NTD8. His story was written in the form of a letter to family and friends almost three weeks after Cyclone Tracy. He lived in Houston Street, Larrakeyah.

Sadly, not long after writing his letter, Jim flew to Melbourne to begin treatment for melanoma. A long and torrid course of chemotherapy in Darwin followed, before he was flown to Brisbane in November to be with his parents. They subsequently withdrew treatment to spare him any further suffering and Jim died on December 12, 1975, just days before the first anniversary of the cyclone.

It all started off very casually indeed, with much less importance placed on Tracy than on Selma some weeks earlier. Both the ABC Radio and commercial station, 8DN, were broadcasting regular cyclone warnings.

As usual, no-one took much notice – although I don't attribute the disastrous outcome of Tracy to this complacency as those who took precautions as instructed suffered the same fate as those who didn't.

After the first cyclone of the season, Selma, however we at NTD8 decided to be prepared for the next. At that time, we had no warning slide or siren, so I proceeded to organise some, and as far as we were concerned, we were prepared. Little did we know.

Christmas Eve was busy because we were preparing for the Christmas break with three days of programs to be made up.

During the afternoon the Weather Bureau was sending in reports on Tracy, and both Assistant Program Director Peter Miller and I were deciding whether to transmit them as warnings, which required the siren to be used, or just reports – which were more a weather report. There had been so much talk about Selma's false alarm that we felt duty-bound not to worry people unduly.

We put out several reports up until 7 pm when I decided I would push off home. The latest bureau telex message reported Tracy as 120 km from Darwin and moving closer. Peter recorded that one and continued to use it with the warning siren about three times an hour.

By this time the edge of the storm had reached us, and it was an effort to go anywhere. Nevertheless, Peter went back to the station later in the evening, after the duty technician advised another bulletin had come in. He recorded a further warning.

I settled down at 14 Houston Street to weather what I thought would be 'a bit of a blow'. By now it was teeming, with rain splashing in through the louvres. The wind was high but not enough to cause me concern. There was obviously some sort of leak from upstairs because a few spots began to come through my living room ceiling.

I gave up trying to mop up the water and just as I was contemplating leaving things until the morning, the power went out. I decided the best place was bed, at least the bedroom was quite dry.

A short time later the phone rang. It was my friend, the Anglican Bishop of Darwin, Ken Mason, inviting me to spend the night at 'The Lodge' if things got any worse.

When I heard glass breaking in the flat above, water began cascading through the ceiling and the wind was truly howling, I decided to move to the Bishop's Lodge in Larrakeyah.

Wearing only a pair of swimming trunks, I sloshed through the water now covering the floor and went outside to move my car into the driveway. Debris was already flying about, and some small trees had been uprooted. I could hear roofing iron crashing, but I wanted to try to save some of my possessions.

Struggling to keep the car door open against the wind, which was howling like a thousand banshees, I manhandled two large speakers onto the back seat followed by the newly purchased amplifier, speakers and cassette deck bought by a friend, who was on holidays down south.

I grabbed a pair of shorts and a shirt, climbed into the car and began making my way to the Bishop's place. Just around the corner, I suddenly remembered that I'd left my watch on the bedside table, and as I couldn't face being without it, with great difficulty returned for it, a decision which was probably stupid but seemed logical at the time.

Having recovered the watch, I resumed the short drive to Bishop Ken's only to discover a tree across the road and power lines down in the vicinity of the hospital. I skirted the tree, driving over the wires and reached the Lodge without mishap. On the drive Susie, my cat, was absolutely terrified, and I had to hold her as well as drive. There was much mewing and wild-eyed looks but, on entering the Lodge, she seemed to quieten down a little.

The Bishop was to leave on Christmas Day for a nine-months overseas study tour and John, who was to look after the place in his absence, had been to a Christmas party and was a little the worse for wear, and sound asleep.

While the ABC Radio remained on air it gave news that was anything but heartening. Reports on which streets were impassable seemed to pop up with monotonous regularity and then it was reported all police cars had been withdrawn to Casuarina to help residents there who appeared to be most in need.

Around 2 am the wind, which had been steadily increasing in intensity suddenly leapt into high gear, the Lodge began to shake and with the sound of flapping iron, the wind screamed at such a pitch as I had never heard before (nor wish to hear again). At this time the bishop woke John, who was a mite hazy initially, but was soon wide awake, shaking like the rest of us and very sober indeed.

Together, we descended to what we hoped would be the safety of the study.

The following three hours were the most harrowing I've ever experienced. Water pouring into the study; the terrific noise of the wind; the building shaking; and the crashing and banging of debris flying about outside is all implanted in my brain. For three long hours the elements did their best to destroy the Lodge. Just when we thought the wind couldn't get any stronger another gust would make us hold our breath and wonder if this was 'it'.

Speaking was impossible, so for that time we sat there as three dejected heaps. I'm sorry to say that Suzie disappeared during this period, and I haven't seen her since.

As dawn broke, the wreckage we saw of the house next door in Myilly Terrace was just a prelude to the devastation we were to see later on. The wind was still howling mightily and to venture outside nothing short of stupidity, so we retreated to the study again to await developments.

By about 7 am the wind had abated sufficiently to allow investigation wider afield. We ascended to take stock of the lodge and ourselves. I fully expected to find the car with windows broken and water inside but to my surprise and unbounded relief found it was practically unscathed, save for a few scratches and paint chips.

During the short walk to the hospital, we saw three cars upside-down with roofs crushed and bodywork dented beyond repair. They had been rolled over and over by the wind until they came to rest against something solid. Others had been damaged to varying degrees by flying debris.

Ken went to see what had happened to church property while I wandered to the hospital to see if I could lend a hand and see if there was anyone I knew. Peter Miller and his sister, Jane, were there after spending a harrowing night under the stairs in his block of flats. Jane, a teacher from Victoria, had arrived a few days earlier to spend Christmas with Peter. She was doing what she could to assist and as it appeared I was not needed I decided to go to my flat in Houston Street to see how it had fared.

Again, I fully expected to find nothing left. The gang from upstairs were sheltering in a car and preparing to evacuate. The building's roof had completely gone. All the windows upstairs had blown out, the front door had blown in, and some tins of paint left by a painter a few weeks before had burst open. The flat was covered in splatters of white paint.

There was nothing I could do there, so I returned to the hospital. Peter Miller was still wandering around in a bit of a daze, so I suggested we hop in the car and see what had happened to the TV station. Jane remained at the hospital.

Getting to NTD8 studios was a major exercise as the usual routes were blocked by trees and other debris.

My heart sank as we approached the building. The front doors and my office windows had been blown in and a large part of the roof was missing. The full extent of the damage became clear as we scrambled though the front entrance and over the pile of debris that had once been a television station.

The film department was completely demolished with not a dry item to be seen. Everything was saturated and even then rust was beginning to show on what equipment still existed. New equipment worth many thousands of dollars, bought in anticipation of the conversion from black-and-white to colour, had been utterly destroyed.

Peter and I looked at each other and neither of us could hold back the tears as we realised that all the work of those months and months of planning, the extra hours which we had both given was all for nothing, gone in a few hours. What had once been a thriving television station was now a mass of rubble and twisted metal and at 8 o'clock on that fateful Christmas Day the situation looked so hopeless that neither us would have given any odds at all on one single item being salvaged.

Postscript. In the days that followed, Jim, Peter Miller and his sister Jane moved into the damaged home of the station manager, John Lewis and his family in Drysdale Street, Parap. John's wife, Maxine, their children, and Jane were later evacuated. Jim, Peter, and John managed to make the house mostly waterproof, then set about the task of sorting out the television station. NTD8 was back on air ten months later, on October 27, 1975.

Ray Vuillermin

Ray Vuillermin was a pilot with Trans Australia Airlines (TAA) one of the two major domestic airlines then operating within Australia. With First Officer Tony Burgess, he is credited with flying the first significant airline flight into Darwin on Christmas Day, 1974. He had previously lived in Darwin, spending 1965 to 1967 on secondment from TAA to the NT Aerial Medical Service.

Our flight to Darwin on December 25, 1974, began as a normal TAA scheduled service from Melbourne to Darwin. The schedule had us departing Melbourne in the early morning with passengers on a jet service to Adelaide and Alice Springs where we would change to a Fokker F27 Friendship (VH-TQT) for the so-called 'milk run' to Darwin with stops at Tennant Creek and Katherine (Tindal).

Arriving in Alice Springs we were alerted to 'something unusual' happening in Darwin but it was not until Katherine that we started hearing suggestions that there had been a catastrophe in Darwin, though with no specific detail.

TAA instructed me to leave my passengers and take medical staff into Darwin. I had my daughter Nicole, aged nine, with me as she was to spend Christmas in Darwin with her grandmother, Alice Carter. Alice had been in the Territory for some time living with the aboriginal group who had walked off Wave Hill Station to camp at Wattie Creek and was making her way home to Melbourne. I couldn't abandon Nikki, so took her on with me.

Approaching Darwin, we could not contact the (air traffic)

control tower so circled around Darwin looking with amazement at the destruction. As a former Darwin resident, I simply could not believe the damage I was seeing.

As we circled the radio suddenly came to life with the speaker identifying himself as a RAAF officer in a radio-equipped vehicle. He asked what distance we needed to land and I told him 3000 feet (just under 1 kilometre). He advised that Air Force personnel had managed to clear half the main runway of debris for a distance of about 6000 feet and said he would wait at the end of that area of the runway in his vehicle, a bright yellow VW Kombi, to lead us through the debris into the terminal area.

We landed about 5.30 pm and upon shutting down I was surprised to find that my guide, Flying Officer Perry Matthews*, an RAAF special duties air traffic controller, and I had lived just a few hundred yards apart in Macleod, Victoria, had gone to the same school, and had been members of the same air force cadet unit.

Although there were reports some light aircraft had already landed, I believe we were the first 'heavy' aircraft to land after Tracy and were followed shortly by an Ansett F27 Fokker Friendship with a friend, Ron Neve in command. Ron subsequently told me he had been circling because he couldn't make radio contact with Darwin.

My daughter had been looking forward to staying at the Travelodge, where TAA normally accommodated staff, and I had promised her we would be spending some time in the pool. Nikki was disgusted to note as we circled before landing that there was a car in the pool.

Later in the evening, Major General Alan Stretton, head of the National Disasters Organisation, arrived in a RAAF C130 Hercules. By that time, Nicole, the crew, and I, had managed to get to the Travelodge and found my mother-in-law, Alice. I left Nikki with her, knowing then that she planned to drive south in her VW beetle.

---

* Flying Officer Perry Matthews' story also appears in this book.

When Stretton arrived, I told him the F27 was fuelled and ready to go. He instructed us to get some rest and report back early in the morning to take women and babies from the maternity ward to Brisbane.

We didn't get much sleep. We wanted to stay in contact as there was a strong rumour that the cyclone was doubling back, and we thought we might have to move the Fokker. The cyclone, of course, did not come back. On the ground we were well looked after by TAA staff most of whom stayed to help with the evacuation despite their own cyclone experiences.

The next morning, Boxing Day, we were preparing for departure when a QANTAS Boeing 707 arrived unannounced overhead, carrying equipment, supplies and relief personnel to allow the evacuation of QANTAS staff.

We needed in-flight supplies of food and water and although QANTAS didn't have catering facilities they opened their damaged catering section and told our flight hostesses, Marie Willis and Debbie Marker to 'help themselves'. Marie and Debbie loaded up with biscuits, drinks and as much in the way of towels and pads as they could find.

We finally departed with 57 passengers – 30 traumatised women and 27 newborns – an RAAF doctor and crew, aboard a 36-seat aeroplane. From the cockpit the two-hour flight was uneventful, but the cabin was like a war hospital with Marie and Debbie flat-out the whole time, putting their first aid experience to good use offering succour, medical, and hygiene assistance.

There was still almost no news of Darwin reaching the outside world so, when we called our company representative before descent into Mount Isa to arrange for catering to be made available, he didn't believe us, but nevertheless, drinks and sandwiches were ready when we landed there to refuel.

The doctor agreed the best course would be to get the women and babies to Brisbane and the best care as quickly as possible, so we made a quick turnaround and flew another two hours to Brisbane, arriving in the afternoon.

After our passengers were taken care of we all collapsed at our Lennons Hotel accommodation, having just enough energy for a quick beer before we headed off to sleep.

I then resumed normal flight duties and made no further flights to Darwin during the evacuation.

Nikki and her grandmother, Alice, became part of the convoy of people leaving Darwin by road and they arrived in Alice Springs a few days later. Two tyres had been replaced free of charge following an inspection at a checkpoint as they were departing Darwin. Nikki remembers them being billeted for a night in a house with a man with a huge beard and two snakes.

In Alice Springs they put the car on the Ghan to Adelaide, again free of charge and enjoyed a sleeper compartment. From Adelaide they were flown home to Melbourne.

Rob Wesley-Smith

By 1974, Rob Wesley-Smith had become recognised as an activist supporting causes including the Land Rights movement started by the Gurindji people's walk-off from Wave Hill, and opposition to the Vietnam War. His occasional brushes with the law colour some of the attitudes reflected here. During the cyclone he was living in a two-storey block of units on the corner of Foelsche and Woods Street, in the city. He claims to have been the first to visit the CBD with a camera after the storm.

I don't think anyone much in Darwin took impending doom seriously, as we had had a serious cyclone warning a few weeks earlier which had fizzled out, anyway it seemed to be heading – as usual, to the west or southwest. But Tracy dudded us and turned southeast – right through Darwin town.

I had gone to bed, when I awoke the power was off, and I couldn't find my shoes, or a torch. My early photos and papers were in a small storeroom in this great old solid two-storey block. Its little window was broken, and stuff was flying out. I had trouble shutting the door due to the wind pressure but when I finally got it shut I fell backwards and stepped on some broken glass. Then, of course, the door flew open again – was the building moving? I dunno.

Anyway, I thought caution was the better part of valour and looked for two walls to sit between. Such a spot was hard to find because the unit had glass louvres on both sides and a plank had already flown right through. I settled for backing onto the fridge with the kitchen wall not far away, found a bottle of Canadian Club and had a few calming sips, and waited until the grey light of early dawn allowed one to see.

Looking out I saw the elevated house that belonged to friends over the road was demolished. There was a plank through the windscreen of a car – can't remember if it was mine, and the roof of my two-storey block was damaged – but the building and similar others were in good basic shape. I grabbed my German Practika camera and walked up to Smith Street, past the Victoria Hotel, past the remains of the Anglican Cathedral, and on to look over the wharf, taking photos as I walked until my film was finished. (In retrospect, I curse the invention of digital photo taking coming too late!)

Anyway, these photos were the first, they show cars strewn around Smith Street, so no one could drive through. I gave these pics to the NT Library, where a photography expert, I think named Butcher, copied them onto their computer systems. Years later I found them listed as 'photographer unknown'. I had that changed, and also told the staff at the time how they came to be, which they didn't know. I also was interviewed after Tracy, and the photos are listed in 5 or more segments.

The occupants of the floor above me came down, and sat around, shocked. I said to the bloke – "use your axe", which he'd brought down "and chop some of the fallen wood for a fire." He just sat and mumbled he couldn't. So, I contacted the evacuation people and got them on a plane out of here. For those who stayed, in the first few days, food was not a problem, as fridges were stocked for Christmas dinners. Water in the pipes ran out, but the alert few went to the main water pipe and bathed under the spray and collected water for home use. I later had another shower under the runoff from a friend's roof. My flat accommodated several extra bods for a while.

I got a stitch in my foot, but with no anaesthetic and a tough sole, but perhaps not a tough soul, I bailed out of a second one. When the roads allowed driving, I went to the house of the only bloke who reported to me in the Department of Primary Industries.

Figure 20: Damage to shop fronts, Smith Street, including Star Theatre and Victoria Hotel (Rob Wesley-Smith Collection, LANT ph0244-0053).

Figure 21: Smith Street, Victoria Hotel on the left (Rob Wesley-Smith Collection, LANT ph0244-0036)

I found his house wasn't even floorboards, and that he had been killed. His wife had received a big cut over the scalp. A local nurse stitched it so well it amazed the doctors.

Their VW was 'sand blasted' and I was asked to sell it, but car dealers, who probably had plenty, offered a pittance, so I gave her twice the best offer, took it home and using bright yellow full-gloss paint, brushed it to a respectable finish.

I went into the police HQ in Mitchell Street and saw the initial tranche of bodies lying there. I can't remember if I could provide any new identifications but the cops, knowing of my connections with Aboriginal people, asked me to find individuals and groups to see if any wanted evacuation on flights south. I agreed but stipulated I wanted an escort, a police car, and an officer to show some authority, so it didn't happen.

A friendly highlight for a while was going to Darwin High School to get a delicious hot meal, and chat to other locals. Also, I remember the first time we could use a public phone to alert family we were still alive, and just as bonkers. There was a distribution of some small generator sets, which was useful for me.

I found the challenge of living quite acceptable, and when I got a letter from the Housing Commission (my landlord) asking me to 'fill in' my complaints, I didn't reply. But when my rent was doubled, I did complain and a fella came around and said, "your windows are broken, there is no security, so why didn't you alert us?" I said the word was 'complaints' and I didn't want to be a whinger, so just cracked hardy, but I objected to my rent being doubled. He arranged for it to be cut entirely, and back-paid the previous – very nice! I was burgled once, through a busted window, but the only thing taken was food.

I saw many old houses stay intact while most new ones were lost, and I understand the required bracing was not put in newer ones, relying on the 'asbestos' sheeting to hold firm, but flying debris from Tracy broke many of these sheets and the houses collapsed.

Eventually I built my own tropical style house but on the ground and took a great interest in housing construction in Timor.

Of course, thousands of Darwin people were evacuated, and many colleagues were allowed to go and work in their home states for a year or more. Some came back with a higher degree, which got them a promotion, but I wanted to hang around and keep visiting properties as a pastoral adviser.

Figure 22: Stuart Park houses (Rob Wesley-Smith Collection, LANT, PH02440007).

Coming back from one such trip, I was stopped at a roadblock and told no one was allowed into Darwin without a permit. It took me some time to convince a cop I had just left that morning doing my job, so they let me in saying to get a permit. The Department gave me a card saying I was a highly valued employee and needed to do property visits, or some such. I think they regretted thereafter the words 'highly valued'! But I did write advisory stuff using the heading TERNON, or Top End Rural News which proved useful, as staff were so few.

When my accommodation was to be fixed up, they moved me from this great two-bedroom big building to a tiny bedsitter. When I asked why, I was told people had complained that I was a single man living there when it should be occupied by a family. I said, "How dare they, my wife has gone south but we are not divorced". I was told it didn't matter, so I was outta there to a tiny bedsitter, where my books would stand in tall piles. At least I could read the spines and still find things.

After the Indonesian Invasion of East Timor with resistance forces moving to the mountains, I set up a radio with a tuned wire antenna to listen to Radio Maubere broadcasts from the Fretilin resistance fighters. The first time I could hear one, I ran outside wanting to shout to the world, or at least tell someone, or just kick my heels up! But the first person I saw was the (conservative) Catholic Bishop O'Loughlin, pacing near his cathedral, probably practicing his sermon. I said, "Bish, come and hear Radio Maubere in my unit, which he did, and sat on the only possible spot – my bed.

Two Maningrida girls I knew came past to visit but, in the gathering gloom, they saw this white shrouded figure sitting there. They ran for their lives!

The bishop said, "I tell my Timorese parishioners to forget about Timor, their lives are here now". I replied that that was the most unchristian thing I had heard in my life! Many years later, in October 1999, Bishop Ted Collins recommended me to a Non-Government Organisation (NGO)working in Timor for my agricultural skills.

So began another chapter in my life: direct involvement with Timor.

Figure 23: Damage after Cyclone Tracy (Rob Wesley-Smith Collection, LANT, ph0244-0029).

Peter Whelan

Peter arrived in Darwin as a boy in November 1956. He completed all his primary and high school education in Darwin and then studied agricultural science at Adelaide University, graduating in 1972. He began working in the Medical Entomology Unit of the Department of Health in January 1974. He was to lead this organization for decades after the cyclone. Peter, and his then girlfriend Liane, lived in a unit near the racecourse in Wells Street, Ludmilla.

The Christmas Eve after-work drinks were like many others at the end of a working week. I picked up my girlfriend, Liane Schuhen, from our rented flat in Wells Street, Ludmilla, around 5 o'clock, and we drove to the old Fannie Bay Hotel. We had organized to meet a few friends and we settled just under the cover of the overhang at the front bar and began a round of schooners. Our circle of chairs gradually widened but, when the rain began around 6 o'clock, we moved inside because the rain was blowing into the undercover area. Someone said it must be the start of the cyclone, but few had any idea of the expected winds or rain. I didn't give a thought about what 'a possible destructive wind' was going to be.

Four of us decided to play pool, but the game was disrupted by the rising wind and the rain spray coming onto the table. Someone saw a utility with a surfboard on the rack racing along East Point Road in the direction of the golf club beach. It was Ian Melville, one of our drinking friends who had said earlier that, if the winds get big with the approach of a storm, there would be great surfing.

I never found out how the surf was that night.

During our pool game, I heard a car scraping another just outside the window in Bayview Street. Liane said, "I think that bloke just hit your car."

I raced outside and the guy was about to drive off, but after some discussion I accepted $50 compensation for the damage he had caused. The pool was abandoned as more rain drifted onto the table. Liane and I decided that we would go home and have a pre-Christmas drink on the verandah to watch the storm and open presents 'German-style', that is on Christmas eve.

We drove home to Wells Street in increasingly heavy rain and settled on the top step to watch the rain coming down in the darkening sky. Our flat was the front part of a previously elevated house and a part of Blacker's Flats. It had a small living area and one bedroom against the wall of a new two-storey block of flats.

It became apparent Tracy was no ordinary storm. The heavy rain soon drove us off the steps to the inside. We opened our presents and after another drink, decided it was more comfortable to go to bed and read. Liane wanted to finish her latest novel, titled, believe it or not, *Gone with the wind.*

I drifted off to sleep but sometime later Liane woke me. The increasing wind was driving rain through the closed front louvres, so we tried to soak it up with towels. This was futile and we realized how serious it was getting. The wind strengthened. The electricity lines were swinging alarmingly and sparking with each other, and the arcing of the lines became more violent until all the lights went out.

We saw a guy running along the road where the lines were down. I yelled out, "Watch out, all the lines are down there." But he was head down and racing and disappeared into the dark. My voice was lost in the storm noise anyway, but I sometimes wonder if he heard me and what happened to him.

I realized we needed to take some precautions. I thought if it gets worse, our best protection was against the wall of the bed area, which backed onto the solid brick wall of the second storey flats. We sat with our backs to the wall with the bed frame and mattress forming a barrier. All around we could hear the increasing roar of wind and fine rain spray was penetrating to our barricade. We could hear the agonizing sound of iron tearing off the roof and things crashing to the ground. We kept huddled and hoped for the best but were increasingly nervous that the brick wall behind us would collapse and crush us.

Later, there was a sudden stop of the wind and rain. It was the eye. I grabbed a candle, and it lit easily in the stillness. Gingerly, we went down the stairs to the front lawn to look around. Other people from the flats were emerging. When we looked up, we could see stars. There were no clouds. The candle flame burned straight up without wavering. We couldn't see much else in the darkness but could hear a distant roar.

A few comments were exchanged with other tenants gathered on the lawn, but no one discussed plans. After a few minutes, we could hear the roar getting closer and suddenly everyone began running to their own flats. I suggested that we needed to find a safer place than where we were. We ran to the nearest ground level flat and banged on the door. If anyone was there, they would not open the door. We raced to the next door, with the same result. I never knew if they could hear us banging or yelling but maybe they were too scared to open the door. Sheets of tin and other rubbish were now swirling around. Better protection was urgent.

Then we heard a voice on the second-floor flats coming down the stairway saying, "come up here." We raced up the stairway to the closed door immediately at the top of the stairs and tried to open it while standing against the bank of louvres adjacent to the door. A voice inside said "Hang on, I will help." Just as the door cracked, I had a premonition of imminent danger, or I heard something changing.

We were against a lot of glass, and I grabbed Liane and pulled us both down onto the concrete veranda just below the louvre bank.

In a few milliseconds the entire bank of louvres exploded above our heads and jetted out into the air. It was a miraculous escape, but we didn't have time to consider our luck.

All we thought about was trying to get cover. The partial opening of the door had changed pressure conditions inside, and the internal pressure had been helping keep the outer wall intact. This sudden decrease of pressure allowed the whole outer wall to cave-in and the blast had carried straight through to the opposite wall and our louvre bank. The door slammed shut again and I couldn't budge it open.

The guy inside yelled out, "hang on I am crawling to the door." He could only move it a fraction, with the enormous pressure of the wind forcing the door closed. As he pulled, I pushed. The door was an almost immovable object, with the full force of wind against the door. We gradually eased it open with great effort, just enough for Liane and I to duck in before it slammed shut again. But this room was obviously no place to be, so we followed the guy into the second bedroom. It was still barely intact, but at least it was shelter.

Three blokes sat on the floor with their backs against the cupboards. I said a brief "thanks mate". It was still looking dangerous, as sheets of iron or other debris could still easily fly in. Only the guy who helped with the door was able to talk – it seemed like everyone else was shell-shocked or stunned. Later Liane said that she thought they were stoned.

We decided we should get into the cupboard. We dragged the double bed frame towards the wardrobe, and with the mattress, it offered protection against flying debris. There was only room in the wardrobe for three to stand at once, so two had to crouch down to make room. Through the crack of the cupboard door, two held the bed and mattress at the top and the two below helped grasp the bottom.

The other one standing was tasked with keeping inwards pressure on the cupboard door with enough room to allow our arms out.

We could still hear iron roofing being torn and twisted, and the absolute roar of wind shrieking all around us. There was a loud tearing sound and the collapsing crash of tin and heavy stuff falling on the ground close to us. I thought, "there goes our verandah… it probably just squashed the car at the bottom of the steps."

There was a loud rhythmic banging above us which we assumed was the ceiling or the roof rising and falling on the walls. Liane said she could see some sky, so maybe the roof was gone. At least the ceiling was offering some protection from penetrating rain, but I could feel a mist on my arms when they were outside the wardrobe.

We spent the time in silence, partly because of the noise, but also because we were lost in our own fear. I was shivering. The air around us was cold, and a T-shirt and shorts were not ideal to keep warm.

I remembered I knew one of them. I had seen him coming and going before the cyclone and knew he was gay, as were his two flat mates. After the storm was over, we laughed about me spending the cyclone with three gay guys and, literally, coming 'out of the closet' we had sheltered in.

The long hours were spent in rotation: two squatting and three standing and changing positions to prevent cramping. At one stage, one of the guys yelled out in a heavy European accent and began panicking. He tried to get out, but we grabbed him and pulled him back. We told him, "It's too dangerous outside mate! You must stay here. The iron will cut you to pieces." We had to physically restrain him until he stopped struggling and seemed to calm down.

All during the darkness we could hear the violent roar of the wind and shrieking of tin and the collision of debris. The ceiling creaked and banged intermittently above our heads but seemed to be holding together. At last, it became partially light, and we heard the wind decrease considerably.

When Liane and I finally ventured out, we returned to our flat. My first concern was my car, but luckily the Morris had escaped damage – just. The verandah had landed next to it on the sodden lawn. The walls of our flat were intact but blasted with holes, and the banks of louvre windows were just gaping holes. All the roofing iron was off, exposing bare timbers, but the back wall had remained intact. Our refuge on the second floor had a blasted wall facing the west, with most of the louvres and parts of the wall missing.

I could see all the way across the racetrack, towards what should have been trees and the wall of mangroves of Ludmilla Creek. There was now just a level expanse of tree skeletons. All the leaves had been stripped. It was like the Hiroshima bombscape. The few elevated and ground level homes in Wells Street were missing or just low ruins. I thought all of Darwin must be flattened and expected thousands to be dead or injured.

Other people emerged from their shelter too and looked around. Everyone had experienced a miraculous escape and, apart from a few minor cuts, no one was seriously injured in our vicinity. Our first concern was immediate survival. We salvaged what we could and started to dry things out, hanging wet clothes and bedding on the low brick fence, and putting other possessions onto the lawn.

After an hour of light, my brother John turned up in his utility from the city. He lived in Shepherd Street with my mum and dad. He told me our parents were fine, and so were their two dobermans.

"Although the house is soaked," he said. "It is mostly ok, and we can stay there underneath the piers. All the town is wrecked, and I had a real problem trying to find where I was. There are no landmarks anywhere. There is debris all over the roads through Parap and Stuart Park. You can drive on the footpath and bits of road to get around debris."

We loaded the Morris with as much of our gear as we could fit – mostly clothes and a few items like the record player and speaker boxes. It wasn't much. Then we drove in the direction of Fannie Bay Gaol and the coast. John was right. It was hard to orientate where we were, even though I had lived in Darwin most of my life. The radio was dead, the street signs were missing, and the trees were down or leafless. Sheets of iron and timber trusses, splintered like match wood, were strewn everywhere, mangled in with clothing and the remains of entire households. Most houses were just elevated floorboards or roofless shells. Cars were abandoned at the side of the road, gravel peppered and with dented panels. Liane said "Great you got $50 from that guy at the pub for your car. You would have Buckleys getting anything for car damage now."

When we arrived at my parents' house in Shepherd Street, we could see the house was mostly intact, except for a few blast holes in the front wall and broken windows. There were also holes in the roof, but its structure was sound. It was one of four 'Burnett-style' 2-bedroom houses in Shepherd Street. There was no power or water.

My parents both looked shell-shocked, although a bad hangover was also to blame for both, as they had needed a few stiff drinks during the night. Upstairs there was an incessant dripping from the bulging ceiling. Dad bored a few holes through the ceiling with his old hand drill to let the water through and stopped the ceiling from collapsing.

In mid-morning, John and I went up on the roof and decided we could block the holes with salvaged roofing iron and make the place relatively waterproof. We then wandered around the nearby streets and dragged as many good-looking iron sheets as possible back and banged them on over the gaps.

One concern was the lack of sanitation and the need for water. We could live downstairs while the top of the house was organized and dried out, but using the downstairs toilet was going to be a potential problem. I gathered all the buckets and tins I could find, and we organized a store of rainwater. Two clean plastic buckets were kept apart for drinking water and the rest were for flushing the toilet. Each day it rained a little, and we refilled containers from the roof drainpipe.

Late on boxing day, two prawn fishermen came past with a huge bag of prawns in a wheelbarrow. They said they couldn't store them so were giving them away. A couple of kilos of prawns was a huge morale booster. Mum also had a huge smoked ham in the fridge. With no power, the fridge kept cold for a bit of the first day. We collected any salvageable food, and that fed us for a few days. Dad unpacked an old kerosine fridge he had under the house from our time in Ceduna, pre-1956 and got it going, so we could then keep some things cold.

On the Sunday I went to Moil to see how my boss in Health Entomology, Neville, was getting on. He was originally from Sri Lanka and had little in the way of practical skills, so I thought he might need a hand. He and his doctor wife had two young daughters and rented in a block of flats off Rothdale Road. They had survived under a table covered with a collapsed gyprock ceiling, and he and his family were ok.

I helped him pack a few things in boxes, particularly his prized Katazan pottery from Borneo, and he asked me to organize the forwarding of his stuff to the south later. He was going to get evacuated to Canberra asap and, as a result, I was promoted to take over the medical entomology unit.

Rumours were everywhere: all dogs were to be shot! looting was rife! hundreds were killed! there were still bodies in houses! there was a mass grave being prepared!

As a family with two dobermans, we decided we were not leaving so that we could protect our dogs. We soon had radio reception, but many confusing messages were broadcast.

Eventually, Major General Alan Stretton came to Darwin and told us not to believe anyone else. "I will tell you the truth of what is going on. Only listen to me," he said. This brought great comfort to us about the government's ability to get things organized for the stayers.

On Monday morning, I went to my work at the MLC building in Smith Street. The Head of Health, Dr Charles Gurd had experience of post cyclone events from Fiji, so he knew what to expect. He assigned roles to each of the section heads.

I oversaw entomology and was to monitor the flies and mosquito situation. An inspection of the sewage system was necessary, especially the outlets from the maceration plants in various spots around the harbour. Our main problem for mosquito breeding was broken pipes discharging sewage into the edge of the mangroves. They needed fixing. We were able to appropriate all the usable insecticides from pest control businesses and transfer them to a stockpile at the airport.

My unit went from house to house, including through blocks of flats, to see where the flies were breeding, and report any infested fridges and deep freezers to health inspectors for action. Later, sailors from HMAS Melbourne, and then the army, did the dirty work.

A few days after the cyclone, low flying planes sprayed malathion over residential areas to control the flies. The first was a crop-duster from Katherine, flown by Stuart Cox, and then two more came from Kununurra. Ironically, one of them was registered as VH-DDT, so there was a rumour that we were using DDT.

We set up fly killing trays and large wet wheat bags sprinkled with red sugar-based dipel insecticide granules, at all the free food kitchens. We counted dead flies every few days and reported the numbers to Dr Gurd. They were mostly the blue blowfly, *Chrysomyia megacephala*, which feeds on protein based rotting food and dead animals.

We also monitored the mosquito population to locate problem areas. We located sewer pipes broken by tree roots that were discharging sewerage into a hidden dense bush area. I used a big, motorized fogger from down south for the immediate treatment of these areas.

The smell of wet and rotting carpet, decaying food, dead animals, and maggoty rotten fridges and freezers was a constant for months in every wrecked house and in many occupied houses. Our inspections revealed some people had left with a Christmas eve meal still on the kitchen table and had just abandoned the premises and everything in the house, without recovering anything.

Liane and I slept in an old caravan in my parent's yard until she was evacuated four days later. The authorities confiscated all the grog from the port buildings and dug temporary trench dumps in Coconut Grove and Lee Point. Not surprisingly, the trucks ferrying the grog for dumping were diverted to other places. My friends and I had free beer for months.

Other memories I have of the aftermath include the free food supermarket at Darwin High School, where there were many tins of Irish stew! There were also food centres at Parap Hostel and the old Esplanade Hostel. There was a generous distribution of generators to provide power; an emergency water pump set up on Kimmorley Bridge over Rapid Creek to put water into the mains supply; lines of people queued for bags of ice from ice machines; and emergency payments of cash went to the survivors.

We were given an airfare out after 6 months for respite, and for a long time, everything before the cyclone was referred to as BC and afterwards was AC. It was a life changing event, and a time reference and milestone in my life.

Sandra White

Sandra and her husband, John, moved to Darwin in November 1971, with Mark, then aged three, and Karen 11 months. John worked at Detroit Engine and Tool Company, and Sandra was a dressmaker who could stay home and look after the children. They lived in a Housing Commission home in Carstens Crescent, Wagaman.

Christmas Eve. Decorations up, presents wrapped, and food prepared for the next day. There had been cyclone warnings for a few days and the weather was very wet and windy but, not having experienced a cyclone before and thinking that everything would be okay, we went to a Christmas Eve party.

During the evening the weather got so bad that we decided to go home. We went to bed but couldn't sleep because the lightning and the noise of thunder and the rain was so frightening – even though it was mild compared with what was to come. Very soon water was pouring through the louvres in the hallway, so we laid down towels to soak it up. What a joke that was!

We eventually realised that a cyclone was imminent, the only question was: 'How bad? Tracy hit us at 1.00 am on Christmas morning. By this time, we had collected the children from their bedrooms and the four of us were together. Where to go to stay safe?

We climbed into a wardrobe. When that bedroom crashed down around us we moved to Mark's bedroom and hid under a mattress that we had put on a slant against the wall. Soon the ceiling crashed down on top of the mattress, so we crawled out and managed to get to the bathroom where once again the ceiling crashed down. Our toilet was separate from the bathroom, and this seemed to be our last option.

We sat on the floor, in our nightwear, with our backs braced against the door and arms around Mark and Karen to protect them as best we could. We needed protection in case the louvres smashed, and glass flew into our faces. 'Lilac' and 'fluffy 'was popular for toilets and I would love to have a photo of John with the fluffy toilet seat cover on his head and the fluffy mat on mine!

The louvres along the hallway behind us shattered and crashed against and under the door. We were soaked with water from both the ceiling and under the door. So, sitting in water and broken glass, we shivered uncontrollably from cold and fear, huddling together as close as we could.

It is impossible to describe the noise of the house being ripped apart and the continual flashing of lightning and the noise of the thunder. Surprisingly, we managed to stay calm for the sake of the children. Ever since that day I dislike it when people say 'I would do this, or I would do that'. I firmly believe that unless you are faced with a situation, it is impossible to know how you will react.

Around 4 am the eye passed over Wagaman, and it was calm for about 30 minutes. John clambered barefooted over the rubble to find some shoes and blankets, and I was terrified he might not come back. He did! With shoes and blankets. We had no option but to sit and wait, not knowing how long it would take to pass and not knowing whether we would be dead or alive, or perhaps severely injured, when Tracy finally left us.

After six terrifying hours it was an indescribable relief when it was finally calm enough for us to assess the situation and to find that none of us were physically injured.

We looked out of the only louvres in the house that weren't shattered. When I saw the total devastation I couldn't imagine how anyone could have survived. I said: 'My God everyone must be dead."

What on earth do we do now?

Figure 24: Sandra and John White's Wagaman Home.

To our amazement, neighbours started to emerge and climb over rubble to check on each other. Just knowing we weren't the only people still alive was an unbelievable relief.

Our cat was safe, but terrified, in the washing basket with the ceiling over the top giving him protection. We had to leave him behind, but we found him months later and he lived until he was 18 years old.

Casuarina High School was our nearest and best option, but Mark was a student at Wagaman Primary School so, in our confused state we made our way there to find it too was badly damaged and flooded. But it was comforting to find lots of people there all trying to survive just like us.

Army personnel set up a soup kitchen. A neighbour and I made our way back to our houses and filled my pram with food. It was so frightening being out in the open as we pushed, pulled, and lifted that pram until we got to the doorway of the school, just as a wheel fell off! Luckily, help was at hand to help us pick up the contents.

We also collected brooms and a chain gang was formed to continually sweep the water out.

The children wore dry shirts we found in the school's dress up box. At the end of the day, we found a couple of wooden doors to lie on out of the water. Every bit of floor space was taken up by families feeling, as we were, fortunate to be alive and safe.

By the next day a lot of roads had been cleared and our friend

Garry found us. He lived in Stuart Park where houses were not as badly damaged as in Wagaman. I was so overcome with joy and relief to see him, that was the first time I cried.

Garry drove us back to our place to see if we could salvage some clothes. It was devasting to see the utter destruction of our home.

Later, with no power or water, there was risk of disease, so we joined long queues at the Darwin Aviation Club to get vaccinated.

At Darwin Airport, a tin shed with no air-conditioning, we waited in queues every day for evacuation. On the fourth day, Mark, Karen, and I boarded a RAAF Lockheed C-130 Hercules transport plane bound for Adelaide. John stayed behind and lived at his workplace.

With all communications cut, my brother and sister-in-law had spent day and night at Adelaide Airport hoping we might be on one of the planes full of evacuees and they were there when we arrived. Once again, I was overcome with joy and relief, and I simply hugged them and sobbed.

I flew back to Darwin in mid-March, leaving the children with my brother and sister-in-law. The few things we salvaged from the ruins of our house were stored at Detroit, and we drove the 3,000 kms to Adelaide to pick up a 24ft caravan. John had never towed a van before, so he put a sign in the back window that said 'Beware: Nervous Darwin Novice.'

The road was not sealed between Port Augusta and Alice Springs in those days, so we had to travel on the old Ghan with the car and caravan. There was no platform at Alice Springs Railway Station, so a crane and forklift had to be used to lift them off the train.

The caravan was our home for the next 18 months. A tarp was put up over the open-air toilet in the ruins of the house next door, and as there was no plumbing, we used a bucket of water to flush it.

We set up the van at the side of our block while the remains of our house were bulldozed, and a new house built. John and I still live there today.

Ted Whiteaker

Ted Whiteaker was an air-traffic controller at Darwin Airport. He went through the cyclone in his home in Goldsmith Street, Fannie Bay, which fortunately suffered less damage than most of the city.

I left work at the Operations Control Centre shortly after 7 pm on Tracy Eve. The wind was blowing strongly, and it was gusty and wet. I had a bite to eat at home, and a little later went to my regular watering hole, the public bar at the Fannie Bay Hotel on the corner of Bayview Street and East Point Road, directly in the face of the elements howling in over the sea. I was not there for long – the heavy plate glass doors kept blowing open in strong gusts, with near-horizontal rain driving into the bar and making it very wet and uncomfortable.

At around 10pm, I left and went to a friend's house in Hinkler Crescent, Fannie Bay and we played scrabble and listened to the ABC radio reports of the intensifying cyclone. Around 11.30pm, a fellow who was living in a caravan in the yard opened the back door to bring his dog inside. We were surprised to see the extent of garden debris piling up in the darkness outside, and considering the seriousness of the situation, I decided to go home.

After a wild drive through blinding rain, I found Goldsmith Street by the lightning flashes and got home just before midnight. Four us were in the house when the power failed. We sat in the dark in the lounge room (there was plenty of flickering lightning to see what was going on) and listened to the ABC on a transistor radio as the wind strength intensified relentlessly. Then, at 2.30 am, the radio station went off the air. Our glass louvre windows were bowing seriously under the wind pressure and the rain was being driven inside. The floor was awash in a few inches of water – a novel situation in an elevated house.

The lounge room was very wet, so we moved, with my expensive stereo system, down the other end of the house. We were lucky. Half-a-dozen louvres exploded in a particularly savage gust, spearing shards of glass across the loungeroom just after we left. This allowed the pressure inside the house to equalise more harmoniously with the pressure outside, and while there was a continuous deluge of driven rain inside the house, no more damage occurred.

The eye came at about 3.00 am and lasted about 20 minutes where we were – it was deathly quiet and still. I wandered out with a torch to see what was happening in the street. The family on one side of us were away, and their roof was starting to show signs of peeling, while the fellows across the road had already lost part of their roof. They were a bit nervous about their prospects, so the five of them joined us. As the eye passed, the wind started to pick up again from the opposite direction. It could be heard approaching from the surrounding blackness in a rapidly increasing roar of fury, building from nothing to maximum intensity in what seemed a few short minutes.

The house had always been a bit tender on its steel piers. Walking up the stairs was enough to send a gentle shudder through the building at the best of times; if a breeze came through the open louvres and offset the balance of the ceiling fans, the house would quiver in sympathy. Now it was rocketing about like a runaway railway train on steroids, and the noise was indescribable; the wind was howling and shrieking and there were bangs and clatters as airborne debris whirled about outside.

Sometime around 4am, I sensed a slight reduction in the wind strength, and at 6.00 am the winds had died down to around 70kph.

The grey dawn light revealed the gobsmacking sight of widespread devastation around us. There was wreckage everywhere, the trees had lost all their leaves, and a few people were slowly stirring in the landscape. Apart from a couple of holes in the external fibro cladding and a few dents in the roof, my house had miraculously been spared from the destruction we could see all around.

I set off on my 350cc Honda trail bike, weaving around the debris on the roads to the Conway's, where I had been the night before. Their property was a mess; the roof was gone, and the house was uninhabitable, but Ken and Carol were OK. They subsequently moved to my place for a month or so.

The extent of the destruction in Fannie Bay was awesome, but nothing compared to the progressively worse picture that unfolded as we drove along Bagot Road and on to the northern suburbs. Incredibly, a couple of front-end loaders were already busy clearing debris off Bagot Road as we passed.

I checked on some displaced friends in the northern suburbs and arranged for a motley bunch of refugees to join our household. I then looked for my parents who were living in Carpentier Crescent, Wagaman. It was a new suburb, only recently settled and on the edge of developed suburbia at the time. Navigation was a real problem, with all the vegetation and street signs gone, and no familiar buildings left as a guide but eventually I found the right street. This area had copped the worst of it, and there was nothing left of the houses but piles of debris and bare floorboards. I found my parents' place, and with some misgivings entered the rubble looking for signs of life. They weren't there, so I went to look at the local school.

The congregation of survivors at the school were a depressing sight; a crowd of people huddled in whatever clothing they had salvaged and looking very miserable among the drips from the leaking roof. The usual leadership candidates amongst them had commandeered the chalk and blackboards, and were trying to instil some organisation in regard to personal hygiene, drinking water, food and medical attention etc. I was relieved to find my parents, looking a bit shocked but at least alive and uninjured.

I got home around 10 am. The wind had died, the leaden skies were overcast, and it was stinking hot and humid without electricity for fans. People gradually arrived to settle in. I was fiddling around with my transistor radio, wondering if anyone in the world outside was aware of the situation in Darwin, when I tuned in to the OIC of the RAAF Base transmitting an assessment of the situation to the wallahs in Canberra. The communication was via the radio of the Connair De Havilland Heron, VH-CLT, which had survived the cyclone in the shelter of a hangar. It was oddly comforting to know that word was getting out.

Later, in the evening, I went to the MLC building in town to see if I could help with the initial disaster response, which was being undertaken by the Education Department under the leadership of the director, Dr. Hedley Beare. The MLC offices were a hive of activity as planning got under way for the air evacuation that was to start in earnest the following day. In the absence of phones or any other communications, I volunteered to act as a courier, ferrying written communications between the MLC and the people at the airport who were starting to organise themselves. As the night unfolded, I drove out to the airport and back a couple of times.

The scene at the airport was shocking. The blacked-out main terminal building, an old, corrugated iron hangar with administration offices, airline counters, and the airport lounge; was a shambles. Its roof was badly damaged, and water was everywhere. It was intermittently raining, and a large crowd of desperate survivors were huddled in the areas of least wetness, waiting for the following day and hoping for a flight out on any aircraft that might arrive.

The next morning, I fronted up at the airport again. I ran around finding out what aircraft were due and where they were going when they left and helped marshal evacuees off the arriving buses into groups according to their destinations.

The evacuees were a sorry looking lot, dressed in whatever clothing they had salvaged and clutching a few belongings in bags, or perhaps a suitcase. Many had nothing, and many were injured.

Most were in a state of calm shock, while a few were weeping and having a hard time of it. The Salvation Army set up a kitchen, and sandwiches and drinks were available to all. It was heartening to observe the co-operation and kindness between everybody. The injured, women and children, and older folk were prioritised for boarding, and then others filled any spare capacity remaining on the aircraft.

I had always wanted to drive a truck, and now seemed like a good opportunity, so the next day I tried my luck at the Department of Works depot at the two-and-a-half mile. A supervisor looked me up and down and said they needed a 5-ton Bedford driven to Ludmilla School to assist with delivery of food supplies. As I was about to hop in the truck, he asked me if I had a truck driver's license. I didn't, and said so, thinking that under the circumstances it shouldn't matter much, but apparently it did. The supervisor let me drive the truck to the school, but that was the end of it, much to my disappointment. I stacked boxes of food for an hour or two, and when the job dwindled to hanging around again, I went home.

Organisation quickly settled in all over. People generally were willing to pitch in and do whatever was necessary at the time, and the quick availability of food, fuel, gas, and generators made life a little more bearable. The Air Traffic Control system had been knocked out and various components of the system were carried out from other interstate centres, leaving me to my own devices with a bit of free time. Trips through the police roadblocks to waterfalls out bush were a great escape from the bleak reality of the Darwin landscape post-Tracy.

Air Traffic Control resumed operations sometime around the New Year. My first shift was at night. I sat in the dark with a torch at a communications console covered in plastic sheeting with a few blinking buttons flashing feebly underneath (but non-functional nevertheless), and a single telephone line. No tea, no coffee. There was no air traffic, just rainwater dripping all around. It was a long shift.

We were among the few fortunate households with only minor damage, but no-one who went through that night will ever forget the experience.

Robert Woodward

Bob was the Business Manager for Territory Ford. He and his wife Erica and their four children – Mark 7, Darren 6, Kerry 4, and Robbie 3 – were living in a house in Conigrave Street, Fannie Bay. Also with them was Bob's father, on his first visit back to Darwin after being seriously injured in the first Japanese air raids in 1942 and being evacuated. The family went through two house destructions.

My family and I arrived back in Darwin on Christmas Eve. My father had come back to Darwin with me after the funeral of his second wife that we had attended just a few days earlier.

The weather was overcast. There was a drizzly, light rain as we went into town to pick up some last-minute Christmas gifts. There was discussion about a cyclone around, but everyone was shrugging it off.

We had experienced the Cyclone Selma warnings just weeks before, and that was a fizzer, turning into a rain depression. In preparation for that, we still had our campervan roped down onto star pickets driven deep into the ground, and the yard was all cleaned up.

After dropping my dad and the family off home in Fannie Bay, I returned to the city to the Territory Ford Christmas party at the dealership on Daly Street. During the party, the boss of Westco Mazda, who was with us, got a phone call from his wife. Their home near Casuarina Shopping Centre, "was vibrating, then shaking in the strong wind gusts, and could he come home?"

The air was perfectly calm, and very still, in the city.

Anyway, we all packed up the party and went home, though not without incident – the dealer principal, Colin Hurley, told us days later that he was nearly blown off the road near the McMillans Road turn off on his way home to Nightcliff.

At home in Conigrave Street, Erica was still wrapping presents and the kids had just gone to sleep. Warnings on ABC Radio were becoming more alarming and they were interviewing people who had dropped into the studio and giving out advice on what everyone should be doing. I remember, I think it was Allan Stuart, a tour operator, talking calmly but seriously… one had to listen.

We followed the advice and opened all the louvres on the opposite side of the house to the incoming wind direction. We filled our kitchen and bathroom sinks and the bath with water, but later had to empty the bath to put the kids in there when it all got terribly worse. We also put a single bed mattress over all of us, three adults lying on the floor. The bathroom we had been advised was the strongest room in the house.

The ABC said that the cyclone, now named Tracy, had become stationery off Charles Point for about an hour, and this would likely increase the projected wind speeds.

Then came those fateful words. "A cyclone is imminent."

When the power went off, and the ABC went off the air, we were alone in the dark. The house started to vibrate and shake in the stronger gusts as the wind built to a roar, and came again and again in waves, even louder than the constant never-abating tumult.

Then the horrific curdling sound of corrugated iron being torn and ripped off the roof battens, accompanied by banging and crashing, and glass breaking. There was an almighty roar as the ground level house next door exploded completely, sending pieces of material through our house like spears through paper. It was the house of the Tom The Cheap supermarket manager, but they were fortunately away. The noises were terrifying. Then the eye arrived. Total calm.

I took a look with a torch. The internal staircase was covered in debris and broken glass. The roof had gone, and the entire northern side of the house had crashed to the ground. We heard a voice:

"Are you all OK? Hello, hello can you hear me?"

"Yes" we answered.

"I will try to clear a path on the stairs to get you all out, and into my place".

It was Jack, our rear neighbour. I don't remember his surname, but I think he worked for Attorney General's Department. He had already got out two other neighbours' families, including Trevor Millikan, who also worked for government, and his family.

We climbed through fallen Mango trees, alive with multitudes of excited green ants and soaking wet gardens to get onto his property. Then all four families were in Jack's lounge. He had a gas lamp going and started to open a jeroboam of champagne and just got out the words "merry Christmas" when the wind came back like a freight train roaring through a level crossing. The end wall of the lounge tore out and we all saw it, in the light from the gas lamp, go upwards and away in another almighty roar over the screaming wind.

We all then scrambled to shelter on top of each other under their dining table. And as the house was mercilessly torn apart, we protected ourselves by placing chairs, lying on their sides like lion tamers' chairs, against flying debris. Before it died down at daylight, the wind was zinging jarrah floorboards off the bearers at the western end of the building.

As the sun rose, we could see all the way to the new hospital under construction – way out near Lee Point, as most trees had gone. Their gnarled remains had no leaves. There was corrugated iron wrapped around bent over steel power poles. And there were no houses – just the concrete stilts of what once were elevated homes.

My first thought was that it looked like a nuclear bomb had been dropped. It was hard to accept Mother Nature could be so powerful as to destroy a whole city. It was the most dreadful night of my life and I consider it a miracle we survived.

The front showroom of the Ford premises had been destroyed but the roof was still on the service department and, miraculously the telex was still working. We told the police that, and as a result the ACT police took over the building, when they arrived.

Over the next few days, we picked up some kids toys, and Erica and I found a few clothes at our home in Conigrave Street. We moved into the service department of Territory Ford. Dad set up an oxyacetylene rig to boil water and made tea – and that made us a point of call for many of the clean-up workers.

Investigating noises out front a day or two later Dad and I went out to check. We were suddenly accosted by a Department of Civil Aviation screaming security guard, waving a pistol at us very nervously, and sweating profusely. I explained who I was and that my family were out back in the service department, and he ordered us to go around back and followed us to check. Dad offered him a cup of tea and he calmed down – he was a volunteer from Victoria, we learned later. After that, he and others called in every night for a cuppa. We set up a barricade at the front entrance and if anyone came looking for parts, we gave them away. Later, Emergency Services commandeered all the new car stock and some late model used cars.

I went to the Police station to advise we had three new Transit vans that could be used as ambulances if they could get my family out, as we were sleeping in them. The police looked like they had not slept for days. I also asked about getting my dad out of Darwin, because he had the only keys for the Bata Shoe Company factory in Seaford on him, and it would have to re-open in the new year. But the answer was no, only women, children and the injured were being evacuated by air.

Erica and our four young kids were loaded onto a semi-trailer flat-top at Ludmilla Primary School, and taken to the Airport. They flew to Melbourne on a TAA 727 with just a plastic bag of personal items and the clothes they stood up in. Luggage was not allowed so each aircraft could carry more passengers – and they took world record numbers. All regular domestic flights were stopped to enable the evacuation of Darwin. My brother-in-law says a Department of Civil Aviation guy in Melbourne, who was helping the Salvation Army receive the evacuees, told him that the authorities "had one eye closed, and the hand over the other eye, at what was being achieved with the aircraft loading numbers, all bets were off, and rules lapsed to get all the women and kids out of Darwin."

The family's leaving was a very emotional parting, but a great relief that they were getting out. Dad and I then set off to drive to Melbourne and we were looked after well by the people in every town. We slept in the Catholic Church in Katherine the first night, after having been stopped for hours at flooded creek crossings. In Alice Springs every vehicle was checked, and the Lions and Rotary Clubs gave us emergency ration packs.

A surprise was the government opened up the Woomera Rocket range to refugee traffic. It was weird to see a commonwealth copper standing in the middle of the corrugated, dusty South Road, waving us to turn left and telling us "stay on the bitumen road, take no photos, and don't stop until you get to the Woomera Township." We saw a British Blue Streak rocket on the launch pad.

It was really cold and on arrival at Woomera, we entered a large hall and were given food to eat and drinks and more cans of food to take with us. An American came up to me, took off his beautiful white polo-necked jumper, and gave it to me. "You need this more than me." I was ever so grateful, and still become emotional years later when I tell that story.

After our arrival back in Melbourne, Ford went to work to gain a permit for me to return to Darwin to help re-organise the business and recover water damaged records. It took a few days as places were scarce, but I flew back on an Ansett 727 via Brisbane and Mount Isa. Back in Darwin, leaving the aircraft we were immediately hit by the stench: wet bedding, rotting, stripped vegetation, and other odours.

Entering the terminal building was just like a scene from a war movie, with military and interstate police everywhere. I fronted up to a long desk and was interrogated about why I was entering Darwin. They checked my permit papers, and recorded the details about where I was staying and who I was employed by. Fortunately, I had a letter from the CEO of Ford Australia.

I was picked up by a fellow staffer who had remained while I took my dad back to Melbourne. We occupied a block of flats in Nightcliff, loaned to Ford by the owner. There were no windows or doors, it was just a shell of about three floors, and no power meant we endured long sweaty nights.

We worked in the unroofed office at Ford during the day under tarpaulins. On one occasion we experienced a lightning strike on the steel roof trusses of the show room and that fried the switchboard and the phone handsets.

The Victorian State Electricity Commission workers, who had come to help, suffered terribly from the heat and humidity while up the ladders outside. They ran electrical wires along Daly Street. Men from the Townsville Electricity Board straightened all the bent over steel poles along Bagot Road.

We bathed in Rapid Creek and showered at the water main on the Stuart Highway on the way into work, just up from where the overpass is today. Light aircraft sprayed the northern suburbs to keep the flies and mosquitos down.

We helped our friends at the Travelodge – our old Friday night drinking spot – pull up all the wet carpet. We threw it out the glassless windows, with all the curtains, bedding, and anything else that had been wet. For this we were fed, but we also dined at a Commonwealth Hostels set up named Block 8, and at Nightcliff High School. There were some boozy, all men, drinking sessions at the Sand Pebbles Restaurant at the Rapid Creek Hotel. It was just like a wartime movie, with a guy belting out tunes on the piano. With beer cans stacked high on the piano, it was a very jovial scene.

Everyone worked so hard cleaning up and re-establishing Darwin and its empty suburbs of cyclone wreckage, they deserved to play a little hard too.

Could It Happen Again?

By Derek Pugh

It has happened before.

Big storms and squalls are not unusual in the Top End but three cyclones, including Tracy, have been big enough to cause the deaths of Darwin residents in the 155 years since settlement. Even the very first settlements in the north experienced their wrath and in 1839, the British settlement at Port Essington was also destroyed by a cyclone.

By 1897, most old Territorians had already experienced some of their ferocity. In December 1893, Palmerston was hit hard by what seems to have been a tornado:

> … It came up from the eastward on Sunday afternoon last, wind and rain, thunder and lightning, and a spray that looked like nothing more than sleet. It came along in a body, and long before it was within reach, townspeople who were watching it had made up their minds that it was going to be something unusual. It was truly an extraordinary storm. The whole town felt the force of a stiff squall, but it was only within a very limited radius that the severest of the wind was experienced.

Then, on 6 January 1897, the tiny colony was struck, for four long hours, by the full fury of a tropical cyclone that became known as the *Great Hurricane.*[*]

---

[*] Palmerston's 1897 cyclone was called the *Great Hurricane* as cyclones were not named in the 1890s – except in Queensland where a meteorologist named Clement Wragge, named them using the Greek alphabet, mythological characters, and politicians. Wragge retired in 1908 and the naming stopped, but in 1964, the Bureau of Meteorology began using female names, starting with Cyclone Bessie, and the practice became worldwide. In 1975, the Australian Minister for Science,

The telegraph line south was down, but Post and Telegraph Master, John Little could still use the undersea cables to Broome:

… 4 am – Hurricane here. Barometer 28.784. Line and station buildings damaged, also considerable damage to other buildings in township. Everything possible will be done to restore communication quickly.

7.30 am – Lines all broken by hurricane; nearly every building in township wrecked. Barometer rising, but still blowing very hard.

All but one or two shelters in the town were destroyed. The *Times* described the scene:

… strongly built houses collapsed like houses of cards; roofs blew bodily away; lamps and telephone posts were bent or torn up; immense beams of timber were hurled away like chaff; trees were uprooted; in many instances large houses were lifted bodily from their foundations and deposited ten or twelve feet away; and in short the night was one of terrifying destructiveness that made the stoutest heart quail.

The *Adelaide Observer* reported on 9 January 1897:

… The distress among the residents is simply appalling, and a large proportion of the people are absolutely ruined by the terrible visitation. The bodies of ten persons who met with their deaths through the collapse of the buildings in which they resided at the time of the cyclone have already been recovered, but a great number of people are missing and have yet to be accounted for…

The railway sheds at 2½ Mile, Parap, were levelled and the line towards Pine Creek washed away in several places. In Fannie Bay, the botanic gardens were flattened, and the gaol was torn open. The prisoners wandered around, dazed. Any boat caught at a mooring in the harbour was sunk, the lucky few were blown out to sea or into the mangrove forests. All the government offices were wrecked, and government business ground to a halt.

On 10 January, worried southerners heard that the weather was

---

Bill Morrison, objected that only female names were used and since then, cyclones have also had male names.

now fine and sunny in Port Darwin, but 'imagination could not paint the wreck and devastation'. Mrs Tack's family was one that was lucky to survive:

> ... we were forced to run out into the street, nearly blinded with the rain. My little children were blown in all directions, their shrieks being heart rending. I fell several times into the water, but by breathing in the dear baby's mouth, managed by God's help and will to keep her above. The little girl, about six years of age, was found in the morning clinging onto a fence, quite exhausted and one little boy took shelter under a piece of iron that had blown off the next house. Mr Tack managed to find the other two children and kept them with him until daybreak. He got his legs cut very badly, the children got cut and bruised, and at present Mr Tack is not well at all. The baby has a severe cold on the chest. I dropped her twice in the water and had to grope about for her in the dark...*

During the storm, families moved from shelter to shelter as each was destroyed behind them. One family said they had moved three times. The *Times* reported that:

> ... it was impossible to tell where to go with the houses disappearing in the way they were and the pitiless rain blinding the sight. To make headway at all against the wind, people had to go down on their hands and knees and lie as close to the ground as possible.†

The immediate needs of Port Darwin residents were shelter, food, and clean water. They also had to bury their dead. The *Times* reported that 28 people had been killed by the storm – 15 of those were on boats in the harbour – but only those bodies recovered were counted. As usual for the era, only the two Europeans who died were named by the papers – Richard Tracey, a gold miner, and M. D. Armstrong. The rest of the dead, who remain nameless, were Japanese pearl shell divers, Chinese residents and Larrakia people.

Armstrong had lived in the Territory for 16 years and was an import/export businessman, cattleman, and butcher, with his business

---

*   In James, 2002.

†   *NTTG*, 25 January 1897.

partner, William Lawrie. At the time of his death, he was 'a prominent and useful member of the community' with many 'intimate friends'. He took 10 days to die of internal injuries brought about by being 'a good deal exposed during the night of the storm and on the following day'.[*]

Figure 24: Corner of Smith and Knuckey Streets after the 1897 'Great Hurricane'. Victoria Hotel in the distance (LANT, ph0840-0001).

The injured were gathered up and taken to what was left of the hospital. Mr G. H. James, landlord of the Hotel Victoria, broke his arm by falling from the hotel balcony to the ground the morning after the cyclone[†]. R. F. Fox, an accountant who had taken shelter at the E.S. and A. Bank, was severely injured by some rocks falling on his head[‡]. The *Times* reported that 'the exposure to the elements brought

[*]   *NTTG*, 29 Jan 1897.
[†]   *NTTG*, 25 January 1897.
[‡]   Frederick Reginald Fox J.P. lived in Darwin for many years. In 1913 he was running a store and other businesses in Smith Street.

on attacks of fever, and half of the European population complained of illness'*.

The town was nailed back together – many houses were only shanties anyway – the railway was repaired, and the telegraph lines restrung. The rebuilding was remarkably quick. By early February the Hotel Victoria was already in a 'very finished state' and:

> ... Allen and, Co. have now quite a pretentious store erected again. Rundle Bros. and Co. we understand, intend erecting spacious premises, in good time; and Mr. Jolly, who arrived here on Wednesday, will proceed at once with the erection of new buildings, in the place of those blown down[†].

Following several near misses, such as a cyclone that caused much damage to Darwin but mostly skirted around the town in 1917, residents may have hoped that lessons learned from the Great Hurricane were enacted. But they meant nothing on the night of 10th March 1937. It happened again:

> ... Darwin has been devastated by one of the worst cyclones on record. Many persons are homeless and injured, one death has been reported and grave fears are felt for the safety of pearling fleets which have been caught in raging seas. Cable, wireless and telegraphic communication with the stricken town is interrupted, and only meagre details of the disaster have filtered through.
>
> The cyclone, bigger than that of 1897, crashed on Darwin last night. Raging through the night the fierce storm wrought havoc in the town. Houses were razed to the ground, and extensive damage was done to Government House and other administrative buildings. Pearling fleets were out on the pearling grounds when the storm burst upon Darwin. Today grave concern was felt for the safety of their crews.[‡]

An unnamed Aboriginal man, sleeping under Sergeant Rawling's home, was killed during a cyclone on 3 March 1937[§]. The winds were

---

*   *NTTG*, 12 February 1897.
†   *NTTG*, 12 February 1897.
‡   *Daily News* (Perth), 11 March 1937, page 1.
§   *Northern Standard*, 12 March 1937, page 10. A small child who was with him had a 'miraculous escape'.

strong enough to blow the 'spokes from the wheels of a Howitzer gun'*, said the *Herald*, and just like the survivors of Cyclone Tracy, the residents were amazed that there were not more fatalities.

Figure 25: Darwin: damage from the 1937 cyclone (LANT, ph0110-0434).

The Top End of Australia hosts the full fury of tropical cyclones every year. Every settlement has their stories of being hit, or "just missed"†, but in its first 80 years, the capital had experienced damage and loss of life *twice*. Perhaps now the authorities would make plans for the future of Darwin and 'cyclone proof' its reconstruction. Unfortunately, no.

World War Two interrupted everything, and by the time the city became one of the fastest growing cities in Australia in the 1960s and 1970s, the cyclones of yesteryear had all but been forgotten. As a result, hundreds of thin-skinned houses on matchstick legs were raised in long lines along the streets of the new suburbs. Looking at them from a distance, the young Cyclone Tracy must have rubbed her hands together with glee...

---

* *Sydney Morning Herald*, 16 March 1937: page 12.
† See Kevin Murphy, 1984, *Big Blow Up North*, bom.gov.au.

Index

Printed in Australia
Ingram Content Group Australia Pty Ltd
AUHW010844150524
394393AU00006B/12

9 780645 737417